The *New* Family?

The *New* Family?

edited by

Elizabeth B. Silva and Carol Smart

SAGE Publications
London • Thousand Oaks • New Delhi

First published 1999. Reprinted 2001, 2002

SAGE Publications Ltd
6 Bonhill Street
London EC2A 4PU

SAGE Publications Inc.
2455 Teller Road
Thousand Oaks, California 91320

SAGE Publications India Pvt Ltd
32, M-Block Market
Greater Kailash – I
New Delhi 110 048

British Library Cataloguing in Publication data

A catalogue record for this book is available
from the British Library

ISBN 0 7619 5855 X
ISBN 0 7619 5856 8 (pbk)

Library of Congress catalog card number 98–61272

Typeset by Mayhew Typesetting, Rhayader, Powys
Printed and bound in Great Britain by
Selwood Printing Ltd., Burgess Hill, West Sussex

CONTENTS

CONTRIBUTORS

Joanna Bornat – Senior Lecturer in the School of Health and Social Welfare, The Open University.

Julia Brannen – Professor in Sociology of the Family at the University of London and Senior Research Officer in the Thomas Coram Research Unit, Institute of Education, University of London.

Mary Chamberlain – Professor of Modern Social History in the School of Humanities, Oxford Brookes University.

Brian Dimmock – Lecturer in the School of Health and Social Welfare, The Open University. Chair of the National Stepfamily Association.

Catherine Donovan – Lecturer in Sociology at the University of Sunderland.

Gillian Dunne – Senior Research Fellow in the Gender Institute, London School of Economics.

Brian Heaphy – Research Fellow in the Faculty of Humanities and Social Science, South Bank University, London.

Sarah Irwin – Lecturer in Sociology in the Department of Sociology and Social Policy, University of Leeds.

David Jones – Lecturer in the Faculty of Applied Social Sciences and Humanities, Buckinghamshire University College.

David Morgan – Emeritus Professor of Sociology in the University of Manchester.

Sheila Peace – Senior Lecturer and Sub-dean for Research in the School of Health and Social Welfare, The Open University.

Elizabeth Bortolaia Silva – Senior Research Fellow in the Department of Sociology and Social Policy, University of Leeds.

viii THE *NEW* FAMILY?

Carol Smart – Professor of Sociology in the Department of Sociology and Social Policy, University of Leeds.

Jeffrey Weeks – Professor of Sociology and Dean of Humanities and Social Science, South Bank University, London.

1

THE 'NEW' PRACTICES AND POLITICS OF FAMILY LIFE

Elizabeth B. Silva and Carol Smart

Our focus in this book is the changing nature of intimate and familial relationships in the context of shifting normative frameworks. While our enterprise here is essentially sociological, we recognize the extent to which issues to do with families have become immensely controversial and politicized. There is ongoing both an epistemological and a moral debate about what the family *is* and what the family *ought* to be.

For some it is easy to define what the family should be, namely a heterosexual conjugal unit based on marriage and co-residence. The main purpose of such a family is often thought to be to inculcate proper values in children and to remain independent of state support (Morgan, 1995; Phillips, 1997). In contrast with this *ought*, the actualities of how families work and organize themselves is often perceived as sadly wanting. Thus this framing of how families *should* be, is often juxtaposed with statistics on divorce, lone-parent households, delinquency and so on, to produce a picture of the family in decline or as disintegrating with a range of disastrous consequences for the rest of society.

For others, it is less easy to articulate what families *should* be like. There is, for example, an emphasis on diversity of family practices which need not emphasize the centrality of the conjugal bond, which may not insist on co-residence, and which may not be organized around heterosexuality. This diversity is not interpreted as a sign of decline or immorality. Rather, change is understood in relation to evolving employment patterns, shifting gender relations, and increasing options in sexual orientations. In this model the family is not expected to remain unchanged and unchanging. It is seen as transforming itself in relation to wider social trends and sometimes it is seen as a source of change itself which prompts changes to occur in public policy and provision.

In this book we lean towards the latter approach. Our contributors consider current diverse practices in families and the risks taken by individuals consequent upon their choices about how to live and relate to others. However, we are concerned to reveal that, while personal choices appear as increasingly autonomous and fluid, they are in fact closely connected to social conditions that continue to produce tensions and anomalies. There is a lack of congruence between policies based on how families *should* be and how they actually operate. But this does not mean that we want to abolish institutional supports for family life. Rather, we see the need for many forms of family experiences to be supported by policy frameworks in order to enhance autonomous choices in living arrangements. But for this to happen it is necessary to take seriously fluidity and change in family arrangements, rather than seeing change itself as something dangerous and undesirable.

We see the approach taken in this book as contributing to the development of recent theories on the family, notably by Giddens (1992) and Beck and Beck-Gernsheim (1995). While their interpretations of changes in family life have certain limitations (for example, Giddens's tendency to ignore the significance of children and Beck and Beck-Gernsheim's exclusive focus on heterosexuality (see Smart and Neale, 1999)), they establish families as agents of self-reflexivity, actively interacting with the wider environment. In their work families are not just a passive bedrock for wider structures in society, but a re-defined, fluid context for intimate relationships. This perspective is also close to the one outlined by Morgan (1996) where he develops the concept of 'family practices' as a way of expressing the de-institutionalization of the family and the blurring of the boundaries which have been assumed to separate families (or the private sphere) from other social institutions (or the public sphere). We discuss our understandings of families within this framework under three themes: (1) the stability of political rhetoric; (2) the diversifying practices of family life; and (3) the destabilizing of existing policy and research frameworks.

The Stability of Political Rhetoric

In the last decade, both in the UK and in the USA, there has been a growing public concern over what is happening to the family. This concern has been fuelled by conservative politicians and commentators who have seen changes in family life as bringing social disorder in their wake (e.g., Murray, 1990; Dennis and Erdos, 1993; Phillips, 1998). While there is a widespread consensus that society is undergoing a process of rapid and radical change, political rhetoric tends to claim that the family is an institution which must not change. The family is still supposed to stand outside and above economic restructuring, market forces and financial, legal, technological and political change, as a pillar of supposed stability. This political mantra on the family is not peculiar to Conservative governments but has also become a theme of New Labour in Britain. In his first major Conference speech after winning the General Election in 1997, the Prime Minister Tony Blair stated:

> We cannot say we want a strong and secure society when we ignore its very foundations: family life. This is not about preaching to individuals about their private lives. It is addressing a huge social problem. Attitudes have changed. The world has changed, but I am a modern man leading a modern country and this is a modern crisis. Nearly 100,000 teenage pregnancies every year; elderly parents with whom families cannot cope; children growing up without role models they can respect and learn from; more and deeper poverty; more crime; more truancy; more neglect of educational opportunities, and above all more unhappiness. Every area of this government's policy will be scrutinized to see how it affects family life. Every policy examined, every initiative tested, every avenue explored to see how we strengthen our families. (*The Guardian*, 1.10.97)

Strong families are, of course, seen as conjugal, heterosexual parents with an employed male breadwinner. Lone mothers and gay couples do not, by definition, constitute strong families in this rhetoric. On the contrary, they are part of the problem and part of the process of destabilizing the necessary fortitude of the proper family.

Blair's speech is typical of the political approach which acknowledges social change, while striving to hold fast to a model of family life which is associated with a particular cultural and economic moment in British history. Yet his emphasis on lone motherhood, absent fathers and a cycle of deprivation is clearly more a rhetorical device than a good reflection of typical family patterns. This point is important, because although family practices are changing, particularly over the life course, the amount of change within and across families is often exaggerated in popular rhetoric to achieve a specific political goal. We might, for example, be forgiven for imagining that the conjugal nuclear family was on the point of extinction. Yet in 1996 73 per cent of households were composed of heterosexual couples (with just under 90 per cent of these being married), 50 per cent of these households had children, and 40 per cent had dependent children (i.e., under 16 years). Only 9 per cent of households with dependent children were headed by lone parents (Office for National Statistics, 1997).

Notwithstanding the fact that family life may not have changed that dramatically, the political rhetoric sees this change as the slippery slope. Moreover, this alarmist device is potentially supported by changes in behaviour which may, in time, become trends which do signify major changes. Thus statistical indicators show that, although most people still marry and have children at some point in their lives, the average age at marriage has increased, and people have fewer children and become parents later in life. Women are now better educated, have greater control of their fertility, and may be becoming less enamoured of the triple burden of paid work, housework and childcare. The number of families living solely on a man's wage has dropped significantly in the late 1990s, with fewer people thinking that a wife's job is solely to look after the home and the family (Scott and Brook, 1997). As Blair suggests in his speech, it may be changes in attitudes, rather than in household composition, that are seen as so alarming and destabilizing.

Ultimately, statistical trends are contradictory. We might say that there is both continuity and diversity in family life at the end of the twentieth century. This means that although there is a numerical dominance in the form of two-parent families, this organization no longer defines so exclusively what it is like to live in a family, or what a family *is*. We live in a context where the normative European model of the conjugal couple living in a nuclear household is losing force. It is this ideological slippage that the political rhetoric seems to address just as much as actual shifts in family practices. Indeed, as Fox Harding (1996) has pointed out, government policies on families are contradictory in their implementation. The meaning of a family, the significance of marriage and the importance of genetic parenthood, for example, may all be treated differently in different areas of policy. Thus the Children Act prioritizes parenthood over marriage, but immigration law gives priority to legal marriage; laws regulating assisted reproduction repudiate the possibility of gay and lesbian parenthood, while adoption policy will allow for gay or lesbian (or single-parent) adoption. Yet at the rhetorical level there is little tolerance for this kind of diversity and although policies are contradictory, the lack of political commitment to diversity means that newer family practices cannot assume, or rely on, policy support. What support there may be, happens almost by accident. It is therefore, part of our argument that policy formulation needs to be more open to diversity, rather than, as Blair would have it, focusing on 'strengthening' the family which inevitably means prioritizing the conjugal heterosexual couple and their children.

New Family Practices

We have suggested that statistical trends on family life are contradictory and that statistical data does not reveal the complexity of the changes which may be occurring. This is both because family forms have moved away from a fixed or rigid notion of the 'proper' family and because, even inside traditionally structured families, new normative guidelines are emerging. At the turn of the twenty-first century in Western societies, most people no longer follow rigid set paths of living. Thus, because our biographies are not pre-given, new types and qualities of relationships have supplanted fixed models.

To account for changes in these fixed or rigid notions of the proper family, Morgan (1996 and in this volume) has proposed that a more appropriate focus should now be on *family practices*. This implies that individuals are *doing* family, instead of simply passively residing within a pre-given structure. For Morgan, these practices are routines that are not random and do not change suddenly. They are located in culture, history and personal biography and they change according to circumstances. Practices do not imply an opposition between structure and agency, but he acknowledges that there can be tensions between different and conflicting practices. Certain historical, social, cultural and policy contexts may increase tensions and the risks associated with certain family practices.

From our analysis of new family practices we argue that, contrary to those interpretations that insist that family links are being weakened, families remain a crucial relational entity playing a fundamental part in the intimate life of and connections between individuals. The more recently accepted narrative of the dynamics between family life and wider structures acknowledges that in the last half-century or so families have lived through considerable transformations in their composition and in the conditions under which they accomplish domestic labour, in the labour associated with the emotional growth and sociability of individuals, and in their forms of intimacy. The discursive construction of the *Happy Home* (Good Housekeeping Institute, 1955) in the 1950s placed the traditional family as the ideal model of how things were, supposedly before change (namely, decline) began. But, as Nicholson (1997) has argued, the 1950s' family was itself quite a new model where households were slimmed down to contain only spouses and 2–3 children, and where the home was constructed as a site of leisure and consumption (Cowan, 1983). The fordist model of production which dominated production throughout most of this century was based on male labour with earnings high enough to enable the purchase of consumer durables and equipment for the home, and to allow housewives to stay at home in order to do the caring activities needed by husbands and children (as producers of the future and consumers). This model was based on an unequal interdependence of the conjugal couple and on women's lack of autonomy (Lefaucher, 1995). The 1970s' feminist debate on domestic labour focused on this particular social dynamic and revealed the hidden disadvantages for women (Gardiner, 1997). This model of labour and the wage system has been gradually superseded, giving rise to new forms of analysis of the changes taking place. In the 1990s, formerly core socio-economic analytical categories like *the capitalist* and *the worker* lost their analytical significance as feminist critiques developed and as the labour market itself changed in relation to changes in the domestic sphere. Terms such as service workers, professionals, flexible and casual labour, have become key categories in a new context where the physical components of the workforce are being replaced by intellectual, cultural and relational components. In the discourse of economics, the need for 'physical reproduction' demanded by the fordist model has given place to demands for the 'reproduction' of intellectual and emotional 'capital'. It has become increasingly important to achieve qualifications, to obtain diplomas, and to upgrade and update one's labour skills. In this transformed context, the importance of families as agents of emotional support and transmitters of cultural capital has increased. On the other hand, these transformations have reduced the pressures for the maintenance solely of a legal, conjugal link. In a way, it is not just that the power of economic structures to shape family practices has changed, but that the ways people live and how they make their living (as well as who makes that living) have also shaped economic and social structures. Thus we have come to transcend the old sociological presumption that the institution of the family changes only in response to primary changes in the economic sphere. Now we are more inclined to look for the interplay between sections of the labour market or welfare and changing forms of intimacy. For instance, women's social and economic status has become less dependent on the status of her husband (if she has one). For a woman to have a professional lifestyle she does not need to marry a professional but only to obtain a suitable degree or diploma. More and more women have understood that this is a much more secure route to a decent standard of living than marriage can provide. And if this woman found that her marriage did not provide the expected satisfactions in terms of identity, affection, and sexuality, she could leave the marriage. She might lose her illusions, her home, and some of the time she might have wanted to spend with her children, but she would not lose her job, her pension or the vital currency of her professional qualifications.

In this new scenario, the family appears as a context of fluid and changeable relationships, as well as a site of intimacy and emotional growth not only for children but also for the adults. In a world where the individual becomes a central reference point (Beck, 1992), families help in the constitution of personal autonomy. Post-modern (or post-fordist) families are positioned to provide for the satisfaction of emotional and material needs (even though not all families do this). Families endure, or are transformed, according to whether they continue to serve these needs. Of course choices about whether to sustain or to transform intimate relationships are not unconstrained or inconsequential. The possibility of satisfying the desire for personal growth and autonomy varies according to the available cultural and economic capital possessed by each individual, in terms of age, gender, professional qualifications, position in the labour market, sexual preferences, parental obligations, and so on. Personal scripts are written in the context of the different social and economic locations of families, as well as individuals, within wider social structures. But there is now more than one normative guideline to provide the context for these choices. Moreover, social class, gender, sexuality, age and ethnicity no longer operate as inevitable or one-dimensional pre-determining aspects of these normative guidelines.

Only recently has mainstream sociological analysis of family life and intimacy begun to reject the traditional presumption that the family is an institution which is separate from other social institutions. This boundary has been referred to as the boundary between the private sphere and the public sphere. Certainly feminists in the 1970s and 1980s were highly critical of this false analytical distinction but only in the 1990s has it become more widely accepted that the family is not best analysed as an 'institution' and that it is not in practice separated from other social processes. This newer understanding has clear repercussions for what is meant by family and for our understanding of the supposed boundaries between families and the public sphere. We want to explore these issues by reference to the contributions in this book in order to show how they take forward this new understanding in a range of empirical and theoretical work.

'Doing' Family Life

As we suggest above, there has recently been considerable debate about the usefulness of the concept of *the family* as a category of analysis (Morgan, 1996; Bernardes, 1997). The studies in this book corroborate the growing consensus that diverse patterns of family life exist and that notwithstanding this, people still define particular aspects of their lives as 'family life' and feel committed to families (Bernardes, 1987; Finch and Mason, 1993; Morgan 1996). A major change in the concept of family is that it has come to signify the subjective meaning of intimate connections rather than formal, objective blood or marriage ties. This subjective appreciation binds together people who live in separate households for part of the time, or all the time, as well as people who have legal links, or people who simply choose to belong together as a family.

In this context of fluid and changing definitions of families, a basic core remains which refers to the sharing of resources, caring, responsibilities and obligations. What a family is appears intrinsically related to what it does. All the studies in this book suggest that while there are new family forms emerging, alongside new normative guidelines about family relationships, this does not mean that values of caring and obligation are abandoned. On the contrary, these are central issues which continue to bind people together.

The traditional sociological understanding of the family as a separate sphere is challenged by the data and the literature analysed here by Sarah Irwin. The intermeshing of family practices and patterns of paid employment is reflected in the re-ordering of gendered positions in the 'caring' activities in households (referred to by Irwin as 'social reproduction'). It is essential to look very closely at the interiority of family life to understand how these relationships are shifting. But the context in which new forms of intimacy emerge has broader connections. One such connection is with technologies in the home. Elizabeth Silva identifies housework firmly as a caring activity, and she argues that those who carry out the activities of care-as-housework have changed historically, both in terms of social class and gender. While this has changed the activities of individuals within families, the social devaluation of care has influenced the pattern of innovation of technologies for the home. Household technologies may be regressive in that they valorize such ideals as the doting, dependent wife and mother, but they can also create alternative patterns for relationships in households.

The focus on the idea of 'doing' family as opposed to 'being' in a family demands participation and renewed commitment from individuals. While it is recognized that male power in the family has not changed significantly and that men's share of housework-as-care remains very small, the sharing of housework and parenting exemplified by normative heterosexuality appears to be increasingly challenged by lesbian and gay relationships. Those outside the heterosexual matrix may more often tend to be conscious agents of change. In gay and lesbian intimate relationships there are no traditional normative guidelines about gender inequalities and differences. Gill Dunne is concerned with the negotiations in lesbian households and how everyday living can be shifted towards more egalitarian arrangements. Of course she acknowledges that lesbians need to negotiate differences to avoid inequalities, but she argues that, in the context of greater recognition of women's traditional areas of work and influence, more harmonious ways of living are possible. Along the same lines, Weeks, Donovan and Heaphy find that chosen and consciously created intimate relationships are part of a process of self-invention, in a context of negotiated arrangements for everyday living. The distinctiveness that they find in same-sex households may increasingly be shared by newly emergent patterns in heterosexual relationships where commitment may be a matter of negotiation, rather than ascription.

A particular site for the exploration of how relationships between couples, kin and children are shifting is in the forms of parenting developed in post-divorce families. Here the idea of family as nuclear is dissipated as parents and children live in different households. Carol Smart shows that the kinds of parenting relationships desired by recent legal and family policy are extremely difficult because shared parenting does not usually exist prior to relationship breakdown. These policies underestimate the difficulties of establishing joint parenting after divorce in a context where it is virtually impossible for the majority of women and men during cohabitation. She argues that more attention must be paid to issues of responsibility (who takes it?), identity (are motherhood and fatherhood changing?), and ultimately to the question of citizenship and the extent to which caring for others diminishes citizenship status.

The idea of negotiating relationships challenges the very conception of *broken* families. The family ties of step-kin explored by Bornat, Dimmock, Jones and Peace indicate that feelings and emotions towards particular individuals count more than formal or legal links. But they argue that the labour of care needed to sustain these relationships is basically done by women. Obviously there are various languages of care employed by women. While some emphasize independence, others stress connectedness, and more than one idea of how one *does* family life emerged in their interviews. The choice of investment in caring is a moral choice, and women typically exercise their moral agency by building and sustaining family ties.

Different ways of building and maintaining family connections are a particularly significant feature of Caribbean families. Mary Chamberlain argues that for these families the conjugal relationship is not always the most important organizing principle of family life. Yet it has been the very primacy of this conjugal tie in dominant white rhetoric and policy which has led to the stigmatization of Afro-Caribbean families as anarchic and dysfunctional. Chamberlain's work therefore shows the importance of shifting the focus of analysis away from the conjugal relationship on to siblings, aunts and uncles, in order to illustrate the significance of other dynamics in family life. At the same time she reveals the narrowness of popular and political visions in contemporary Britain of how families *ought* to be lived.

Blurring the Boundaries of Families

It has become a popular methodological tool in research on families and childhood to ask respondents to draw maps of their families, or to locate family members on a set of concentric circles. This method has its roots in both psychometrics and social work practice and it was meant to be a diagnostic tool to measure social integration and family relationships. The adult who placed friends closer than kin might be defined as having some kind of pathology, and the child who drew more than one family would certainly be seen as incipiently problematic. However, these tools are currently being used in less prescriptive ways in contemporary research. The identification of 'friends' as 'family' is not seen as a pathology but as a reflection of how the subjective meaning of family is changing and how individuals may be shifting their locus of intimacy and support away from kin towards other people. In some instances the maps which are produced are a long way away from the idealized picture of mother, father and two siblings, and even where the standard stock of kin appear within the circles, others now may find a place, disrupting the taken-for-grantedness of primacy of blood and marital relationships.

From these maps appear new arrangements such as 'families of choice' (Weston, 1991), parenting across households (Maclean and

Eekelaar, 1997), single-parent families, step-families, and many more. We do not yet have names for many of these arrangements. What, for example, is the name for the relationship between a sperm donor (/ biological father) and a child with whom he does not live but with whom he has a good, companionate relationship? What is the name for the relationship between the children conceived in prior relationships but who live together under one roof because their parents have decided to cohabit (but not to marry)? What is the name of the relationship between a child and the woman who provided the genetic material to her birth mother to allow her to be conceived? It is interesting that a new vocabulary is not in fact emerging to deal with these new relationships. Rather, what seems to be occurring is that the notion of family is being stretched to cover everything. This can be understood in two competing ways. Using the concept of family to cover such a variety may simply obscure the changes which are occurring and create an impression that little is really happening. On the other hand, as Morgan argues, it could be that there is a resistance to giving up the qualities associated with the idea of 'family' such as caring, responsibility, intimacy, and loving, particularly in a culture which still devalues other kinds of relationship. But this stretching of the concept of the family also means that the sharp boundaries which are presumed to exist between *proper* families and less desirable families can no longer operate, either conceptually or politically. Using the concept of family in this new sense may ultimately carry wide political connotations by dissolving the idea that only one kind of family (namely the heterosexual, conjugal family) can produce moral, autonomous, but caring citizens. Accepting diverse forms of intimacy and caring as legitimate forms of family life will de-centre the nuclear family through a process of gradual cultural change.

Everyday experiments in family practices have thus begun to challenge the normative structures of family life. The sort of changes identified in this book reflect shifting moral subjectivities and moral rationalities both at the level of individuals and at the level of wider cultural significance. Normative guidelines are thus developing at the level of personal experiences of intimacy, often framed against more traditional established 'rules'. The question that this then raises is what are the implications of these new family practices for policy?

'New' Families/'New' Policies?

The contributions by David Morgan and Julia Brannen provide vital reflexive chapters which frame the debates arising from the empirical work featured in the intervening chapters of this book. Morgan focuses on questions of theorizing the family and allows us to begin to ask different questions in our future research. His work reveals how important it is to refrain from asking the same old questions about caring, relationships, intimacy and kinship at a time when society is undergoing substantial change. Brannen focuses more on questions of the politics of research and the problems of allowing a policy agenda to frame research questions. Her focus is on children and childhood and, while she acknowledges the importance of recognizing children's agency in families, she cautions against an uncritical acceptance of a 'new' interest in the lifestyles of children which may obscure longer-standing concerns about child poverty and the growing restrictions placed on children's lives by urbanization, inadequate educational provision, impoverished housing stocks and so on. Why, we might ask, is so much attention given to researching the consequences of divorce for children and so little on the effects of poverty on child health?

The questions raised by Brannen are pivotal. While family practices may be diversifying and while childhood too may be being transformed by these changing experiences and patterns of intimacy, we cannot ignore the broader policy context in which these insights arise. We have pointed out above that political rhetoric from left and right has tended to idealize a particular family form. The extent to which policy in practice carries through this rhetoric is another matter however. Various fiscal measures, divorce laws, protections against domestic violence, the abolition of illegitimacy and so on, have all produced a complex picture which makes it difficult to identify a clear policy (or even set of policies) for families. This ambiguity has arisen in part as a consequence of the diversification of family practices and yet it is clear that the moral rationale for most family policies remains rooted in a Beveridge-style model of a male breadwinner with dependent wife and children.

The question that is posed by reframing our conceptual apparatus such that we come to accept diversity in family life is, of course, what should the future policy agenda look like? How long can policies on family life go on imagining the nuclear family as the only relevant form or legitimate basis for policy measures? How long can politicians go on hoping that family life will revert to a model based on the 1950s, before it becomes apparent that a newer conceptualization and concomitant moral rationale is needed for the welfare state?

We have suggested that families 'are' what families 'do', rather than relying on an institutional definition of The Family. This might start to provide a new basis for policy and welfare measures. Thus, instead of linking benefits, taxes and pensions to marriage, they might be linked to practices of care. Rather than dividing the population into categories of 'the self-sufficient worker', 'the dependent carer', and 'the dependent recipient of care', we need to recognize that one person might be each of these things during the life course. Thus what is needed is a welfare provision which smoothes the transitions and does not *fix* the individual into one supposedly discrete category. We might start to wonder why it has become so economically risky for an individual to engage in caring and why we have developed a labour market which is so intolerant of

caring activities. What moral values underpin a system of paid employment and welfare provision which inflicts future poverty (in the form of
inadequate pensions and low pay) on those who care for others or who
need care themselves at some stage in their lives? The economic and
cultural transformations of modern post-industrial societies mean that
marriage cannot resume its former location as a structural support for
the provision of care. It is increasingly vital for individuals to have direct
access to an income for at least part of their lives and it is increasingly
risky for women to imagine that marriage offers any kind of economic
security at all. It is clear that men are increasingly unwilling to support
dependants, at least if they live in other households, and there is a
growing intolerance of mothers who wish to make childcare their 'job' if
they do not have a partner to support them.

Framing questions for policy in this way enables us to move away from
an analysis of social transformation which locates the 'blame' for
changing family structures in the emergence of 'new' families. Popular
rhetoric blames lone mothers, working mothers, gay and lesbian families
and so on for undermining the *proper* family. It does not understand that
the idealized nuclear family simply cannot work, either across the whole
of the life course or on a universal basis, any more (if it ever did of
course). Moreover, this rhetoric adds to the negative evaluation of diverse
forms of family life by linking them with the abandonment of traditional
morality and ignoring the extent to which they continue to operate within
the moral realm of care and care-giving (Tronto, 1993; Sevenhuijsen,
1998). If we return to the theme of Blair's speech which we outlined at the
start of this chapter, we can see the extent to which he was presenting
ideas immersed in the assumption that only the nuclear family produces
moral citizens. He therefore concluded that the (nuclear) family needed
strengthening. It might have been more appropriate if he had concluded
that economic and cultural supports for 'caring' needed strengthening. In
that way he might have started to address more accurately the issue of
what families 'do' rather than the increasingly less significant issue of
what form they take. This in turn might have led to more radical policy
discussions about how to sustain diversity in family life rather than
continuing the negative rhetoric about 'new' families.

2

RISK AND FAMILY PRACTICES: ACCOUNTING FOR CHANGE AND FLUIDITY IN FAMILY LIFE

David H.J. Morgan

Modern family life is often characterized in terms of flux and fluidity and this may be a matter of concern or a cause for celebration. This chapter explores two ways of conceptualizing this fluidity, one which looks at family living in terms of practices and the other which starts from a perspective which emphasizes risk. Both of these approaches stress that while the idea of the family or the lived experiences of family life may well be useful points of departure, they should not necessarily be seen as points of conclusion as well. In the case of the analysis in terms of practices, I argue that the use of the term implies, among other things, a recognition that family life can be considered through a variety of different lenses and from different perspectives. Thus, family practices may also be gender practices, class practices, age practices and so on. This point is made in order to stress that family life is never simply family life and that it is always continuous with other areas of existence. The points of overlap and connection are often more important than the separate entities, understood as work, family, politics and so on. This approach departs from the more functional or systems-theory analyses which require the family to be a relatively bounded unit exchanging with other, equally relatively bounded, units.

In the case of the approach which began with considerations of risk, the initial point of departure was not a conceptualization of the family, but rather a reflection on some of the distinctive characteristics of a late modern society. Here the idea of risk, often global in its scope, seems to subsume traditional bounded family units while individualization, another feature of late modernity, would seem to undermine such entities from within. Yet the outcome is not necessarily a simple and stark opposition between the individual and the risks created by an

increasingly globalized economy. Out of the double erosion of conventional models of the nuclear family-based household, there emerge
more fluid ways of understanding and transcending this opposition
between individual and collectivity. The tendency towards 'do-it-
yourself' biographies does not necessarily lead to the parallel life courses
of sets of relatively atomized individuals. Rather, these biographies are
woven together, often loosely and for short periods of time, in the face of
the fluidities and uncertainties of what Beck (1992) has described as 'risk
society'. Again, while family and household may be points of departure,
we need to follow up the various leads that take us from the family
networks and households into wider and more flexible networks.

In contrast, many more popular or policy-orientated accounts of
modern family life lack this sense of openness and fluidity. Such
accounts often begin, and sometimes end, with lists. These lists include a
variety of elements: increasing rates of divorce and cohabitation;
increasing proportions of lone-parent and single-person households;
decreasing rates of marriage and so on. The elements included and their
ordering may vary although it is likely that the above-mentioned would
appear on most such lists. When confronted with such an array, the
reader is invited:

1   To view the items on that list, taken separately and especially in
    conjunction, as being in some way problematic.
2   To view the items as belonging together, as forming some kind of
    overall package. In other words they are not a set of more or less
    random facts about the modern family. In some cases there might be
    causal linkages between some individual elements (divorce rates
    and re-constituted households and lone parents, for example) but
    more generally we are invited to view these items as signifiers of
    some underlying set of causes (or perhaps a single cause) or as a
    series of symptoms of some deeper social disorder.
3   To identify the analysis of the modern family with the assemblage of
    such information, information that can be readily tabulated and
    quantified. Scientific family analysis is presented as the establish-
    ment of trends and generalities, at some distance from their
    individual manifestations. In a true Durkheimian fashion, it is not
    your divorce or my divorce but divorce rates that count.

Such constructed facts pervade a wide range of writings about, and
pronouncements on, the family, from public religious or political statements, through the summaries that accompany the relevant sections in
Social Trends into and including more theoretical analyses of modern
family life. The more theoretical accounts both reflect and constitute the
changes under consideration. The choice of whether to write about
'change', 'decline' or 'de-institutionalization' does not simply arise from

the facts as presented but goes a long way towards constituting such facts and their subsequent interpretations.

The 'facts' about modern family living thus presented provide a notion of a unified topic, where the items coalesce in some form of coherent whole and where this constituted whole, 'the family', implicitly rules out a range of other possible considerations. Thus family living is 'about' relationships between spouses (including divorce), between parents and children, close or distant, or the responsibilities that individuals take, or refuse to take, for their kin. Conventionally, in these list-based accounts, family living is not about hospital waiting lists, size of classrooms or the availability of public transport. Yet such matters, in the experiences of individual members, may be at least as much to do with routine family living as the matters subsumed under the statistical tables. These approaches, in terms of 'practices' and 'risk', seek, in different ways, to overcome the gap between some of the more formal or statistical analyses of family life and everyday experiences and understandings.

Practices

My themes, therefore, deal with flux, fluidity and change. It is important, however, to realize that these themes exist at two related but theoretically distinct levels. In the first place, I am talking about actual practices on the part of family members and those accounts which present themselves as aggregations or statistical summaries of these individual practices. In the second place, I am talking about accounts or descriptions of such practices. I am immediately aware of the difficulties of such a distinction, in particular the question of whether practices can exist apart from their descriptions. To talk, say, about 'family rituals' is in part to constitute such rituals as sets of linked and repeated activities which are somehow linked to families. However, it seems important to preserve something of what is implied by such a distinction. Thus, if we were to argue that modern family living is characterized by considerable diversity, this diversity might refer to different modes of living (different life courses, different household compositions and so on) or to diversities in accounting for, describing or presenting modern family life. Thus one group might talk about decline, another of change, another of de-institutionalization and yet another might refer to both continuities and changes. It is important to preserve such a distinction and a sense of the flow and interchange between the two aspects. Some accounts of post-modernity would seem to collapse or conflate the levels of everyday experience and practice with the more abstracted descriptions of these practices.

In the conclusion of a recent book, I attempted to develop the idea of 'practices' as a way of looking at modern family living (Morgan, 1996).

Such an approach derived from a range of scholarly influences – inter-actionist, feminist, post-modern theorizing and so on – and was designed to develop what Stones was later to call a 'past-modern' sociology, in this case applied to modern family living (Stones, 1996). The kinds of list relating to family life cited at the beginning of the chapter, together with much of the theorizing that derived from or commented upon these lists, could be seen as an illustration of the kind of modernism which has, by and large, dominated much writing on the family. In such lists, the reader is invited to make a relatively untroubled passage from the statistics, charts, pie-diagrams and what-have-you to the realities of modern family life. Such an approach is 'modern' in its apparent direct appeal to scientific knowledge and facts as against anecdote or prejudice. A 'past-modern' sociology of family life would see such an approach as failing to do justice to the complexities of modern family living while being wary of a post-modernism that would threaten to empty sociological enquiry (of any kind) of any content. Thus, the assemblage of carefully collected 'facts' about family living is not to be despised but neither is it to be seen as the culmination of family analysis.

My elaboration of the notion of family practices was related to trends that I noted in the development of family theorizing and researching (e.g., Gubrium and Holstein, 1990). In place of an approach which defined a clear object of study – 'the family' – and sought to develop hypotheses and theories in relation to this object, I argued for something much more open. In this alternative approach, family was to be seen as less of a noun and more of an adjective or, possibly, a verb. 'Family' represents a constructed quality of human interaction or an active process rather than a thing-like object of detached social investigation. It should be possible to take a variety of other foci of social enquiry such as work, gender, stratification, the body and so on, and explore the ways in which these areas could be seen to have a family dimension to the mutual enrichment of both areas of study. My approach was to see 'family' as being rather like a primary colour, interesting in itself in a somewhat limited way, but achieving its real significance in combination, under-going repeated variation, with other colours. Such an approach might go some way to avoiding the reification which Bernardes, among others, has identified with much writing on the family and which, it has been argued, has not only smoothed over the complex realities of family living but has sometimes had adverse consequences for policy discussions (Bernardes, 1997). In at least some political usages of the term 'family' there was a kind of slippage, deliberate or otherwise, from the use of this single term to the construction of some kind of normative standard of family living, compared with which other family practices may be seen as being more or less deviant.

At the same time, the continuing use of the word 'family', albeit in a somewhat transformed way, recognizes the fact that 'family', however conceived, is still a matter of some importance for large sections of the population. This importance is not confined to those for whom 'family' might be part of their stock-in-trade, such as journalists, clergy, politicians and various professionals including family sociologists. The importance lies in the fact that family matters remain popular topics of everyday conversation, conversations which themselves reflect abiding concerns with some of the most joyful and the most painful aspects of everyday living. To abandon talk of 'family' altogether would be to deny the realities of these experiences and the importance which social actors assigned to them.

In very general terms the use of the term 'practices' is intended to convey a range of related themes:

1   *A sense of interplay between the perspectives of the social actor, the individual whose actions are being described and accounted for, and the perspectives of the observer*. The addition of the latter to the former serves as a reminder that there are, potentially, a range of different perspectives, interpretations or understandings available. I see a man, a woman and two children playing together in a park and I constitute them as a family. Later observations or questioning would reveal that they were indeed parents and children (and not neighbours who were taking the children out while their actual parents were out Christmas shopping) and that they did understand themselves to be 'a family'.

2   *A sense of the active rather than the passive or static.* Whatever the topic, the emphasis is upon doing class, doing gender, doing family. Even something apparently passive, such as sleeping, might be constituted as 'doing' family in that the sleeping arrangements, shared or separate beds or bedrooms, both constitute and derive from notions of family and proper conduct between family members.

3   *A focus on the everyday.* With practices we are concerned with the relatively routine or trivial, not necessarily to the exclusion of more weighty matters but rather in the realization that it is often in the routine or the trivial that some of the wider concerns are understood or constructed. What you had for breakfast today and how you consumed that breakfast may tell the observer as much about your routine understandings of family living as the more dramatic events such as weddings and funerals.

4   *A stress on regularities.* This is linked to the previous point and also reminds us of one of the other meanings of 'practice' in the English language, that is of repeated activities designed to improve a particular skill. However, it should be stressed that, in contrast to the deliberate and conscious improvement of skills implied in this usage, many of these regularities with which we are concerned constitute part of the everyday taken-for-granted worlds of the social actors concerned. The breakfasting practices referred to in the previous point may initially be the response to guides to healthy

eating but later become woven into the everyday and unexamined flow of normal family living.

5   *A sense of fluidity.* Practices, routinely, are not bounded. They flow into other practices of the same kind or mix with other practices that might be differently described. Thus a family outing might consist of a variety of different family practices while also blending with gendered practices, leisure practices and so on. Further, the family outing may well be linked in the perceptions of the participants to other such outings, to anticipated future outings and the planning involved in each case.

6   *An interplay between history and biography.* While the account of practices up to this point might seem to focus too much upon the here and now, it is also important to realize that practices have a societal and an historical dimension as well. For example, 'family outings' are part of the interwoven life courses of individuals but are also located in a wider historical framework to do with the development of leisure, transportation and shifting constructions of parenthood and childhood.

This discussion so far could apply to practices in general or to any specific sets of practices which might be described as work practices, gender practices, leisure practices and so on. Illustrations have been provided of what might be assumed to be 'family practices'. Yet what is 'family' about all these diverse activities? In other words, what work does the word 'family' do in the context of talking about 'family practices' as opposed to practices in general?

First, we are concerned with those practices which are constructed as being about family. We may consider three sets of agencies that might be said to be involved in the business of constructing family practices, although not necessarily equally. In the first place, there are the social actors themselves – the parents, spouses, kin, children – who see their activities, individually and collectively, as having something to do with family. This is not simply a recognition that such activities are to do immediately or directly with 'their' family, however that may be defined. It is also that there are some linkages made between their activities and more general notions of family. A fictional illustration comes from the soap opera *EastEnders* where characters frequently state 'but we're family' (May, 1997). A classic sociological example comes from Voysey's account of couples with handicapped children and how they routinely deploy notions of normal family living as they go about their day-to-day business of coping (Voysey, 1975). In a somewhat different context, persons in non-heterosexual households may deploy the label of 'family' while simultaneously expressing the distance between their situation and 'normal' family living (Weeks et al., this volume). In this case we see that notions of 'family' are rarely static but are constantly subjected to processes of negotiation and re-definition.

Also involved in the work of family construction are more abstract agencies such as professionals, writers of advice columns, people who frame or enact legislation, feminist and other critics, religious leaders and so on. These agencies, who do not necessarily speak with a single voice, make distinctions between family and non-family, between true and false or between functional and dysfunctional families. These accounts and the work of the various political and moral agencies have their own histories, often drawing upon the actual or ideal experiences of families in the past. Such accounts may be influential in the practices of individual family members, or may become the cultural resources upon which they draw in giving meaning to their own activities. Thus part of the 'reflexiveness' of modern life (the subject of the next section) is the explicit monitoring of one's own routine practices against some standard of normality. These standards might be constructed by these various professionals and others and mediated through repeated discussions in newspapers, magazines and radio or television programmes.

The construction of family practices involves another agent, one often forgotten in discussions of social constructionism. This is the observer, in this case the sociologist. Routinely, the expectation is that these observer constructions should in some ways match and derive from those of the actors whose practices are being constructed in this way. Thus, if a sociologist describes a set of activities (bathing a child, cutting a hedge, telephoning a doctor) as 'family' practices, we would expect that the actors would see these activities in this way also. However, there are occasions when such convergence is difficult or impossible, where, for example, we are dealing with historical sources. Further, even where disagreement is both possible and present, it does not necessarily mean that the sociological account is invalid. The perspectives of observers and observed will necessarily differ in some respects since they are engaged on different projects. What is important is that there should be some free flow between the two.

Thus, 'family practices' are those practices described as being in some measure about 'family' by one or more of the following: individual actors; social and cultural institutions; the observer. However, while this might satisfy the cognitive dimension of family living, it less adequately deals with the more emotional or evaluative side which is involved when the word 'family' is used. Put crudely, family practices are not just any old practices; they are also practices which matter to the persons concerned and which are seen in some way as being 'special' or 'different'. To 'mean' something to somebody is not simply to be able to identify, but also to invest that object of identification with a degree of emotional significance. It should be stressed that this emotional/evaluative aspect need not be positive; in family matters, as many have noted, we are dealing with love and hate, attraction and repulsion, approval and disapproval.

The sources of this 'special' character of family living might be discussed at length. In part we are talking about 'the families we live by', the ideological constructions of how family life ought to be and is re-enacted in family myths and rituals (Gillis, 1997). These images of the family, in contrast to the 'families we live with' are often presented as having a timeless quality although their historical origins, often quite recent historical origins, can frequently be traced. The close links with life, death and sexuality, traditionally also matters of concern to the church and state, are also part of the story although again it has to be stressed that these seemingly changeless events exist, and are given meaning, within particular historical contexts. We may also point to the particularly strong location of families and households in time, linking across generations and creating bridges between individual times and life courses and historical time (Morgan, 1996). In numerous ways, therefore, family practices come to have strong, but not unchallengeable, associations with our wider understandings of the world and the way in which individuals live their lives.

One implication of a shift to talking about 'family practices' may be added. This is that family practices are not necessarily practices which take place in times and spaces conventionally designated to do with 'family', that is the home. It is possible to see paid work outside the home as constituting part of family practices. Further, a gendered under-standing of 'family practices' might recognize that these are being done by men as they absent themselves from family settings or responsi-bilities. Such practices, even if they seemingly have nothing to do with the family (working late in the office, attending a union meeting, drinking with mates on the way home from work) are family practices in that they reinforce certain constructions of fatherhood and, by implication, motherhood as well.

This recognition that 'family practices' may take place outside the home may be linked to frequently made assertions about the centrality of the family in society; such assertions, after all, maintain that the family is not a concern of its 'members' alone. The first point to make about such assertions is that they are, themselves, family practices. In other words, claims about the centrality of family life are practices which address themselves in a strong way to the idea of the family and which are intended to be influential and persuasive. Further, such assertions may often become part of the routine understandings of individual actors as they go about their family practices. This is not in the crude sense of ideological indoctrination. Rather, it is more in the sense of social actors using culturally available rhetorics about the family in order to account for their own practices. 'The family comes first' is frequently a powerful argument with few effective counters (Jordan et al., 1994).

The use of the term 'practices' is not, of course, entirely original. Its usage may be found in other writings, most notably in the work of

Pierre Bourdieu (1977, 1996). The influence of Bourdieu in my own writings was somewhat indirect, although I find that there are some overlaps in the usages. His concern is to transcend what he sees as an unhelpful divide between objectivist and subjectivist social anthropological accounts and to shift from research projects which focus upon modelling rules of social action to one which is much more concerned with everyday strategies. Thus a sense of honour is distinct from the more abstract rules of honour. Reading the 'Highway Code' is different from routinely reading the actual road and other road users. In the area of kinship he is concerned with a contrast between official and practical kin, the latter being 'continuously practised, kept up and cultivated' (Bourdieu, 1977: 37). While his approach might seem close to that of ethnomethodologists, he argues that he does not wish to confine his analysis to inter-personal activity. Such relationships are never just individual to individual; 'the truth of the interaction is never entirely contained in the interaction' (ibid.: 81). Family interactions may contain a lot of improvisation but the props and resources that facilitate such improvisation derive from outside the immediate interactions of family members.

What comes across strongly in Bourdieu's writings (despite some obscurities) is a sense of the lived-in and taken-for-granted world. This world, in families as in anything else, is constantly being created and reproduced through the day-to-day activities of the members. The account is dynamic and complex:

> Thus the family as an objective social category (a structuring structure) is the basis of the family as a subjective social category (a structured structure), a mental category which is the matrix of countless representations and actions (e.g., marriages) which help to reproduce the objective social category. The circle is that of reproduction of the social order. (Bourdieu, 1996: 21)

What is perhaps missing here, and in other accounts, is a sense of the possibility of alternative or challenging formulations. Family life is not simply reproduced through its everyday practices; it may also be undermined. And one way in which this undermining may take place is through the fact that, in a modern society, there are frequently alternative ways of viewing the same practices. Family practices may be reformulated as gender practices, not only by the observer but also by those engaged in those routine practices. Thus to re-describe low levels of participation in domestic labour on the part of a husband as gendered activity, as part of the behaviour of men, rather than as behaviour routinely associated with the head of the household, is to present some kind of challenge to the domestic order which sustained the latter set of perceptions.

Various other usages may be indicated. Dorothy Smith's fusion of ethnomethodology and feminist perspectives, for example, makes use of the term: 'The emphasis is on the "how", and the notion of practices is intended to capture the ongoing of our doing what we, generally, know how to do' (Smith, 1987: 212). In a slightly, but only slightly, different vein, Gubrium and Holstein emphasize practice. 'It is *practice*', they write, 'that unifies ideas and things' (Gubrium and Holstein, 1990: 157, original emphasis). Yet again, Rodger's discussion of family paradigms and the way in which families construct their own realities has some affinities with the approach being suggested here (Rodger, 1996: 100–1). Doubtless, these examples could be multiplied. The point would seem to be that there is some kind of converging need for approaches that focus on the range of issues being discussed here and consider their points of overlap and intersection. Another approach which that seem to be more removed from the considerations outlined here is one which emphasizes risk.

Risk and Family Practices

If I am attempting to reformulate my discussion of modern family life in terms of family practices, this is not simply a consequence of developments in my thinking in isolation. As has already been suggested, the notion of 'practices' has been around for some time and several people, with different influences and different projects, may be found to be using the word. My usage derives, in ways which are both recognized and unrecognized, from these wider usages. At the same time, this increasing usage of the term 'practices' reflects, in some measure, real changes within the wider society. As with all social enquiry, there is an exchange between the developing theories and terminologies and the changing societies within which this terminology has evolved, partly in order to understand these self-same changes. If I wish to develop a terminology which attempts to capture a sense of fluidity and openness, this is not just a personal project but one located within a society which already manifests some of these characteristics.

As has been suggested, another word which is being used with increasing frequency and which reflects some similar issues is the word 'risk'. In his *Risk Society*, Ulrich Beck considers two aspects of what he calls 'reflexive modernization' (Beck, 1992). The first is to do with a long-term shift within societies where a former dominance of and preoccupation with wealth production has given way to the increasing dominance of 'risk production'. This has been an uneven shift but it may be seen in all kinds of manifestations. The heroic and spectacular achievements of industrial capitalism in terms of wealth creation, development of new cities, increasing applications of science and technology and so on have given way to increasing concerns about pollution, numerous risks to health and life, and apparent deteriorations of the quality of life. On the day when I am drafting this section, my copy of the *Independent* (5 August 1997) has on its front page the headline '6000 heart attacks a year from car fumes'. Turning to page 3, I find stories on 'CJD' and 'Alcopops'. There are, of course, also stories to do with wealth creation and distribution on later pages but the theme of risk is certainly a very prominent one.

The focus on risk deals with the more structural aspects of reflexivity (Lash, 1994: 116). By this is meant those processes and events within society that bring about a wider discussion of the character of the society which produced those events (the food scares, the pollution) and the kinds of interventions that might reduce the incidence of such events or modify their impact. At the level of self-reflexivity we have the familiar theme of 'individualization'. A variety of critical perspectives on modern societies have highlighted this aspect, although with different emphases and evaluations. At its simplest, the term refers to the growing stress on individual projects and the idea of the individual as the yardstick against which all projects and programmes are judged. Whether we are considering work, the family, leisure, sexuality, health or education, the stress would seem to be increasingly on the individual as the key unit and with this individual comes an emphasis upon the self, fulfilment, choice, rights and freedom. Such individualization should be seen as a social product and is therefore to be distinguished from the more philosophical idea of individualism.

The notion of reflexivity is linked to these themes of individualization in that the self and the individual become objects of self-monitoring. In some senses this may be seen as a secular equivalent of the 'moral bookkeeping' of the early puritans. Manifestations include calorie-counting and weightwatching, numerous popular psychological tests which monitor one's skills as a lover, a parent or an employer, and regular health checks. There may be links between this self-monitoring and wider societal processes of reflexivity, as, for example, where individuals consider their consumption or tourism in ethical terms.

This is not the place to develop a detailed critique of Beck's ideas of risk and 'reflexive modernization'. Much of his argument may seem familiar, some of it obscure, and there are questions to be raised about the connections between the various themes which he develops in this book. The links between the growing significance of 'risk' in modern society and the theme of individualization, for example, are hinted at rather than systematically explored. However, the idea of 'reflexive modernization', a sense of modernity which includes within itself a constant monitoring of its own practices in terms of risk and the individual, does have some affinities and overlaps with some of the ideas of practices being developed here.

Sometimes these overlaps may be fairly obvious:

But to determine the relationship between the sexes solely by what they appear to be – relations between the sexes involving the topics of sexuality,

affection, marriage, parenthood and so on – is to fail to recognize that besides
that, they are also everything else at the same time: work, professions,
inequality, politics, and economics. (Beck, 1992: 103)

Perhaps more striking is his reference, in a recent publication, to the
artist Kandinsky's discussion of the word 'And' (Beck, 1997a: 1). The
idea, which Beck elaborates at several points, is that the nineteenth
century was the century of 'Either/Or' whereas the twentieth century is
the century of 'And'. 'Either/Or' is associated with an early modern
scientific sensibility, stressing structures and classifications and sus-
picious of ambiguity. 'And' hints at the possibilities of alternatives, of
openness and fluidity. This sense of rigid structures and oppositions
being dissolved into overlaps and ambiguities has considerable affinities
with the usage of 'practices' being developed here. It is recognized, as
has been argued, that the description of a set of activities as 'family
practices' does not preclude other ways of describing or accounting for
these activities.

There are various other points in the argument where these connections, with family and family practices, may be traced or suggested.
Thus Beck writes of the 'negotiated provisional family' (Beck, 1992: 129).
This is a family life which depends less on traditional or external
prescriptions and more on the expectations and aspirations of the participants. One of his major themes is the overall shift from the 'standard
to elective biography', or the development in late modern times of a
'do-it-yourself biography' (ibid.: 135). In other words, one's life transitions are less frequently dominated by the stable regularities of
courtship, marriage, parenthood and so on, regularities which, for the
man at least, are, or were, woven into the orderliness of a career or a
working life.

No doubt other, specific, links and overlaps may be traced through a
careful study of Beck's writings. This is not the aim of this chapter.
Rather, it is argued that, despite some omissions and obscurities, the
ideas of individualization and risk, the twin themes of 'reflexive
modernization', help us to think critically about family practices.
Before proceeding with this exploration it may be useful to distinguish
between 'actual' risks and perceptions of risk, a variation of a point
made at the beginning of the previous section. The two are clearly
inter-related and there is, of course, a sense in which risks cannot be
detached from the perceptions or constructions of them. Debates about
the fear of crime, related to but not identical with actual crime, may be
taken as an illustration. In the case of risk more generally we have a
diffuse sense of risk perception and there are few areas of life now
untouched by a sense of calculation of the risks involved. Again, as in
the case of air travel, this diffuse sense of risk may contrast with more
sober or specialized analysis of risks. It may be a possible criticism of
Beck's argument that he failed to make an adequate distinction

between this diffuse sense of risk and actual risks and threats. However, both of these are implicated in this exploration of risks in relation to family practices. This exploration takes off from some of Beck's observations rather than simply re-formulating them in terms of the family.

First, it may be argued that risk, in both senses, serves to undermine more traditional, solid, established solidarities. This might be seen as the dominant way in which risk is implicated in family practices. Here, among any list of 'traditional solidarities', we would include a strong sense of 'family'. Risk, contaminated food, nuclear fall-out, acid rain or global warming, does not recognize the authority of the more established boundaries of nation, neighbourhood or family. A report by the 'Compassion in World Farming' group writes of the health risks associated with modern farming in these terms: 'It's no good blaming the poor housewife or whoever cooks the food. The problem is at source on the farm' (quoted in the *Independent*, 16 August 1997). Beck seeks to show how reflexive modernization undermined the close, interlocking links between family, class and social order, characteristic of early modern societies (Beck et al., 1994: 13). We may, as Beck does, contrast risk with wealth. Wealth can be seen as being mediated through family practices such as inheritance and family businesses. Even at some of the poorer levels where questions of property seem minimal, it may be argued that family or household-based strategies help to preserve whatever resources are available and to gain access to further, if limited, resources. Such family-based strategies would seem to be of little relevance in the face of the kinds of global risks with which we are increasingly familiar. Later in this section I shall qualify my argument. However, at this very general level, it does appear to be a plausible contrast between a positive and reinforcing set of inter-connections between wealth and family practices on the one hand and a tension between family practices and risk on the other. Repeated claims about the family as a fundamental unit of society would appear to refer to social orders where considerations of wealth and property were more dominant considerations.

It is worth noting the temporal dimension to this tension between family and reflexive modernization. What we sometimes call traditional families (although Gillis has reminded us that many of these traditions are of relatively recent origin (Gillis, 1997)) were clearly located in time, looking back to family-based heritages and, increasingly, forward through children and their hoped-for developments. It could be argued that the family constituted an important basis through which individuals came to understand temporality. Reflexive modernization calls into question the relevance of the past and raises even stronger questions about the future. The links between family and temporality become weakened through reflexive modernization.

Secondly, reflexive modernization may encourage individuals to invest more in inter-personal relationships:

> Individualization may drive men and women apart, but paradoxically it also pushes them back into one another's arms. As traditions become debated, the attractions of a close relationship grow. (Beck and Beck-Gernsheim, 1995: 32)

As against this, Giddens, in his analysis of intimacy in modern society, is critical of a simple reactive model whereby the quest for intimacy is seen as some kind of retreat from the threats and uncertainties of modern life (Giddens, 1992). His overall assessment and evaluation of the desire to invest more in pure relationships is generally more positive. To see the desire to invest more in inter-personal relationships as being simply a reaction against risk would run counter to Giddens's overall stress on the importance of individual agency.

There is certainly a difference of emphasis between Beck and Beck-Gernsheim and Giddens on this point. Nevertheless the apparent contrast between the uncertainties of the modern world and the reality, however fragile, of what Giddens calls 'pure relationships' does appear to be a popular one in modern culture. The relationship, as Beck and Beck-Gernsheim point out, is a paradoxical one since the dyadic character of the pure relationship does have its own inbuilt instabilities. The twin forces of reflexive modernization, risk and individualization, produce a need for the apparent securities of a relationship based upon the perceived characteristics of the other and the relationship itself, apart from any external or functional considerations. Yet it would appear that these same influences also suggest the real limitations of these possi-bilities. If risk and individualization together seem to encourage a search for pure relationships, those self-same forces can threaten and undermine those relationships.

In relation to the wider discussion of family practices and risk, the pure relationship does present certain problems. The inherent instability of the dyadic relationship is augmented by the fact that the pure relationship as constructed by Giddens is purely an adult relationship. Hence notions of relationships, in this strong sense, contrast with the complexities of family practices which cut across households and generations and which frequently include children as well as adults. If Giddens is correct, and pure relationships have become a central goal in late modernity, then this provides further evidence of the margin-alization of the experience of childhood in that society. Hence, in a risk society, the pursuit of individually based adult relationships may pro-vide further sources of instability for family-based practices. It is possible of course, that the idea of pure relationships, and their centrality in late modernity, is over-stated, and in this case the evidence points to a marginalization of children and childhood in sociological thought.

The third set of linkages between risk and family practices revolves around an argument that risks may be mediated through family prac-tices. The strongest argument here is probably one which focuses upon patterns of consumption, especially as these are practised within households. Indeed, it can be argued that patterns of consumption are intimately linked with the structure and distribution of households. Generally, it can be argued that it is not simply individuals who consume but, to a large extent, individuals as members or on behalf of households. This remains true even where the household under consideration is a single-person household.

The ways in which consumption practices are linked to issues of risk are numerous. They contribute to the use, and possible depletion, of the earth's resources and energy sources. They affect the spread of particular risks and hazards such as food impurities and contaminations. The disposal of packaging or obsolete models presents further environmental problems and risks. And certain aspects of consumption, especially the consumption of forms of home entertainment and information, may help to spread the perception of society as being risk-based. The developing understanding of a risk society requires a perception which sees overlaps between family, household and consumption practices and the way in which these contribute to the mediation of risk and the perceptions of risk.

However, fourthly, the perception of family and household practices as mediating risk also reminds us that, as was suggested earlier, individuals and households do not passively respond to or act as conduits for wider societal risks. The more personal lifestyles and individualized biographies may themselves include some element of deliberate risk management or action against sources of risk. At one end this may include support for, or membership of, groups or organizations opposed to some of the corporate or governmental sources of risk in our society. Middle-class support for opposition to the export of live animals or the extension of motorways has been the subject of some media comment in recent years and may perhaps be understood as part of the greater fluidity of everyday practices which has been the focus of this chapter. Older polarities between individualism and collectivism are not necessarily being transcended either through the choice of one end or the other or through the development of ideas of community or friendship, but rather through the steady development of a kind of fluidity in everyday practices that embraces, while transforming, both.

Risk management, of course, may not take the form of full-blown activism but may, instead, be more a question of responding to sources which may be trusted (books, newspaper articles, etc.) and adjusting one's lifestyle accordingly. This may be especially the case in the avoidance of, or expressed preference for, certain kinds of food but may also include other forms of ethical consumerism such as investments or travel. Modern recipe books, for example, not only produce recipes for meals which are exotic or tasty but include advice about food values, diet, organic food and sometimes about the wider ethical or political implications of one's food choices. This is not a dimension which quite fits into Warde's analysis of the 'antinomies of taste', although the polarity between 'health' and 'indulgence' captures some of the concerns of risk and food practices (Warde, 1997). In a variety of ways routine and evolving household practices might shade into consumption and politics at the same time.

It may also be noted that patterns of risk management within households and families may also undermine some traditional family-based practices or structures. The social distribution of knowledge, as Mannheim recognized, includes a generational dimension as well as a class and a gender dimension. Younger members of the family may be the source of knowledge about food additives or the global production of risks and households may have to adjust to the introduction of vegetarianism being adopted by younger generations. Vegetarians are more likely to be female (Beardsworth and Keil, 1992) and probably found among the younger age categories. Warde notes that there are few completely vegetarian households (Warde, 1997: 121), a finding that supports the idea of the individualization .of lifestyles as well as suggesting possible divisions within households along the lines that I have suggested.

Finally, the very idea of risk encompasses one particular way in which people talk about or understand their family and domestic practices. Knowledge about the proportion of marriages ending in divorce or about the impact of lone parenthood or divorce upon children's life chances are widely publicized and are presumably woven into individuals' biographies. Understandings of risk, whether accurate or not, are probably becoming part of the way in which individuals talk about or understand their family practices. Family practices, therefore, include a different kind of future orientation, one less optimistic and perhaps more fearful than the future orientations of the classic modern bourgeois family. The future is understood in terms of risks which may be identified as the responsibility of parents or partners or where, as in the case of drugs, alcohol abuse or AIDS, family members may perceive some degree of responsibility even where they are unable to provide a completely effective barrier.

Conclusion

Both the ideas of risk and the ideas of practices emerge at a time when there is an increasing need to capture the fluidity of modern life without abdicating the responsibility to attempt the imaginative understanding of the linkings of history and biography. It has also been suggested that there are widespread perceptions that family life is in some way important and distinctive and that these perceptions are not necessarily the property of moral entrepreneurs. The idea of practices ought to be able to take on board this understanding as being part of the way in which family life is routinely understood without signing up to any one normative model of family living. For social actors, the importance of family life lies in the actual practices, practices which inevitably overlap with other areas of life and other practices, rather than any supposed unit or structure. Family practices exist in the routine talk about family – family obligations, family duties, family constraints, family burdens and so on – as much as in any particular piece of activity, and more than any definitive structure. Family talk is family action, re-affirming or modifying the entity under discussion.

The idea of risk, on the other hand, would seem to belong to a different order of seriousness. It deals with issues of global significance which transcend not only family boundaries but also national and communal boundaries as well. But the idea of a society increasingly dominated by considerations of risk (considerations which include perceptions of an increasing riskiness of everyday life) is frequently and necessarily mediated through frameworks of understanding based upon individuals in households and social networks. Some of these may have family-type characteristics, while others may not.

There are two possible qualifications that needed to be inserted at this point. One is that it is possible to overstate the degree of fluidity and change in modern family living. The kinds of list referred to at the beginning of this chapter can readily be modified to present a picture of relative stability. An Editorial in the *Independent*, referring to an HMSO publication, *Social Focus on Families*, writes: 'Let it be shouted from the rooftops that the majority of children grow up in a family with two parents, that four of every five dependent children live in a "family" with a mum and a dad' (7 August 1997: 11). This is a useful corrective to the more popular jeremiads. But what we are perhaps concerned with are perceptions and modes of understanding. It is likely that fluidity has always been part of family living; in a sense, such fluidity is a necessity not an optional extra. It is perhaps that our modes of understanding family living have come closer to the realities of everyday experience and perception than some of the earlier models of functionalists or marxists.

The second qualification is that, as the above quotation suggests, there are always alternative versions as to what is going on and what should be going on. Beck refers to the trends of counter-modernization which seek to assert or solidify societal boundaries in the face of reflexive modernization which seeks to abolish them (Beck, 1997a: 62). These are sometimes not just differences of opinion but contested versions which are mobilized and which have real effects: versions of the 'moral majority', 'ethical socialism', assertive claims on the part of fatherhood, anti-abortion pressure groups and so on. The movement on the part of some American men called 'The Promise Keepers' is an apt reminder of these counter-modernizing tendencies. But this is what we might expect and notions of risk and ideas of practices seek to capture this sense of contest not just in terms of versions of what is, but also stronger claims about what should be.

The presence of risk in society and the increasing perceptions of the risks associated with everyday living provides, perhaps, one of the main reasons why nostalgic calls to recreate family or community will have little real effect. The flexibility of action and understanding required under conditions of reflexive modernity have little room for stable or traditional family units or communities if, indeed, these ever really existed. Yet there is no doubt that ties that extend beyond individuals will continue to be necessary as ways of coping with, responding to and perhaps exercising some measure of control over the risks with which we are all confronted. These ties will not necessarily be described in ways which correspond to conventional ways of understanding family, friendship, community or whatever, although they may have elements of all of these. The notion of practices attempts to capture a sense of family woven into the wider networks and practices of everyday life in a society characterized by risk and uncertainty.

3

RESOURCING THE FAMILY: GENDERED CLAIMS AND OBLIGATIONS AND ISSUES OF EXPLANATION

Sarah Irwin

A key development in the family in contemporary society is the modification of male claims to a breadwinner wage and a growth in the prevalence and importance of the financial co-resourcing of households. This development reflects important changes in women's and men's relations to paid employment and to the family and is suggestive of a re-ordering of gendered positions in the reproduction of social and economic life. Research in the area reveals two rather different perspectives on these changes. One is that they are bound up with a significant transformation in the nature of social relationships and ties. Here a rise in individualism and a decline in traditional gender status constraints are important aspects of social change at the turn of the twenty-first century. The other perspective specifically addresses women's position in employment and the family and concludes that continuity is the most salient feature of female experience in both those domains. However, processes underlying continuity and change in gendered positions in the family and in employment have not been satisfactorily addressed.

Recent decades have seen significant developments in family demography, including trends to deferral in the timing of family formation, declining fertility, a growing incidence of childlessness, rising divorce rates and an increase in the incidence of lone parenthood. A range of perspectives, popular, sociological and demographic, converge to suggest that new forms of diversity in family arrangements can be understood in terms of a growth in individualism and a change in the nature of the social, or moral ties that bind individuals and groups in contemporary society (e.g., Aries, 1980; Beck, 1992; Dennis and Erdos, 1993; Lesthaeghe, 1995; McRae, 1997). In these approaches it appears that we are witnessing an increase in individualism and that this is generating a new kind of marketized family in which prior social, or moral, arrangements are dissolved. The emphasis on individualism, or the changing relationship of the individual to the contemporary social environment, is seen to help account for new forms of diversity in family structure and, for some writers, a greater autonomy of individuals and freedom (or a new need) to be authors of their own biographies and lifestyles. Traditional status constraints with respect to gender are weakening and, in some versions, the commodification of female labour is paralleled by a growing contingency of family relationships. In conjunction, it appears that cultural changes have undermined traditional expectations about appropriate gender roles, and that female claims to independence have altered women's position, and relative power, within the family. A paradox which emerges from within the literature is that, while the initial emphasis is on the 'ties that bind' individuals and groups in the reproduction of social life, these social relations tend to recede in explanatory significance, either as economistic, marketizing processes become general, or as a new set of cultural norms come into play. Arguments of individualism suggest a diminution, or a growing contingency, of social ties.

The second approach takes women's relations to employment as a specific focus (e.g., Arber and Ginn, 1995; Glover and Arber, 1995; Harrop and Moss, 1995; Ward et al., 1996). Here there is a continuation of longer-standing concerns with the mutually reinforcing nature of women's position in the family and their position within employment. Again these spheres are seen to be interacting, but in a way which generates continuity in women's social location. Despite changes in some women's position within employment, the general experience of women is of relative economic disadvantage and vulnerability. The literature here emphasizes continuity in the shape and general extent of female disadvantage, and is a valuable corrective to assertions otherwise. Further, the notion that there is a weakening of gender status constraints looks less convincing in the light of this research. However, because research agendas are shaped by a concern with continuity in women's disadvantaged position with respect to employment rewards and opportunities, there has been relatively little engagement with changes in gendered *relations* in the organization of social reproduction. These comprise changes in women's and men's position with respect to household resourcing, and their relationship to patterns of access to and rewards from employment.

Within much research on gender and employment the domains of the 'social' and the 'economic', or family and labour market, are treated as distinct but interacting spheres driven by different dynamics. It is an argument of this chapter that the division between social and economic processes, as a description of family structure and employment organization, generates explanatory problems which are not readily addressed within current frameworks. An alternative approach challenges the view of social and economic processes as 'distinct-but-interacting' and theorizes the 'labour market' as itself a system of distribution which is predicated on social processes. In other words, people's differing social locations, and the patterning of claims and obligations that reproduce these locations, are embedded in the structure of access to and rewards from employment (Garnsey, 1982; Peattie and Rein, 1983; Humphries and Rubery, 1984; Irwin, 1995a, 1995b). Here change in divisions of labour in family resourcing and change in claims to employment are aspects of a single, coherent, dynamic. Drawing on such an approach, it is an argument of this chapter that we are witnessing change in the position of women and men in the reproduction of social life. A fundamental aspect of change in such family arrangements is the increased significance of female employment in the formal economy, and the associated modification of the breadwinner mode of household resourcing or more precisely a modification of male claims to a breadwinner wage, as the earnings of women as well as men become increasingly necessary to the resourcing of households. These developments do reflect important changes in the relative social position of women and men. However, they reveal not the ascendance of individualism or a triumph of market processes, but change in the relations of women and men to the reproduction of social life, both day to day and across generations.

Individualism and the 'New' Family

Across a wide literature on change in family demography people are either seen to become authors of their own fates, or they are seen to be experiencing fundamental changes in the kinds of constraint and social process which shape their choices and actions. A decline in traditional status constraints, and increasing female participation in paid employment, either together or apart, contribute to the transformation of familial and household relationships, and new forms of diversity emerge, for example the growth in the relative proportion of step-families, lone-parent families, childless couples and single-person households.

In a recent review of developments in demography and in the labour market, McRae suggests that one of the major causes of recent trends in cohabitation, marriage, fertility and divorce is '"the individualizing tendency" of participation in the labour market, together with the cultural values of individualization that both facilitate and reinforce this participation' (1997: 385). In concluding her review, McRae advances an outline agenda for research which should examine the trend towards individualization in both households and labour markets, an agenda which reflects the two 'spheres' which are foregrounded in many discussions of individualization and change in the family. McRae alludes to the approaches of economic and social demographers as a pointer to general themes which could help in the ordering and interpretation of recent trends in fertility, divorce and other aspects of family demography. It is pertinent to address some of the literature here, since it directly addresses the relationship between change in family demography and gendered claims to employment and independence.

Within economic demography, the approach of the New Home Economics school is of interest, given its advocates' engagement with the consequences of change in female employment patterns and earnings for changes in family demography (e.g., Ermisch, 1983; De Cooman et al., 1987). Here the gender division of labour in the household is understood as a strategy for maximizing well-being in the context of differential earnings between women and men. As women's wages rise relative to those of men the gain from the domestic division of labour diminishes and, for women, the opportunity costs of marriage and childbearing rise. This narrowing of wage differentials is consequently seen to generate demographic changes, including declines in fertility, trends towards delay in family formation, and increasing rates of divorce. Changes in the labour market thereby produce change in family relationships. As the advantages of the domestic division of labour diminish so the economic logic which ties men and women into given (breadwinning and unpaid caring) roles within the family dissipates and the conventional family form looks increasingly tenuous.

The approach is helpful in so far as it develops a framework which foregrounds the interaction of productive and reproductive processes. However, it is notable that the causal direction is all one way, from the former to the latter, and the approach elides the potential importance of demographic processes in the structuring of gender inequalities within employment. For example, long-term declines in family size, and the compressing of the period of women's lifetimes spent in childbearing are essential to understanding the increased participation of women in employment. It is therefore problematic to treat changes in employment processes as themselves independent of change in family structure (Irwin, 1995a, 1995b). Another associated problem is that the New Home Economics models take the domestic division of labour as a starting point, rather than as something requiring explanation. It is 'given' by an economic logic of differential earnings of women and men. However, if such differentials can be explained (at least in part) by women's and men's differing relations to childrearing and the family, then the economic logic is predicated on *social* processes. Changed earnings differentials may be as much a consequence as a cause of change in domestic divisions of labour. Omission of this consideration is of some consequence, since there is evidence to suggest that changes in gendered relations to the family are of especial importance to understanding change in gendered earnings inequalities (Irwin, 1995a).

Interestingly, the perspectives of several writers within social demography and sociology share more with the approach of the New Home Economics than might be expected. A standard challenge to the model of utility maximization and rational self-interest on which New Home Economics theorists draw is to highlight the fundamental importance of norms, values and institutional constraints on human behaviour. However, a recent stress on a decline of traditional constraints and a liberalization of ideas about appropriate gender roles appears to align sociological approaches more closely with the economists' models. A striking statement of such convergence emerges from a piece of American research into intergenerational influences on the labour force participation of women (Mott et al., 1982). The authors argue that as gender roles become more liberal so women will be able to make more economically rational decisions about whether or not to work. As attitudes become less constrained by traditional gender role expectations, neo-classical theory will become increasingly appropriate as a framework for analysing female employment participation (Mott et al., 1982), a curious displacement where deficiency appears to reside not in the theory but in current social processes. More recently, in his cross-national analysis of factors associated with recent trends in a wide range of demographic variables, Lesthaeghe (1995) concludes that the 'second demographic transition', a series of developments including declining fertility, increasing cohabitation and increasing divorce rates, can be located within cultural traditions which promote individual autonomy and self-fulfilment. From the 1960s on, the conditions were set for a new demographic transition. Lesthaeghe proposes that: 'The origin of social orientation became less a social etiquette, a religious duty, or an act of patriotism than in the past. It had to come "straight from the heart" of the individual' (1995: 26). Here the importance of self-fulfilment within marital unions raises expectations, rendering such unions more fragile than in the past. It is interesting to note that the stress on individual self-fulfilment again appears to suggest a renewed significance of the self-interested figure of conventional economic theory. For example, Lesthaeghe describes cohabitation in terms of a combination of two individual utility functions (Lesthaeghe, 1995). Another associated strand within the demographic literature is to see change in family demography, including the decline of fertility, in terms of changed consumption preferences. A choice between having children or consuming goods is increasingly resolved in favour of the latter (e.g., Aries, 1980; see also Van Krieken, 1997). Interestingly Van Krieken concludes that much of the literature on reproduction and declining fertility manifests a tendency to see contemporary individuals as being in charge of their own destinies while people in the past are seen as social products (Van Krieken, 1997).

Reviewing literature on changing fertility patterns in the American context, Oppenheimer (1994) draws our attention to a paradox which emerges from the growing emphasis on cultural explanations of change in family behaviour. In such explanations modernization is seen to have underlain a growth of individualism with its emphasis on self fulfilment. Oppenheimer notes that,

> there is a general erosion of family norms with the result that marriage and family behaviour is becoming more discretionary and less important in people's lives. This perspective takes us beyond the economist's narrow individualistic decision-making concern with the gain to marriage and into the sociological realm of norms and values; but, in a sense, the cultural argument is that the self-interested man (or woman) of traditional microeconomics is what has been emerging from the more tradition-bound conformist of the past. (1994: 309)

Across much of the literature, then, it seems that the declining salience of economic or status-based constraints on individual behaviour, and a liberalization of values, has also dissolved some of the standard sociological objections to the assumptions of neo-classical theory. However, an alternative and increasingly influential view within sociology is to see the decline in traditional constraints as only one aspect of a more general transformation of social relationships. Here traditional economic and status-related constraints have been displaced by new modes of social organization and a newly emerging set of processes which shape and constrain behaviour. Two writers who have generated much interest here are Beck and Giddens. Though writing from different perspectives, both argue that there is an increasingly contingent nature to the ties that bind people in family relationships. It is with Beck that I will pause since his thesis of individualization and gender relations directly addresses issues of change in the labour market as well as in the family. Of course he maintains that his thesis is inapplicable in the British context given the continued resonance of class inequalities and identities in Britain. However, his thesis has had an influential, although mixed, reception in the British context (e.g., Chisholm and du Bois-Reymond, 1993; Scott, 1997; Smart, 1997; Van Krieken, 1997; Morgan, in this volume). I will make some observations on his arguments concerning change in family and gender relationships since they share some interesting parallels with the positions outlined above.

Beck (1992) posits that individualization is an aspect of both family and labour market relationships. In most Western industrialized nations capitalist organization has delivered not general immiseration but wealth and, for the most part, presided over a dissolving rather than a hardening of class divisions. Further, there has been a weakening of traditional gender status divisions, increasingly drawing women into the realm of paid employment. In this way there is a pressure towards the marketization of family relationships. Of course, taken to its logical conclusion the trend towards a market family, where individuals are rewarded solely for their labour and thus unable to resource the claims of any dependants, is predicated on its own demise. This is a tension which Beck acknowledges, and whose problematic resolution he sees as part of the modern predicament.

> Thought through to its ultimate consequences, the market model of modernity implies a society *without* families and children. Everyone must be independent, free for the demands of the market in order to guarantee his/her economic existence. The market subject is ultimately the single individual, 'unhindered' by a relationship, marriage or family. Correspondingly, the ultimate market society is a childless society – unless the children grow up with mobile, single fathers and mothers. (Beck, 1992: 116)

The ultimate market society begins to look like the end of society, but Beck is pointing to what he sees as a tendency, a dynamic which generates structural problems. What arises is not the dissolution of the family or of procreation, but a growing contradiction between reproduction and production. As a mode of social organization, the family has been based on an asymmetry and inequality of gender relations through which the tensions between the demands of production and the resourcing of reproduction have been contained. As women have become increasingly drawn into the realm of paid employment, the tensions are increasingly overt and consequential. In the absence of institutional solutions there is a growing pressure on the family. It is within these trends that Beck locates the modern 'negotiated' family, where marital partnerships are increasingly subject to recall. However, a symmetry of gender relations either in employment or in the family is far from being a reality. In consequence there is a growing discrepancy between women's expectations of equality and continuity of gender inequality. Expectations outstrip circumstances. Consciousness, Beck says, has rushed ahead of conditions (Beck, 1992: 104).

Beck gives a limited explanation of the extension of marketized relations in the productive sphere, other than in terms of the logic of capital accumulation or industrial development, offering little discussion of the processes underlying trends in female employment participation. He sees individualization partly as a process of increasing individualism, and partly as a process whereby constraints and social forces re-emerge at a level removed from individual apprehension: secondary agencies and institutions replace traditional ties in controlling and shaping experience, and new dependencies arise. 'The individual situations that come into existence are thoroughly dependent on the labour market. – They are, so to speak, the extension of market dependency into every corner of (earning a) living' (Beck, 1992: 130). General evidence offers some support for this thesis. Certainly it is a general

view that economic restructuring has drawn women into paid employment at low wage rates as part of a general set of moves to reduce labour
costs and increase flexibility, reflected in the significant growth in the
proportion of part-time and casualized jobs. (e.g., Humphries and
Rubery, 1992; Rubery, 1996; Walby, 1997). Women spend more of their
working lifetimes in paid employment, and their obligations to their
children become less of an obstacle to continued labour force participation, indeed in some respects appear to demand it. However, it is
far from clear that these trends amount to a marketization, or commodification, of social relationships. Logically, Beck's argument that
there is a marketization of employment (and family) relations must
require a dissolving of *all* status divisions, and not just gender ones.

Beck claims that the individual becomes 'the reproduction unit of the
social', yet his interpretation is directly contradicted by an important
change in the structure of family relations which has occurred over the
past century and a quarter: the prolonging of the period that children
and young adults remain economically dependent, or partially
dependent, on their parents. Presumably Beck's market society must
be one where children work, since their labour would also be
commodified. Their claims would certainly not be reflected in the
wages of (either one) of their parents. The trend, however, is in the other
direction: as young people's claims to independence at an early age have
been undermined, so their reproduction is (partially) resourced through
claims on their parents (see Irwin, 1995a). This development is itself
integral to change in the age distribution of earnings. Further, recent
decades have seen a compression of the period of people's lifetimes
spent in paid employment, and an exclusion from paid employment of
traditionally cheap forms of labour (young people and senior citizens). It
is therefore difficult to sustain the argument of commodification as a
description of twentieth-century capitalism. This has important
consequences for Beck's argument since it suggests that we are
observing change in the position of women and men with respect to
social reproduction, and not the individualization of social reproduction.

To sum up, across a range of perspectives in sociology and demography there is an argument that changes in gendered (and in particular
women's) participation in paid employment, along with changing
values and expectations about women's roles, are bound up with an
individualizing tendency in modern society which generates a new and
less stable foundation for family relationships. In the next section I
address some rather different perspectives on the issues of change in
women's and men's relations to employment and the family, arising
from recent empirical work. It is of interest that among those
undertaking empirical research into women's position within employment, the emergent consensus is that continuity rather than change is
the defining feature of women's position relative to that of men, in both
employment and the family.

Gender Inequality: At Home at Work

One of the dominant themes to emerge from other recent empirical research into women's position in paid employment is of continuity in women's position of economic disadvantage. In short, while a minority of relatively advantaged women have been both authors and bene-ficiaries of improvements in employment prospects and rewards at the top end of the female jobs hierarchy, those at the lower end have experienced a deterioration in conditions of employment. Along with the majority of working women in 'middle range' jobs, and many women who are not in employment, these women remain in a position of economic vulnerability and disadvantage with regard to their employ-ment prospects. The literature effectively highlights the continued econ-omic vulnerability of women. It also calls into question any suggestion that there is a growing symmetry in gender relations or that it is women's economic position which has weakened their attachment to older forms of family life. However, partly because of the emphasis on continuity in gender inequality there has been relatively little sustained engagement with the processes shaping change in women's and men's positioning in respect of the resourcing and reproduction of families. The area is under-explored and under-theorized.

Some writers have set themselves the task of challenging what they see as general and popular perceptions of change in the employment opportunities and scope for independence available to women. A general perception of significant improvements in women's position is seen to ensue from a combination of cultural, legislative and economic changes, but this is not borne out by the evidence. The shape of gender inequality may have changed somewhat but, in contrast to the per-spectives reviewed above, it is erroneous to read too much into this. So, in the case of women's employment and earnings position, continuity of relative disadvantage is the key to understanding (e.g., Hutton, 1994; Arber and Ginn, 1995). For Arber and Ginn, the issue is one of problems which ensue from presuming that advances made by women in the labour market can be interpreted as an aspect of more general changes in gender inequality. So, they suggest:

> There is a contradiction in contemporary society between the general accept-ance of equality of opportunity and pay for women . . . and the normative structure of the domestic domain in which husbands are generally accepted as the main breadwinner. . . . Western societies have achieved some progress towards gender equality in the public sphere of the labour market, but gender inequality in economic roles in the household may be more resistant to change. Women's disadvantaged position in British society can only be understood by considering the relationship between women's role in the public sphere of the labour market and their economic position in the private sphere of the home. (Arber and Ginn, 1995: 21)

It is interesting to note that for Arber and Ginn advances in the labour market appear to outstrip change in norms and values about women's and men's roles. This provides a mirror image to Beck's interpretation: now conditions appear to have 'rushed ahead' of consciousness. This perceived dissonance appears to emerge from a contradiction between change in gendered differences in the labour market and continuity at the level of households. Arber and Ginn suggest that women have made gains in the labour market, but these have not translated into commensurate gains within the household, this proving more resistant to change. This is the case as women come to carry the double burden, become increasingly time-poor, and have to negotiate the constraints which follow from traditional norms and expectations with respect to gender roles. But furthermore, gender roles, and inequalities in power and quality of life within the family continue because gains in the labour market do not translate into improvements in women's economic position at the household level. What Arber and Ginn argue is that when we analyse earnings inequalities at the level of the household, the improvements which might be presumed on the basis of other measures prove to be without substance (Arber and Ginn, 1995). From this perspective the impact on family demography of change in women's relations to employment is called into question.

It is instructive to reconsider the evidence as presented by Arber and Ginn, and to put another perspective on it by addressing further evidence on change in the earnings relativities of couples. Further analysis of GHS data by the author[1] follows the example of Arber and Ginn by exploring the experience of female and male cohabitees (married and cohabiting couples are considered as one group), and focusing on dual-earner couples where each partner works full-time. Around one-third of women in such couples work full-time, around one-third work part-time, and the remainder are not engaged in paid employment. Arber and Ginn provide a comparison of husbands' and wives' earnings, at the level of the household, with earnings data grouped into £100 (gross weekly earnings) brackets. The patterning of earnings relativities is summarized in the first column of Table 3.1, revealing the entrenched dominance of husbands' earnings at the level of the household. Recalling that we are examining earnings among couples where both work full-time, the evidence indicates that women earn more in 11 per cent of couples and earn the same in 33 per cent of couples, while men earn more in 56 per cent of couples (Arber and Ginn, 1995). My own analysis of 1993 GHS data shows a very similar distribution of earnings.[2] There is a slight 'improvement' in women's position, but this may be to do with demographic differences in the sample structures, rather than with any substantive change in this short period. Let us turn to the 1973 GHS data set. Here earnings were disaggregated into £10 (gross weekly earnings) brackets and the resulting pattern of relativities is shown in the third column of Table 3.1.[3] While

Table 3.1 *Comparison of earnings levels between wives and husbands*

	GHS 1988–90 (Arber and Ginn, 1995)	GHS 1993	GHS 1973
Husband dominant	56.2%	55.2%	82.7%
Equal	32.8%	29.6%	14.1%
Wife dominant	11.1%	15.0%	3.4%

the measure is again a crude one, it is illustrative of a very significant trend over the 20-year period. In 1973, husbands were earning more in 83 per cent of married-couple households, where the wife worked full-time. That this is the case in around 56 per cent of households in the early 1990s reveals a marked change in the relative earnings of partners who are both employed full-time.

Arber and Ginn draw on a theoretical framework which locates patriarchy as operating in the labour market, reinforcing inequalities within the household which in turn reinforce gender inequalities in the labour market. Evidence of change in the order of earnings inequalities in the labour market is not readily accommodated within the model of mutually reinforcing gender divisions at home and work. For Arber and Ginn, the discrepancy appeared to be bound up with a contradiction between 'advances' at the level of the labour market and stasis at the level of the family. However, a reconsideration of the data they present, in conjunction with data from 20 years previously, is indicative of consistency, and not discrepancy, between labour market processes and gendered earnings relativities at the level of the household.

The above discussion pertains to female full-time workers. It remains consistent with the argument of many theorists that some women have improved their relative position in employment but this is the experience of an elite minority. It seems likely that the data will contain a relatively small proportion of disadvantaged working-age women since they are less likely to be working full-time, if at all. However, it is premature to maintain that changes in gendered obligations in family resourcing are the experience of only a privileged group of dual-career households. One especially interesting focus for exploring wider changes in women's and men's economic position is the period of family building since it has long seen the absence of most women from paid employment, yet recent changes in women's employment rates here are dramatic. This development is addressed below as it is relevant to theorizing change in gendered relations to the family and employment.

Women with young children have manifested a striking increase in their employment participation rates over recent years. While the employment rates of mothers with an unemployed partner, or with no partner, have declined, the employment rates of mothers with an employed partner have increased significantly. Between 1981 and 1994 the total employment rate of women with children aged under five years rose from 22 per cent to 46 per cent (Harrop and Moss, 1995, Labour Force Survey data; Sly et al., 1997). All the evidence indicates a continuation, and a speeding up, of the trend to growing participation rates in the period of family building, with women spending less of their lifetimes engaged in full-time childcare (Martin and Roberts, 1984; McRae, 1991; Joshi and Hinde, 1993).

Research on changing participation rates has focused on polarization in women's employment opportunities. There has been a marked divergence in the employment rates of mothers depending on their occupational level and their level of formal education (e.g., McRae, 1991; Glover and Arber, 1995; Harrop and Moss, 1995). So while women with very young children have increased their employment participation rates across the social spectrum, the majority of these employees are in low-paid part-time jobs while a small, relatively advantaged group of women are in full-time and high-status work with participation maintained throughout the family building period. Ginn et al. note that,

An increased polarization of employed women seems to be occurring, in which an elite minority have the financial resources to buy exemption from some of the effects of motherhood on employment while the majority are trapped in a vicious circle of low pay, inability to afford full-day childcare and part-time employment. (1996: 169)

The relative vulnerability of women to poverty continues by virtue of their earning power being structured in relation to assumptions of their (at least partial) financial dependence (Arber and Ginn, 1995; Ward et al., 1996). The general picture which is emerging from research in the area is one of significant change in *rates* of employment amongst women but, for the majority, continuity of their disadvantaged *position* within the labour market (e.g., Humphries and Rubery, 1992; Joshi and Hinde, 1993; Glover and Arber, 1995; Harrop and Moss, 1995; Hakim, 1996).

The general theme of much of the research on change in female employment patterns is that it has not significantly altered patterns of gender inequality in employment or the family for the majority. Most women are subject to the continuing force of institutional and normative assumptions regarding their financial dependence. From this perspective the 'new' family looks much like the old family, where conventional divisions of labour in the resourcing of households remain intact, despite change in female participation rates. While gender inequalities manifestly continue to structure employment opportunities, a growing body of evidence indicates the general salience of change in gendered employment patterns and in divisions of labour in family resourcing. The evidence reviewed above indicates quite significant changes in patterns of female employment participation over the life course, and in the earnings of women working full-time relative to those of men. The trends are suggestive of an increased significance of female earnings in the financial resourcing of households. Changes in women's and men's obligations here are reflected both in the growing extent of co-resourcing as a mode of household organization and in the growing proportion of female earnings within the household income package. Recent decades have manifested a significant increase in the proportion of dual-earner and no-earner households, and a decline in the proportion of single-earner households. The 1980s saw dual-earner families become the majority group among two-parent families, increasing from 44 per cent to 57 per cent of the total. Two-parent families in which only the father was employed declined from 46 per cent to 32 per cent of the total (Harrop and Moss, 1995). The period 1971–1991 saw a shift from 22 per cent to 33 per cent of household income comprised of female earnings (Webb, 1993, FES data; see also Irwin, 1995b; Ward et al., 1996). Between 1979 and 1990 women increased their share of household income relative to men, and did so across all points of the earnings distribution, excepting among those with unemployed husbands. Among low-income households male earnings have declined relative to the average, and women have significantly increased their employment participation rates (Machin and Waldfogel, 1994, GHS data). The growth in levels of female employment rates across the population, most dramatic among women with low-earning husbands, and the novel extent of labour force participation among women with young children, suggests that changing relations to household resourcing are being experienced and authored by a population far wider than a privileged group to whom they are often attributed.

Conclusion

A picture of a 'new market family' has emerged from theories which present current social transformations in terms of a rise in individualism. Here the decline of the breadwinning system is taken as given, the resolution of a long-running contradiction within capitalism, and translated in terms of an end to traditional 'social' gender constraints. Employment and family appear to be increasingly economized or marketized. This argument is directly contradicted by the continued importance of family-related divisions and obligations in the resourcing of dependants, and a prolonging of this relationship in the case of children and young adults. A more inclusive theory would address the decline in male claims to a breadwinner wage while recognizing that social claims remain embedded in the structuring of employment. It seems ironic that while recent decades have seen female claims to forms of social citizenship being pressed with some success, related transformations in employment and the family should be located in a triumph of capitalism or an ascendance of individualism.

Other research, on women's position within employment, stresses continuity rather than change as a key feature of women's experience, both within employment and in their familial responsibilities. Here the 'new family' looks much like the 'old family', where changes in women's employment patterns are seen as an aspect of continued gender inequality. However, the focus on continuity of female disadvantage elides the social significance of changing relations of women and men to family resourcing. The developments are fundamental to theorizing change in family arrangements and to analysing change in the structure of inter-household inequalities.

Recent changes are strongly suggestive of a modification of the single earner, or primary/secondary earner mode of household resourcing, with a decline in the relative sufficiency of male earnings and an increased importance of female earnings across the life course of individuals and families. The idea that there is a modification of the male breadwinner system has met with some scepticism given the continued prevalence of female economic vulnerability and female experience of social disadvantage. However, women's continued positioning as secondary earners remains consistent with a quite different relationship to household resourcing. In so far as there is a decline in the availability of breadwinning or (after Siltanen, 1994) 'full wage' jobs, so it appears that for a growing proportion of the population the family income package is comprised of two component wages, the employment of women as well as men increasingly necessary to household resourcing. From this perspective we might stress the general importance of changing divisions of labour in household financial resourcing, a development not restricted to top earners, but an aspect also of poverty and the sufficiency of a single wage in resourcing households. The perceived significance of change in gendered relations to work and family has generated arguments of an increasing individualism, yet such arguments lose sight of the continued importance of social claims and obligations in shaping family arrangements and patterns of access to and rewards from employment. An adequate theorization of the 'new' family requires an improved understanding of changes in the relative position of women and men in the reproduction of social life, changes which reflect the continued importance of social ties and not their displacement.

Notes

1 Material from the General Household Survey for 1973 and 1993, made available through OPCS and the ESRC Data Archive, has been used by permission of the Controller of HMSO.

2 The analyses are of earnings relativities between married or cohabiting different-sex couples. There are slight differences between my own analysis and that of Arber and Ginn (1995). The 1973/93 analyses exclude self-employed

respondents. No age constraint is placed on the sample, the analysis is of all couples where both partners work full-time. Arber and Ginn limit their analysis to those aged 20–59. The 1973/93 analyses refer only to male heads of household and their partners, and excludes working couples where neither is the head of the household.

3 The distributions are provided in detail in Irwin, 1995c.

4

TRANSFORMING HOUSEWIFERY: DISPOSITIONS, PRACTICES AND TECHNOLOGIES

Elizabeth B. Silva

The separate location of the genders that was the basis of the bread-winner and homemaker model of the family has increasingly been challenged, both in practice and theory. It is no longer taken for granted that everyday structures of living simply result from pre-established and naturally pre-ordained models of family and work. Recent feminist theory has discussed this within a framework of a reconceptualization of care which focuses on the social devaluation of care-givers and care-giving both inside and outside the family. This new framework has been developed in the work of Joan Tronto (1993). She puts forward a broad political argument for change in the structures of power and privilege that have relegated caring to private life. I propose to expand her argument by focusing on a specific concern: that of housewifery as a work of care and the transformations of related caring activities via their relationship to technological innovations in the home.

I diverge from one of Tronto's ideas that, '[c]are is difficult work, but it is the work that sustains life' (1993: 117). While I see merit in this statement, I feel uncomfortable with her prevalent assumption of stability in the human needs for care, which appears to fit uneasily with her central concern with change in the ways societies deal with care. In my view, although the work that sustains life is difficult, it can be made easier and care can be made less of a burden, if various social powers are used to lighten the burdens of caring, not simply in terms of valuation and divisions of labour (the central issues addressed by Tronto), but also in changing the burden of the activities themselves.

My proposition implies recovering one of the distinctions developed by the literature on the reconceptualization of care: namely, care as disposition and care as practice. Tronto argues that while an exclusive focus on disposition allows us to think of care as the possession and province of an individual, and also tends to sentimentalize and romanticize care (such as in mothering, see Ruddick, 1980), a focus on practice suggests a possibility for a more democratic expansion of care. However, exclusive practical care may be 'uncaring' at an emotional level. This distinction allows for the recognition of caring as activities of care, as much as about the emotional investment in care (Mason, 1996). I consider household technologies as a means to explore these links between disposition and practice in caring. I see three reasons for this. First, technologies are both conceived as practical instruments and are used in care activities. The disposition to develop technologies for certain areas of practical care has depended on placing specific human needs at the forefront. Particular designs of technologies may dispose people differently, as well as different people, to use them. This results from social choices, where power and privilege are highly significant (Mackenzie and Wajcman, 1985). Secondly, normal daily care in households can benefit from technological developments, even though homes have often been perceived to be impervious to technological influences (Cowan, 1983; Cockburn, 1997). I argue that technologies in the home have changed the ways care is practised in households and also the disposition to care. Thirdly, newer understandings and reassessments of the progressive influence of household technologies for the practice of, and disposition to, care have the potential to bring positive changes in the lives of women in their homes and in society. I claim that feminist inputs into the current and future regulation of the industry and the developments in household technologies require fresh studies and the development of new analytical frameworks (Silva, 1998). This claim aligns with broader concerns about how research agendas can give a proper account of the transformation of domestic life.

Recent feminist literature has argued that research agendas have failed to give a proper account of such transformations because the kinds of questions asked and the sets of issues observed have not been appropriate. Jo VanEvery (1995, 1997) argues that the very assumptions about empirical definitions of housework discursively turn many 'household tasks' into 'housework'. This is valid for both the schedules of the work and the gendered assumptions made by researchers. For instance, it is always assumed that doing things for other people is housework, while in other areas of life notions of communality have been taken to explain and define households and family life. The assumption is that communal tasks are either done by one or shared (equally or unequally). Thus, in one same household there may be two piles of ironing or none, two ironers or none, or just one pile ironed by the wearer of the clothes while the other wears unironed garments, or finds other means by which clothes are ironed (i.e., through commercial services). Within traditional feminist approaches these different patterns of activities are likely to be collapsed into a presumption of gender inequality. This means that potentially subtle changes towards equality are unlikely to be observed. VanEvery also criticizes such approaches for their inability to conceptualize individuals as both needing and giving care. For instance, children are homogenized into a group who needs care, instead of seen as groups composed of different ages, abilities, needs and capabilities of providing care.

The question, then, is to investigate how inequality may be perceived as 'fairness', without losing a sense of differences. An example of this approach is the work of Andrea Doucet (1995, 1996), who proposes new ways of dealing with the complexity of issues in the household division of labour. She poses questions such as: 'Why is it that research has recurrently confirmed the "outstanding stability" of gendered household labour?' 'Would an understanding from the perspective of the people being researched help to shed light on this issue?' Ultimately she argues that household tasks should not always be defined as 'chores'. This new literature stresses that many of the boundaries identified in earlier research are now being crossed, and this should be accorded attention rather than ignored. But equality in the home is not a straightforward issue. For instance, it has been noted that women have overreported their husbands' pathetically small input into household labour (Brannen and Moss, 1991; Coward, 1992), thus colluding with the unequal domestic division of labour. This has been interpreted as a way of preserving family myths (Duncombe and Marsden, 1996). But, of course, different narratives evolve from different positions. Couples in coupledom define as 'difficulties' what separated couples define as 'problems' (Brannen and Collard, 1982). Narratives also relate to evolving collective under- standings of 'fairness' and 'equality'. Same-sex households tend to define the division of labour as predominantly equal, even when there is a division between who takes care of the home and who does paid work outside the home (see Oerton, 1997; Dunne and Weeks et al., in this volume). They feel that 'equality' is represented by a principle of fairness and not by the actual division of labour. The detrimental connotation of housework as work done by a wife for a man in a private household accounts for much of the theoretical assumptions and findings in investigations in this field.

Giddens (1992) has suggested that gays and lesbians are in a vanguard of change, and perhaps their location in society resembles more recent developments towards the 'risk society', which have arguably altered the nature of marriage to reflect a greater emphasis on the couple relationship as a source of fulfilment rather than social, economic or sexual convenience. Increasingly people do not define themselves by adopting traditional male and female role models, following set bio- graphies and performing normative tasks (Beck and Beck-Gernsheim, 1995). These ideas challenge research to account for diversity and trans- formations in the normative expectations of everyday living in house- holds and imply the need for a reconceptualization of care.

In this chapter I regard housewifery as the performance of a woman in running a home. This woman is sexually related to the male head of the household. Marriage is not a necessary element although it is typical. Standard demographics indicate that such a woman is often also a mother. I begin with a notion that housework is generally done by this woman, but I go on to argue that wider repertoires have increasingly appeared that contest the normative gender role of the housewife. My argument is that housework is a caring activity whose practice transgresses the boundaries of the private realm. Both the disposition to, and practice of, doing housework also bear a relationship to the available technologies. Technologies are also constructed in relation to certain dispositions and practices in society (Wajcman, 1991).

I want to consider some of the more recent debates on the structural changes in family life, and some of the transformations in recent decades in the ways in which housewifery has been performed. I will concentrate on issues of time, and on the ways that technological developments have related to changes in patterns of gender relations in households. I shall explore technological innovations in cooking and washing-up. Could diverse cooker designs make any difference to housewives and families? What do the discussions of time in households and the patterns of innovation in household technologies tell us about a reconceptualization of care? How can we best understand the current role of housework in our private and public lives and contribute to specific transformations?

Issues of Time: The Disappearance of Housewifery?

Who will be left to care for home and family? The proportion of economically active women rose from 44 per cent in 1971 to 53 per cent in 1994 and indications are that this proportion will rise to 57 per cent by the year 2006 (*Social Focus on Women*, 1995). What is to de done with homes when women are increasingly in outside employment? (See Irwin, in this volume.)

According to Arlie Hochschild (1996), in the USA, both women and men are fleeing into work from the tensions at home. Strained relationships at home grow with women's lack of time for emotional work, and have increased in a context of family fragmentation (second families, reconstituted families, former families, and in intact families). Husbands' resistance towards 'helping' is another major source of conflict. This family-life scenario contrasts with that of work, where the individual has been increasingly valued and cared for within employee-centred management programmes. Yet tensions increase in the home because caring work alone does not provide enough emotional nourishment. Together with the issue of lack of time, it seems that we have a strong need for an 'emotional culture at home'.

Childcare is obviously a major problem, and women's growing employment has been linked to later childbearing and part-time jobs. In the late 1990s the majority of working women both in full-time and in part-time employment have children and the employment of those with younger children has increased. Since 1985 the economic activity rate of married women has grown steadily from 51 per cent in 1975 to 59 per cent in 1993 (GHS, 1995: Table 5.2). Also, there was a steady rise during the 1980s in the economic activity rate of women with dependent children. This trend is evident among women with children of all ages but it is greater among those with children under the age of five. For these, the economic activity rate was 30 per cent in 1980 rising to 52 per cent in 1991–93. This reflects an increase in full-time working and particularly rapid growth in part-time working among women with children aged under five (GHS, 1995: Tables 5.10, 5.11). Although the number of childcare nurseries more than doubled between 1971 and 1993, for those under five years of age, this still does not meet demand and there is no state provision for the care of children of school age beyond school hours.

While the provision of childcare either by the state or commercial enterprise has been a key focus of equal opportunities policies, the arrangements that go on inside households are a more private matter and indeed much of the literature on housework has focused predominantly on women as mothers. I do not propose to uncouple this. It is well established that children greatly affect the demands of housework and the division of labour in households. But a focus on children and childcare leaves much untouched, and I suggest that we consider broader matters of household arrangements.

Juliet Schor (1993: 98) has argued that 'housewifery is dying out' because fewer households nowadays can afford the labour of an adult solely to do house-cleaning, cooking and mothering. In conditions in which domestic labour is cheap, there is not much incentive to save it, but when housewives' time is at a premium (because of economic, social or cultural reasons) households have to begin to behave differently. Despite the noted reduction in time spent on housework that has accompanied increased female labour market participation, women are still locked into a household technology and a culture of domestic work that are inefficient, time consuming and onerous. The cause was the low cost of the housewife's labour, which becomes higher as women spend more time in the labour market. In Schor's view, families 'bought' so much domestic labour because it was very cheap and standards and services escalated. Conversely, as a woman's income begins to count, the time she spends on domestic labour begins to shrink.

The time women spend on domestic labour has indeed shrunk. Jonathan Gershuny (1983) noted different patterns for working-class and middle-class households. He found that for working-class women time spent in housework increased slightly from 1930 to 1950. His hypothesis is that the early stages of development of appliances may have led households to engage in more housework. However, time spent on housework decreased quite sharply from 1950 to 1980, possibly because the efficiency of the domestic capital increased. Middle-class housewives in 1930 did about half of the amount of housework done by working-class housewives. However, the time spent on housework by middle-class housewives increased sharply up to 1960. The difference between working-class and middle-class housewives was then minimal. The loss of servants increased the time spent on housework for middle-class women. But, from 1960 to 1980 time spent on housework decreased markedly. This reduction, both for working-class and for middle-class housewives, is likely to continue given that women who are employed full-time tend to spend less time doing housework than the increasingly diminishing number of full-time housewives (Morris, 1990; Gershuny, 1992). It has also been found that men, albeit still in small numbers, become more involved in housework, childcare and cleaning (Schor, 1993; Gershuny et al., 1994), particularly when certain kinds of appliances are available (Cockburn and Ormrod, 1993; Smeds et al., 1994).

On the basis of these trends we can conclude that the persons in charge of carrying out the activities of care-as-housework changed historically both in terms of social class and gender. In addition there have been changes in the time allocated to these activities. But, how far can the economic value of women's time account for these changes?

For Hilary Silver (1987), the value of women's time counts only in so far as it enables them to buy replacement domestic service. In her view, time spent in domestic labour can only be reduced by access to the labour of others. Women can either buy other people's time or force people, through the state, to share the burden of domestic labour. Both these strategies implicate demand from the service industries. The tendency is then for a transference of housework from the private home to the public space of the market. This is why the growing industrialization of housework in the USA in the 1980s is associated with the growth of employment in specific industries such as laundries, eating and drinking, paid childcare, repair services and hotels. Technological improvements would then affect housework only via innovation in the service industries, with the implication that housework would be displaced from the home. Silver does not consider changes in the gender division of labour in households: she presumes that since men do not do housework it is virtually impossible to change the gender division of labour in households.

But others have found that the male proportion of the household's total domestic work has risen because women are doing less domestic work. This emerges not just out of choice, but from a process of 'lagged adaptation' (Gershuny et al., 1994) in which adjustment of work roles in the home takes place through a process of household negotiation over a long period of time. For Gershuny (1983) the gender division of labour in households has nothing to do with economics or technology because it relates to 'role models' and is ultimately an issue of moral values. While I do not agree with a dismissal of the importance of economics and technologies in changing the division of labour in households (see also Gardiner, 1997), I welcome his emphasis on questions of moral values and explore this more below.

While some of these analyses address the issue of the disappearance of the housewife, in a more recent and sophisticated analysis of the gendered experiences of time, Oriel Sullivan (1997) explores the current conditions of housewives' work. She argues that the fact that women's time is both more pressured in the home and more fragmented in terms of leisure than men's bears a strong relation to gender identities. Thus competencies endowed by socialization are most strongly manifested and reinforced by everyday practice. This echoes the earlier concern of Gershuny about the 'moral issue' in the household division of labour. In the context of the home, women and men are 'doing gender' through the accomplishment of specific and differentiated domestic tasks, and women are found to be doing a greater number of domestic tasks simultaneously. How have women attempted to alter these domestic arrangements?

The process of achieving change in domestic arrangements is discussed by Orly Benjamin and Oriel Sullivan (1996), within a framework that considers plurality and difference among households. This is an approach that I adhere to in this chapter. The basic assumption is that there is more than one normative structure. This implies the need to find newer ways of doing gender beyond the traditional dichotomy of female and male 'identities'. This is what increasing numbers of people have been doing, but which research is only now beginning to grasp. It is with this in mind that I consider some technological changes in households as a contribution to an argument for the theoretical and empirical understanding of the transformation of housewifery.

Work in the Kitchen: Feeding the Family and Washing-up

In a beautiful ethnographic study of Canadian women's work in the family, Marjorie DeVault (1991) stresses the connection between feeding and caring gendered work. She makes it clear that while 'doing family meals' women were also 'doing gender' (West and Zimmerman, 1991) against a backdrop of larger economic and technological changes. I want to explore the technological contexts in which work in the kitchen has evolved by looking at the activities of cooking and cleaning. I will show that, contrary to earlier feminist analyses, technologies are not agents of social stability in households and that technological innovations have addressed changes in gender relations. I shall also suggest that we have lost sight of the importance that domestic technologies can have for relations within households. While attributing negative labels to house-work, it seems that we failed to see some of the potential for change. I suggest that the social devaluation of care has influenced the patterns of innovation of technology for the home. I argue that the appliances available would be more efficient if women's time were valued more, if caring work were better valued. Changes in relations between women and men, as well as between people of different social classes, appear to be consistent with transformations in the kinds of household appliances used daily in the home. I do not imply, however, that changes have always occurred in the most desirable directions.

I suggest an expansion of Berk's (1985) assumption that housework produces gender by following West and Zimmerman's proposition that 'We can "do" gender in ways that maintain gender relations, or we can challenge them' (1991: 11). Or, as Benjamin and Sullivan (1996) suggest, these challenges to dominant gender orders could simply be providing alternatives to set patterns of living. How has technology related to normative values or created alternatives in patterns of relationships in households?

Gender, Advertisements and Care

Recent studies arguing for the need to reconceptualize housework and develop new approaches for research have been based on fieldwork empirical studies (Doucet, 1995; VanEvery, 1995; Oerton 1997; Dunne, in this volume). I take a new approach by focusing on advertising as a means to analyse changes in housewifery. I have selected for this chapter advertisements that refer to the core activities of feeding the family: cooking and washing-up. The advertisements refer to activities as pictured in the marketing of appliances. I make a contextual narrative interpretation of the messages carried in advertisements (McCracken, 1993). I treat them as texts, and while I examine them for possible meanings, I am aware that different meanings and uses of objects are negotiated when interpretation is carried out by different actors in different contexts (Akrich, 1992). The information produced by adver-tisements constitutes a reasonably accurate representation of reality, but of a partial reality. I am interested in two particular issues: (1) What realities do advertisements invoke in relation to housework? (2) In what ways are these realities producing gender?

In analysing the patterns of innovation of appliances from the 1920s to the 1990s, I found that the association between care, women and the work in the house has dominated the conceptions in design and adver-tising of appliances. But the care that appeared in the early decades of this century to be overseen by the lady of the house while practically accomplished by her servants was, by the middle of the century, trans-formed into the caring housework of the full-time housewife. Nowadays it is either divided up between two working partners, or it includes some teenagers (male and female), with the woman-in-the-house taking on the majority of tasks and responsibilities.

Of course, these images do not account for the full differentiation of care in households throughout this period. In particular, the woman addressed by designers, manufacturers and advertisers has tended to be white, urban, middle-class, about 30 years old, married and a mother. This is especially consistent with images produced up to the 1980s. However, new images have more recently emerged, picturing unconventional households and a greater diversity of users of appliances. For instance, a series of advertisements for Hotpoint appliances published in national newspapers and magazines in November and December 1997 addressed women in a different light. Thus, an advertisement for a dishwasher (Figure 4.1) presented a page full of stylish cooking and serving plates, pots, trays and dishes of immense variety. Under each is an intriguing caption:

Chicken & Cherries
Tofu & Tapioca
Paella & Pistachios . . .

At the bottom of the page the advertisement declared:

. . . You've got the rest of your life to be reckless. (*Good Housekeeping*, December 1997)

The implication is that while you can be both adventurous and caring in providing for the family, you can still be freed from the onerous labour of doing the dishes. The images of the women appearing in these advertisements, which invite the idea of 'recklessness', appear to be subjects who dare to be unconventional, sexy and different, by taking risks, choosing what to believe in, and indulging themselves. But all of this is associated with making a sensible choice (of household appliance) which is presumed to liberate her from the chores of everyday living. Here are two further similar representations (Figures 4.2 and 4.3):

(1)   47 women's torsos with various hair styles in all shapes, colours and sizes in an advertisement for a washing machine. '[It] offers incredible looks, awesome performance and a host of unique new features as standard.' (*Observer Life*, 28 September 1997)

(2)   39 dessert plates with wonderfully inviting cakes and pies with bits of them eaten and the last plate empty, but with the remains of red sauce and a fork on it. It is an advertisement for a washing machine, dishwasher and fridge freezer. 'It's one of life's more sensible little indulgences.' (*Guardian Weekend*, 11 October 1997)

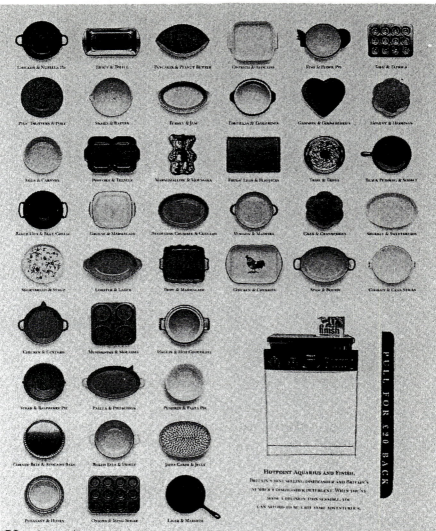

YOU'VE GOT THE REST OF YOUR LIFE TO BE RECKLESS.

Figure 4.1

Addressing slightly different concerns, Whirpool, the world's largest manufacturer of kitchen appliances, issued in 1996 an advertising campaign for its new range of appliances, emphasizing efficiency and quality. In all of the Whirpool advertisements a woman is pictured in the image of the respective appliance: watery (washing machine), wearing a

YOU'VE GOT THE REST OF YOUR LIFE TO BE RECKLESS.

Figure 4.2

smoky outfit (microwave oven), with an ice dress (fridge freezer), and a
fiery dress and hair (cooker). The women look surreal.

Product presentation in marketing creates images that relate both to
the objects they represent and to the uses and users of these objects.
What does this say of gender and care? The advertisements assert
the centrality of women in relation to the household tasks for which the
appliances are designed. While the Whirpool women look surreal and

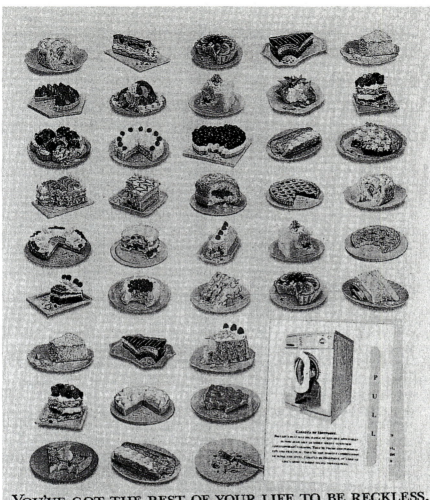

YOU'VE GOT THE REST OF YOUR LIFE TO BE RECKLESS.

Reproduced by permission of Hotpoint

Figure 4.3

magical, the reckless Hotpoint women are equally a fantasy. Both advertising campaigns stress the unconventional, the Hotpoint one in a more
direct language and style. In both cases the machines are designed to
help and are thus presented as efficient and easy to operate. Yet, they do
not emphasize better cooking, or cleaner clothes, in contrast to advertisements in past decades, as I will discuss shortly. The appliances
are designed for, and claim to, take over the work. How do they do it?
By application of 'intelligent' technology, combined with other con-
veniences of modern living, which I call 'technological nexus'.

Cooking

> An oven so intelligent it can remember 100 recipes. (Whirpool advertisement, *Good Housekeeping*, November 1997)

This oven is claimed to be smart, brainy and to have memory.

> My friends want to know how I get him to do all those odd jobs. I tell them it's a piece of cake. The secret's in the Belling. (Belling advertisement, *Good Housekeeping*, November 1997)

The advertiser plays with the idea of gender conflicts over the cooking by referring to the cooker by the personal pronoun him.

> You may have tried to use your old microwave for *more than just heating up food*, but were you really pleased with the results? The Panasonic Navigator Combination Oven has been designed in the UK for *UK foods*. . . . Turning out dishes with a delicious, *traditionally cooked appearance*, all in a fraction of the usual cooking time. (Panasonic advertisement, *Good Housekeeping*, December 1997, my emphases)

There is a tension between the fulfilment of changing needs of saving time and effort, and the preservation of traditional features in the cooking: appearance, taste, and the possibility of 'home cooking'. Even the most modern technology is presented as not disturbing the normal ways of doing things in the home, but just offering the possibility of things being done differently.

Looking at housework activities within an historical perspective gives us a clearer picture of transformations. The advent of the 'intelligent cooker' dates from the 1920s in Britain. Cooker manufacture has obviously always addressed the work of the housewife but in the early stages of the development of appliances, one type of housewife was singled out for special attention: the middle-class housewife who had to run her home entirely unaided because of the growing shortage of servants. The working-class housewife and the working woman, many of them former servants in better-off households, were able to buy only the smaller and cheaper cookers.

The thesis that technological developments for the household have created 'more work for mothers' is based on the substitution of appliances for the loss of servants (Cowan, 1983). Aided by technology the middle-class housewife had to do herself the work she had paid someone else to do for her. In this regard the comparison is between a form of housework that did not exist (servants abolished housework) and one that does. However, for the working-class woman, accustomed to do her own housework, technology improved conditions, increased productivity and made women better off, as demonstrated by Gershuny's (1983) data on Britain. The chore of domestic service suffered by the middle-class housewife and mother was ideologically conceived as the accomplishment of a virtue. The emotional significance of the work of the caring mother and wife reinforced stereotypical aspects of femininity, while technological innovations claimed to make her free effectively to accomplish her caring labour. For example, time liberated by owning a good cooker could be used to bake a greater variety of different shapes of biscuits, fancy and decorated. Yet, when using a cooker with a thermostat control in the 1930s or in the 1950s, the cook was required to accomplish frequent and minute tasks and to perform many varied operations, making it impossible to accept the manufacturer's and advertiser's claim that the cooker was 'intelligent' (Silva, 1997a).

Despite this, innovations made jobs easier. Yet, until the late 1970s, because of a strong identification between women and domesticity, the exploration of unconventional lines of cooking was thought to clash with the conventional role of woman. Developments in cooking technology could theoretically have followed a different pattern but alternatives were slow to be explored. For instance, the requirements of electric cooking developed along the lines prescribed by solid fuel and gas, while other advantages of electric cooking remained unexplored. Just after the Second World War, a 'leading authority' on electricity for domestic use was reported to have said that 'as a matter of policy it was felt that it was unfair to a housewife to introduce her at the same time to new methods of cooking as well as to a new fuel' (Political and Economic Planning, 1945: 66). Although the patronizing of the housewife is an insufficient explanation for the industry's choice of investment, the perception of the needs of women did affect the patterns of technological development. The exploration of far-reaching alternatives, which could have been advantageous in saving labour, time and ease of cooking, were delayed.

With the microwave oven, a newer pattern of cooking technology emerged in the 1970s, combining developments in electricity and electronics. In its early days it was introduced as the ideal saviour of the busy housewife: demands upon the cook were said to be eradicated. It was introduced as the 'super intelligent' machine. Yet, when the claims of advertisers and instruction manuals are deconstructed (Silva, 1997a), the assessment of all the features of the cooking process – ingredients, dishes, temperature, time, operations – are dependent on the cook's tacit knowledge. Tacit knowledge defines what is known without one being aware of it because it was learned through normal living in a particular cultural setting. It is what one does when 'doing gender'. The technologies are thus designed according to particular expectations of 'doing gender' (Chabaud-Rychter, 1994, 1995).

Despite the limits to the technology and the demands placed upon the cook constructed as woman, microwave technology is an extraordinary innovation, particularly in the way it connects with other housework activities such as freezing, cooking, serving and washing-up. Various tasks can be combined, time saved and efficiency achieved. But, what are the social needs for these achievements? How much involvement in the process has been demanded of women who cook? What kinds and images of cooking is this process creating?

In a longer historical analysis of innovation, many elements of class have been dissolved. However, economic and social differentiation is still present in both the kinds of appliances that fit different purchasing powers and on the 'technological nexus'. Because 'proper home cooking' is still the housewife's domain and because it is where labour-intensive activities identify most strongly with caring, the dynamics affecting the technological nexus are very important. The use of restaurants, school meals, hours of employment outside the home, as well as utensils, washing-up demands and so on are also part of the technological nexus. Convenience food is a good illustration of a way in which the techno-logical nexus operates. The convenience food that most closely resembles proper home cooking is more expensive. Less tasty food that presents greater health risks is consumed mostly by the poor. Thus, the main-tenance of the connection between caring and cooking in the context of modern technologies is easier for better-off households who can buy better care-equivalent foods for use in suitable household appliances. Here women are able to care by buying, freezing and leaving to house-hold members the job of heating-up or cooking. This fits well with versatile, flexible lifestyles. In the meanwhile, less well-off households seem to fit more traditional patterns of gender relations with members having less flexibility to share the care required by the needs of feeding families.

It is significant that responsibility for providing meals remains basically with women. As proper cooking remains a female affair, tradi-tional patterns of gender are reinforced (Ormrod, 1994). But it is equally important to note the transformations in the feeding responsibilities of women. The predominant image in advertisements of cookers in the 1930s to the 1970s was of the 'happy housewife'. Recent innovations have escaped from the norm that the cooker 'naturally' belongs to women, as well as from the accomplishment of normal femininity through cooking activities. The call to be reckless is significant in this regard because the disposition to care has changed in terms of the emotional significance of cooking. Also important, both in terms of practices of, and dispositions to, care, is the emergence of newer images of 'cooks': men, teenager boys and girls, and women who do not enjoy cooking. In particular it appears that men are more likely to engage in the provision of meals where enhanced technology is available.

Cooking is one of the most traditional areas of technological inno-vation in the home. Dishwashing is a newer one. Are different issues being addressed in this area? Can we similarly identify alternative patterns of more fluid responsibilities of care, such as the ones that I have identified in the developments of cooking technologies?

Washing-up

A recent advertisement for a Miele dishwasher notes that 8,500 wash cycles is what an average family requires for 20 years. While this indicates the durability of the machine, it reminds consumers of the amount of washing-up that could be avoided. Miele offers 'a model to suit every size of household'.

> And when the children have flown the nest, you'll be glad of the Top Solo option, a programme that washes a half load . . . (*Good Housekeeping*, October 1997)

This flexibility is a new trend in household goods, responding to both changing family needs and concerns for the environment. The German AEG OKO dishwasher (like Miele) is one of the most expensive in the market and according to the Good Housekeeping Institute (October 1997) the 'quietest and most intelligent', with a Sensorlogic system that assesses load size and level of soiling, thus deciding on the amount of water and cycle needs.

An account of change in housework activities has to take into account transformation in a whole range of concerned aspects, which I have called 'technological nexus'. Obviously, dishwashing has varied according to availability of piped water (cold and hot), quality of crockery, washing-up tools (plastic buckets, detergents, drainers, taps, mixers, dishwashing machines, waste disposals), space, number of meals eaten daily in the household, kinds of food eaten and ways in which meals are served. To some extent, who does the job also affects the ways dishwashing is done. For instance, in the interwar period dishwashing was seen as drudgery, with only the employment of servants as a possible escape route for middle-class households. In the magazine for middle-class women, *Woman's Own* (5 November, 1932: 124), I found a story of a (obviously white) young woman who stopped working as a secretary upon marriage but whose husband did not earn enough in England to employ servants. The couple's relationship was portrayed around washing-up. At one point they were given a dishwasher by an elderly aunt but the machine did not work well. Their solution to the washing-up problem was to move to South Africa: 'You have a lady who is as black as your hat and says "yes, Baas," to do it for you.' While the story seems an exaggeration of the dishwashing burden, only in the deployment of another woman's labour was a solution to the couple's conflicts found. And this was no longer affordable for a sole-earner household in the England of the 1930s.

Up to the 1950s the question of who is going to do the washing-up predominates in advertising: 'How often do you face this problem?' (*Housewife*, February 1954). The words caption a picture of a cross-looking man and woman (presumably husband and wife) standing in front of a sink filled with piled-up dirty crockery. The idea was that dishwasher appliances would resolve conflicts. But, apart from dishwashers, other tools and appliances emphasized the freedom from negotiations over who did the job as well as free time: 'Who's washing-up? . . . Dad never minds washing-up since Mother bought a HAPPYMAID plastic cushioned Dish Drainer. What a time saver!' (*Housewife*, October 1957: 119).

Until quite recently, the predominant opinion about machines was that they were too expensive and did not perform well. This is clearly demonstrated in my survey of dishwasher appliances in Britain since the 1920s (Silva, 1997b). Until the 1970s the disadvantages of adopting a dishwasher were considerable both because of the diversity of quality of the appliances and the unreceptive environment. There was a chaotic assortment of widths and depths, some had heaters and some did not, some required to be plumbed in, some had to be fixed on hoses and taps (losing time), the layout was incompatible with most shapes and sizes of bowls, mugs and dishes. Also, not all machines were fully automatic: '. . . you had to stand by to turn taps on and off at the right moment'. Moreover, detergents were hard to find: 'Most suburban shops don't even seem to have heard of a dishwasher, let alone powder to put in it' (*Which?*, December 1968).

Gradually, the relational aspects of washing dishes became less significant in advertisements. In the 1970s and 1980s machines became larger, with removable racks, and economy programmes, while the unfriendliness of high noise levels was tackled with new sound insulation material and design. For the upper market segments dishwashers were transformed from luxuries into necessities. But, obviously, various other washing-up practices co-exist. By the late 1990s less than one-fifth of households in Britain own a dishwasher. This is considerably lower than in Italy and Germany, among other European countries, and a very modest proportion in comparison to the more than half of American households that have dishwashers. Cultural preferences, space, quality of the equipment, and kinds of crockery account for differences in patterns of diffusion. But what have been the technological and relational strategies for 'eliminating' washing-up from housework? There have been three main strategies: (1) better sink technology in the form of tools and chemicals; (2) changes in cooking technology involving different fuels, quality of utensils, reduction in meals, use of ready-made or pre-cooked foods; and (3) involvement by women of the labour of others: male partners and children. Mechanization has progressed very slowly, as if the 'elimination' of the washing-up job were neither expected nor desired.

Is washing-up an area of caring activity where disposition is large and practices unconstrained? There has been an argument that much technology has privatized women's work, isolating them from each other and from the rest of society. This supposed loss of communication and intimacy among women is exemplified in the work of Susan Strasser: a mother regrets the end of her chats with her daughter. If she (the daughter)

> . . . wanted to ask me some questions that were on the sexy side, she didn't have to look at me, because I was at the sink. . . . It was a nice feeling that we had when we were in the kitchen together. (Strasser, 1982: 279)

This romanticizing of times past is also found in Victoria Leto's account of women's memories of doing dishes with their siblings. 'We had fun, sang dumb songs, . . . we played around, acted silly, hit each other with dishrags' (Leto, 1988: 173).

Relationships change along the life course, with the presence of children and employment, and through the different ways in which women introduce change into their relationships or the domestic divisions of labour. Technologies are but one such influence, and their perceived effects are not homogeneous. While in some views companionship compensated for the hard work (Davidson, 1982), others have shown that disputes, gossip and bad feelings erupted among women who had to share common facilities to do the housework (Zmroczek, 1992).

The nostalgia for a romanticized experience addresses some emotional fragments of lost relationships, but not the daily practice of the activity. It refers to particular episodes of disposition but not to the overall emotional involvement contained in doing dishes as an everyday activity. In some ways the nostalgia stresses the essentializing nature of women's work by selectively emphasizing the cosiness of caring. Tronto (1993) remarks that the ways in which we think of care is deeply implicated in existing structures of power and inequalities. While the women, as above, show enjoyment in feeling interdependence in doing the dishes, they also appear to affirm the identification of women with the world of family and friends. The trivialization of the washing-up activity makes it child's play, preventing a more serious concern by substituting for it technical innovations which could more easily fulfil practical needs and other experiences of intimacy. In the structure of what Tronto (1993: 112) calls 'fragmentation of care', within the very devalued housework activities, cooking is more central to the notions of family care while washing-up is assigned very little weight. It is so trivial that it does not require thought, despite its close connection with cooking in the job of feeding families. How do our ways of thinking within academic feminism reinforce or challenge this devaluation of specific activities of household care?

Conclusions

I began this chapter with a reference to the growing shift away from the marital support model of families towards the two-earner model. I asked about the consequences of these changes for the role of housework in people's lives, both private and public. I also explored how the housework activities of feeding the family have changed over time. The main transformations are found in the increasing interdependence and blurring of boundaries between private life in the home and that of public space. The issues of time that I have addressed highlight the vanishing tendency to restrict a woman exclusively to care for family needs, because of both the monetary and moral valuation of women's time. This has had a particularly important connection with the location of genders and gender work in households.

I have argued that the work that sustains life can be made easier and that technologies can lighten the burdens of the practical accomplishment of housework activities. One of the reasons why this has been slow to change is because conceptions of who cares, and what care is, are embedded in the design and operation of technologies. Technological innovations in households still express the structures of power and privilege in society.

As the role of housework in our private and public lives changes, research agendas have to be modified to account for transformations in relationships and practices of daily lives. In particular, newer approaches need to challenge the traditional feminist depreciation of heterosexual housework to consider emergent transformations. My historical account of changes in technologies for cooking and washing-up show that there is some correspondence between technical innovation and change in domestic and gender relationships. But, the negative attitudes to the importance and role of housework in our lives has led to neglect of intervention in technological innovation for care activities in the home.

I asked if cooker designs could have made any difference to women and family living. The picture is complex and non-linear. From my analysis of the relationships between practices and dispositions in the development of technologies, I conclude that while the cooker *per se* can change practices of cooking, lightening the burden of activities, the development of newer cookers has also tended to re-emphasize dominant constructions of the gendered user of the technology. However, newer users have appeared in real life and in the world of advertisements. The image of 'the cook' is now fragmented. Of course, the quality, performance, and design of the cooker makes a difference, and so also does the dishwasher. But machines hardly make any difference in isolation from social contexts.

My analysis of the issues surrounding the innovations in cooking and washing-up suggests that technologies have done less than is desirable and possible for the caring jobs in households. By emphasizing an exclusively female link with housework, technologies in the home have been rendered invisible and devalued. This suggests that there is a lag between the various ways caring has actually been exercised and the ways that it has been perceived. An important area of misperception is in research. In relation to housewifery we are no longer talking of the role of a devoted woman-wife-mother. Yet, the concept of housewifery, with key practices and dispositions assigned to it, still has its meaning attached to a devalued key woman-carer, particularly in the context of traditional feminist analyses of housework and family life. In relation to domestic technologies, we must recover their positive social identities as 'aids' for living. Of course, this implies not relegating caring to private concerns but making it more public, moving away from an 'ethic of care', conceived almost entirely in terms of personal relationships, towards discovering ways in which care can occupy a different location in our lives. This movement for better valuation of care in society calls into question the structures of gender and class values and many other processes of exclusion on which our everyday living is based.

Acknowledgements

The research for this chapter was done under my ESRC award (R000221700). I am grateful to Carol Smart and Steven Tolliday for helpful comments.

5

A PASSION FOR 'SAMENESS'?
SEXUALITY AND GENDER
ACCOUNTABILITY

Gillian A. Dunne

This chapter aims to further theoretical and empirical understandings of household divisions of labour by extending our field of vision to include the experiences of a hitherto neglected and invisible group – lesbian parents. It departs from convention by recognizing that lesbian experience has as much to contribute to debates about gender as it does to sexuality (see Dunne, 1997a, 1998b). I argue that the detailed and critical investigation of divisions of labour between partners of the same gender offers a particularly effective way of revealing those circumstances and practices which facilitate, and those which inhibit the negotiation of, more egalitarian arrangements in partnerships *per se*. Further, by moving beyond the heterosexual focus which dominates empirical research on gender, work and family life (Blumstein and Schwartz, 1985; VanEvery, 1995; for rare exceptions) we are in a position to assess the significance of heterosexuality itself in reproducing the *status quo* (Dunne, 1997a).

The chapter takes as its starting point findings which confirm a tendency for lesbian partners to negotiate fairly equal divisions of labour. It moves on to explore why this outcome is probable in lesbian partnerships but exceptional for heterosexual couples. It will consider this in two ways: (1) through a theoretical discussion of links between sexuality and gender accountability; and (2) by drawing on respondents' observations. I will conclude by briefly considering the implications of my argument for feminism more generally.

Divisions of Labour in Lesbian Households: Some Evidence

When lesbians are asked to describe how their relationships with women differ from their understandings/experience of heterosexual relationships, they almost always make some reference to equality (Dunne, 1997a; see also Heaphy et al., 1997; and Weeks et al., in this volume). There is a small but growing body of research which has focused on divisions of labour between women. The findings suggest that women in lesbian relationships are much more likely than women in heterosexual relationships to describe their domestic/parenting arrangements as equal (e.g., Blumstein and Schwartz, 1985; Peace, 1993; Tasker and Golombok, 1998).

There is, however, a remarkable lack of curiosity about non-heterosexual experience in mainstream accounts of divisions of labour. Implicit in this absence are two contradictory presumptions about the organization of work between lesbian partners: either an unquestioning expectation of equality, or that the processes supporting inequality in heterosexual arrangements are so powerful that they cannot be avoided by non-heterosexual couples (Oerton, 1997). Given that lesbians negotiate their relationships in a context which is a feminist goal (in relation to gender and power), the implications of either of these assumptions for accounts of gender relations and change are profound. If, for example, the arrangements constructed by partners who occupy the same position in the gender hierarchy and share broadly similar gender experience simply mirror the inequalities reflected in dominant trends, then what is the future for feminism?

The Lesbian Household Project

The Lesbian Household Project[1] was designed to investigate whether or to what extent lesbian partners actually manage to operationalize egalitarian ideals in relation to the organization of work. The study draws on the experience of 37 cohabiting lesbian couples with dependent children (mostly of pre-school age). By considering this period in family formation when balanced arrangements are most difficult to achieve/sustain, the study provides an alternative reference point for distinguishing between factors which may support homelife inequalities. Methods employed included a series of two- to three-hour semi-structured interviews with both partners – joint followed several months later by individual. To explore respondents' perceptions of 'who did what', the first interview centred on the creation of a Household Portrait.[2] Data were collected on respondents' work histories and their attitudes to paid employment were explored. To avoid confining the analysis to their perceptions (which may be subject to the desire to present an ideal rather than reality) each participant recorded her activities for seven days in a time-task diary. The second interview was with individual partners, thus providing an alternative context for discussion and clarification of the dynamics of the household and partnership. The study differs from other work on divisions of labour in a number of ways: (1) its focus on lesbian partners with dependent children (the majority became parents via donor insemination; (2) in the range of household dynamics explored (it extends beyond domestic and caring work to include paid employment); (3) in the diversity of methods used to illuminate their arrangements. I now want to outline briefly some of the more interesting findings from the study (see Dunne, 1997b; 1998a, for detailed analysis).

Paid employment   A high level of flexibility and even-handedness characterized the allocation of employment responsibilities in partnerships, regardless of the age of children. Being a birth-mother (or birth-mother of the youngest child if there was more than one)[3] was a poor predictor for employment (hours, status or income) differences between partners. Views dominating accounts of employment were that each partner had a right to, and would benefit from, an identity beyond the home, and that level of pay was a poor indicator of the value of work performed. It was unusual to find one partner's 'career' taking priority over the other's. Their positive attitudes to employment were balanced by a strong sense that caring for a child was important, demanding and pleasurable work. Thus, it was not unusual to find both partners in half-time employment, particularly when they had pre-school children. This situation represented the ideal for many couples in the study. Respondents' decisions about how to balance childcare with paid employment seem to confound 'rational' economic models. It was not unusual for the partner with the higher paid job to reduce her hours to care for a child, or for partners to take turns in developing paid work opportunities. Within reason they were prepared to experience a reduced standard of living, and indeed many did, to enable what they perceived as a fairer, more sensible outcome.

Domestic tasks   On the basis of both how they spent their time (as recorded in their diaries), and their perceptions of who did what, the allocation of household tasks bore no relationship to the gender-segregated patterns that characterize dominant trends for heterosexual couples.[4] Except when differences in paid working hours were extreme (more than 30 hours' difference, N=11), time spent on the performance of domestic work was fairly equally divided in partnerships (81 per cent came within a 60–40 per cent sharing threshold). As childcare was viewed as a valuable job in itself, the reduction in paid working hours to care for a child was rarely seen by either partner as justification for her performing the bulk of domestic labour.

In trying to make sense of why lesbian partners have a far greater chance than their heterosexual peers of achieving balanced employment and home lives my thinking is increasingly drawn to the connections between sexuality and gender. I now want to outline and illustrate my argument that their ability to operationalize their egalitarian ideals can be understood as emerging from the different configuration of gender practices that same-sex interaction facilitates.

Gender as Process

The relationship between sexuality and gender becomes particularly interesting when we conceptualize gender as an active ongoing process, rather than fixed. Gender, as formulated by West and Zimmerman (1987), Connell (1987) and revisited by Fenstermaker, West and Zimmerman (1991) is something that is continuously achieved in our ongoing everyday interaction with others – we *do* rather than *have* gender. The fact that we are doing gender rather than doing personhood implies knowledge of wider social conceptions of what constitutes the 'attitudes and activities appropriate to one's sex category' (West and Zimmerman, 1987: 127). In other words, action is constrained because it is subject to evaluation on the basis of how far it 'measures up' to the gender criteria which are specific to the particular social setting within which the act takes place (Fenstermaker et al., 1991). When we reach the limits of appropriate gendered action there is a sense of being 'up against something' (Connell, 1987: 92).

The fluidity (across time and space) and specificity (from context to context) of gender criteria, together with the fact that our gender identities co-exist alongside a wealth of other social identities, means that we should recognize the existence of masculinit*ies* and femininit*ies* (Connell, 1987: 175–99). However, underpinning the range of meanings and actions associated with belonging to one sex category or another is that our culture recognizes only two. To be a man or a woman rests on the idea of fundamental difference (Connell, 1987: 140; Fenstermaker et al., 1991) As such, the doing of gender must always involve the affirmation of gender difference, and failure to do this can bring censure and may expose the overlapping nature of gender and sexuality. 'Real' women and 'real' men are always heterosexual (Connell, 1987: 186).

We do gender in our mode of dress, through our occupation of and movement in space, in how we manipulate objects and so on. This kind of thinking has been useful for understanding why domestic arrangements negotiated between women and men are so resistant to change (Berk, 1985; Lewis and O'Brien, 1987; Hochschild, 1989; Morris, 1990; Fenstermaker et al., 1991). Engagement with the everyday tasks and objects of the home is not simply about getting necessary work done, it is about engaging in the production of gender (Berk, 1985). As Berk (1985) suggests, the home is a 'gender factory'. The domestic division of labour (one needs to add here – between women and men) is about linking the *musts* of work to be done with the *shoulds* of gender ideals (Berk, 1985; Seymour, 1992).

The way that structure and agency intersect in the doing of gender brings power into relief. As Fenstermaker, West and Zimmerman point out, gender is: '[T]heoretically central to understanding how situated human interaction contributes to the reproduction of social structure . . . both as an outcome of and a rationale for various social arrangements and as a means of legitimating one of the most fundamental divisions of society' (1991: 295). So in relation to household divisions of labour, rather than consciously participating in an exploitative process of labour appropriation, women and men are simply doing what women and men do – in the performance/non-performance of household tasks men and women are affirming their gender difference. The idea that the performance of gender-specific tasks is linked with the affirmation of gender difference is, however, somewhat dependent on this work being allocated between women and men. Presumably when men live alone or with other men they do engage in the performance of laundry, ironing, cleaning the bathroom and so on without feeling that their masculine identity is unduly threatened. The fact that this process of appropriation is somewhat dependent on there being a man and a woman involved illustrates the way that gendered action is mediated by sexuality. Thus, at least in this example, the interaction reproducing the social structure is the doing of gender *through* heterosexuality.

(Hetero)sexuality and Gender (difference)

Sexuality and gender are connected in a variety of powerful overlapping ways. Together they interact to (1) shape gender relations by constructing the conditions by which men and women can relate across gender boundaries, and (2) police the content of masculinities and femininities.

The full meaning of the relationship between sexuality and gender relations becomes clearer when the social origins of this core aspect of identity is recognized. The diversity of sexual meanings that exist across time and space fly in the face of common-sense understandings which link heterosexuality with the expression of some essential sexual nature (see examples in Dunne, 1997a). Instead, how we give voice to and act upon our sexual and emotional feelings is better understood as limited by social, ideological and material forces, whereby heterosexuality and heterosexual relationships are presented as *the only* 'natural', 'healthy', universally socially and morally acceptable expression of adult sexuality.[5] Given that this version of the story provides the logic for drawing women and men together out of their more usually homo-emotional worlds into relations of inequality, a key project for feminism is the understanding of how, why and with what consequences people become heterosexual.[6] This allows us to move beyond an analysis of heterosexuality as practice, to a less divisive position which conceptualizes heterosexuality as a social institution.

There are powerful connections between sexuality and gender content. In contemporary Western societies we do not select partners simply
on the basis of their anatomical sex; we are drawn to them as bearers of
the social and cultural meanings which are attached to the possession of
male or female bodies. The identities 'heterosexual' and 'homosexual'
can only make sense in the context of gender polarization (Connell,
1987). The likelihood that people will form heterosexual partnerships
rests on the social construction of dichotomous and hierarchical gender
categories and practices. As Butler observes: 'The heterosexualization of
desire requires and institutes the production of discrete and asymmetrical oppositions between "feminine" and "masculine"' (1990: 17).
Likewise, Rubin (1975) argues that union between women and men is
assured through the suppression of similarities between them, so that a
'reciprocal state of dependency' will exist between the sexes (1975: 178).
(The suppression of similarities, I would stress, includes skills, competencies, employment opportunities and wages.) As these differences
become translated into reciprocal needs and dependencies they become
eroticized – heterosexuality becomes the attraction of opposites (Connell,
1987: 246) or a passion for a specific configuration of difference.
  If heterosexual outcomes are assured through the suppression of
similarities between women and men, and gender is an ongoing accomplishment, then we should not be too surprised to find that when men
and women form heterosexual partnerships gender *difference* is being
affirmed in the everyday routines of social life. The imperative link and
overlap between doing gender difference and doing heterosexuality
represents an important, but rarely recognized or discussed, contradiction facing the vanguard of women and men who are committed to
negotiating egalitarian relationships with each other. It helps explain
why relationships can be threatened when women seek equality through
challenging the gender differences that structure their partnerships with
men – something much greater than 'fairness' is at stake – a sense of who
one is as a woman or a man. The extent to which individuals can cross
gender boundaries is further limited by the way that gendered territories
give rise to gendered cultures. Doucet (1997) discusses this problem as it
was experienced by the egalitarian heterosexual couples in her study (see
also Dunne and Doucet, forthcoming):

> Even where men cross these [gender] boundaries, as may be the case for
> single fathers actively engaged in 'constructing a different identity', they are
> still perceived, particularly by other mothers as 'honorary mothers' or even
> 'honorary women' (O'Brien, 1987: 241). The majority of women have not let go
> of the overall responsibility for children and men have not yet fully entered
> into this terrain so that [there] still remain . . . 'deeply entrenched' dividing
> lines. (Doucet, 1997: 10)

Collectivities rally to protect gender boundaries from pollution from the
opposite sex: when all else fails men become 'honorary women'. Within

binary thinking there can only be two genders and their existence rests
on the notion of 'otherness'. Recognition of the fluidity of and overlap
between gender categories threatens the logic of difference, and the
raison d'être for compulsory heterosexual coupling.

At the same time, if the social categories heterosexual and homosexual
are dependent upon gender polarization, the boundaries that separate
women and men out as different from each other also provide spaces
and the grounds for solidarity within gender categories (e.g., friendships, feminism). This can give rise to a passion for 'sameness' which,
when acknowledged and acted upon, enables people to question the
taken-for-grantedness of heterosexuality (Dunne, 1997a).[7] Rather than
escaping gender altogether, as Wittig (1992) suggests, lesbian relationships are formed and experienced in a different gender context from that
of heterosexual women. If gender is mediated by sexuality, then it will
have an important bearing on practice.

We can find theoretical justification for this in our more interactive
conception of gender. Gender as a socially situated accomplishment
implies an audience. We can take this a stage further by arguing that *the
gender of the person we are doing our gender with/for and who does it to us*
matters. We only have to think about how differently we can experience
single-sex situations as compared to mixed-settings (schooling, the class-
room, the sports-hall, the pub, and so on) – we can become different sorts
of people (levels of confidence and competence, tasks performed, and so
on). In same-sex settings the compulsion to affirm our gender difference
can be less powerful and, paradoxically, we may be less aware of
ourselves as gendered individuals in these circumstances. Fewer restrictions may be placed upon what constitutes gendered action. Indeed,
circumstances may encourage or force us to transcend appropriate
gender action, as for example, when during the First and Second World
Wars in men's absence women were drawn into male-dominated areas of
production, or when men are bringing up children on their own.

I now want to illustrate this argument by turning to respondents'
accounts and exploring what can be accomplished by women who are
doing gender outside heterosexuality. I will suggest that the alternative
gender dynamic underpinning same-sex relationships is a key factor in
enabling the negotiation of egalitarian relationships.

Doing Gender Beyond Heterosexuality

Domestic Arrangements between Women – 'They're Just Jobs for Us'

What is it about lesbian relationships that appears to turn upside down
many of the assumptions which shape heterosexual practice and
maintain the *status quo*? The answer lies in their similarities as women,
together with the differences that place them outside conventionality,

which provide the opportunity for (and almost require) the re-thinking of household arrangements. This position is summed up by Dolly, who has been living with her partner, Jo, for the past 19 years:

> I suppose because our relationship doesn't fit into a social norm, there are no pre-set indications about how our relationship should work. We have to work it out for ourselves. We've no role models in terms of how we divide our duties, so we've got to work it out afresh as to what suits us. . . . We try very hard to be just to each other and . . . not exploit the other person.

Many respondents had been married or had lived with male partners in the past. When reflecting on how relationships with women differed from their experience of heterosexuality, freedom from gender assumptions around the allocation of household tasks was seen as key. While most viewed their heterosexual relationships positively, because they had usually been involved with men whom they viewed as exceptionally egalitarian, they felt greatly advantaged by the absence of 'gender scripts' to guide their relationships with women (see also Dunne, 1997a). They contrasted the ease with which domestic arrangements emerged in their partnerships with women. Mandy, who works half-time and is the co-parent of a two-year-old boy, describes this:

> *In comparison with heterosexual experience, is there any difference in how you approach and feel about doing housework?* Oh yes! Because it is open for negotiation in a much more real sense, and you are not fighting against anything. No matter how New Mannish or not, there is a prevailing sub-conscious belief that women do housework. And I think a lot of women – I mean, I did – fall into that. I did more than my fair share, or I battled not to. But I didn't negotiate on an equal footing. So yes, I think there is a big difference because it's up for grabs. . . . You are not battling against either overt or covert beliefs in who should do what.

What she is describing here is her earlier experience of being 'up against something' very real (Connell, 1987), in her attempts to resist the 'doing of gender difference'. With persistent regularity respondents identified gender-differentiated expectations mediating the achievement of balanced relationships between men and women. Vicky and June discuss the way their relationship differs from previous heterosexual experience. Vicky is the birth-mother of a primary-school-aged girl and has part-time employment which is home-based. June is the birth-mother of two pre-school-aged children, and has a full-time paid job as a technician:

> *Vicky*: I think it is impossible [to get balance in a heterosexual relationship]. I've had to do so much rebellion against the status I was expected to have in a heterosexual relationship. . . . It's just too complicated. I mean it's difficult for feminists anyway.

What gets in the way?

June: Internalized sex roles and external pressure. . . . I was constantly adding it all up in my head (cooking, cleaning the bathroom, etc.) and thinking this isn't fair. Sex roles get in the way of everything. You can't forget it, you can't just let it go along, which I think we pretty much do really, don't we?

Vicky: Right. If there's a problem then it's between June and me, it's not a problem between men and women like the world over, or history conspiring against us.

The advantages of occupying the same position in the gender order were often stressed, particularly by respondents who had the experience of a heterosexual relationship. In comparing their situation to past experience or that of the heterosexual mothers in their kin/friendship networks, there was a general sense of relief at not having to struggle with the same kind of externally derived sources of inequality which they saw impinging on relationships between women and men. Like Vicky, most understood that all relationships involved difficulties and power imbalances. However, to achieve a 'good' relationship by their definition, imbalances required recognition and working through to some happier medium. When explored in interviews, respondents appeared to understand the term 'equality' to mean this kind of balancing of differences.

Being two women together seems to enable a relaxed approach to the performance of household work. Tasks lost their symbolic value in the disruption of the links between 'the shoulds of gender ideals' and the 'musts of household work' (Berk, 1985; Seymour, 1992). Anet and Mary are both birth-mothers of primary-school-aged boys, and each has full-time employment. They reflect upon their completed household portrait:

Anet: We've put a lot of things 50/50, but within that we divide them up, like at different times, and it's like a fluid thing.

Why do you think it's fluid, where does this come from?

Mary: I suppose it's like an equality on a gender basis.

Anet: We don't have expectations within this set-up on how we should interact. . . . In a heterosexual situation . . . there's this gender inequality which has come with just the way that you've been brought up.

Mary: It's just jobs to do for us, things that need doing and they don't have a value, a sort of female or male value within our set-up, they are just things that need doing and there's none of that gender thing going on.

Mary's idea about tasks losing their symbolic value came up often in interviews, particularly in relation to the performance of 'male' tasks, such as DIY. Judith, birth-mother of a two-year-old boy, comments on this:

I think it's much more acceptable to take on whatever role you want, or whatever you're happy with. I mean it doesn't matter if I want to go and chop down a tree in the garden, that's fine, there's not some man being put out because I am doing heavy work, or if Liz wants to go and fiddle with the car, that's fine. I think it's the whole society man/woman thing. I think there are an awful lot of new men, new relationships. . . . But, I think it's a lot easier for us because we don't have any sort of roles to live up to.

Alternatively, some women who had struggled to achieve more egalitarian heterosexual relationships spoke of their relief from feeling that they had to perform 'male' tasks.

Importantly, respondents' similarities as women, which enabled them to put themselves in the place of the other, facilitated the construction of more balanced domestic arrangements. In discussing their approach to allocating domestic work, respondents spoke in terms of not wanting to exploit the other, or of feeling that one person should not be clearing up after the other, or of just being aware that it was their turn to do something. The balance came because the monitoring of contributions was on the basis of broadly similar criteria. This, together with the empathy experienced, enabled greater transparency in the evaluation of the fairness of contributions. This contrasts with the situation for men and women in heterosexual relationships where gender difference not only structures contributions but hinders change by shaping evaluative criteria (Hochschild, 1989; Gordon, 1990: 97). For example, a mis-match in criteria arises as a man compares his contributions favourably to other men and finds it hard to understand why he fails to satisfy his partner. The ability to be in tune with the rhythm of the household is something that women have learnt. This capacity to notice and anticipate *disadvantages* women in heterosexual partnerships because on the whole men do not do it, but it is a great source of *advantage* for women managing a home together – in the individual interviews, respondents usually spoke of both themselves and their partners as being actively involved in keeping things ticking over on the domestic front.

For two women together divisions of labour in the home were responsive to employment demands. In times of stress the balance could shift. However, there was usually a short-term/long-term distinction made. Respondents commonly challenged the idea that the pursuit of employment opportunities justified the long-term relinquishment of basic domestic and childcare responsibilities. Even in sole-earner partnerships the paid worker entered into the rhythm of the home. Ella, sole-earner, birth-mother to a grown-up son and co-parent of two primary-school-aged boys, explains the situation when she returns home in the evening:

[When I was married] my husband came home from work and his day was finished, in terms of work, whereas when I come home from work I don't have that sense. . . . I take my coat off and assess what's going on and act – get on with it. If they're in the bath I go and get their pyjamas or whatever. You don't have that kind of demarcation line.

Routinely, respondents challenged the logic behind the following statement 'surely, if one partner has a stressful job and her partner is home-based, it is only fair that she should come home to rest?' with comments such as, 'the statement assumes that caring for a small child isn't stressful' or 'getting on with chores at home can be a good way of relaxing'. Again, the capacity for one partner to place herself in the position of the other is key for understanding their views. This empathy was in turn reinforced by the experiential insights gained through lack of specialization. Thus, the performance of paid work, the domestic routine and childcare afforded no mystery. This view is well summarized by Helen. She and her partner, May, each have half-time employment and share the care of their two pre-school-aged children between them:

I think that because you have been through the situation yourself you have a real understanding. If you are at home all day with a baby you cannot think of anything that is more demanding than that or more tiring. But if you have been out at work all day you cannot think of anything more tiring than that. But because we have done both, we can really understand. There wouldn't be an argument about who has had the hardest day because we both had a very clear understanding of the experience of being at home all day and the experience of being at work all day. They are both very demanding in different ways.

The gender dynamics underpinning lesbian relationships enabled women to operationalize their more egalitarian ideals to the extent that most felt that they had managed to achieve a satisfactory balance of power. Most felt consciously involved in maintaining this balance through negotiation and periodic review. Traditional divisions of labour were seen and had often been experienced as restrictive and oppressive, and respondents were keen to avoid replicating them in their relationships with women.

Balance as Default

There were, however, several couples who were less consciously working towards a particular ideal. Because they managed to achieve similar outcomes to those negotiated by respondents with more conscious egalitarian goals, their experience is extremely illuminating of the way that sexuality mediates gender practices. I will illustrate this situation with the experience of Joel and Viv. Each has a primary-school-aged son and they have been living together as a family for just over one year. When married they had both been full-time mothers who held an unproblematic acceptance of the traditional division of labour they experienced with their husbands. Because their uncritical approach to traditional arrangements is so unusual in comparison to the rest of the sample, it is worth exploring in some detail the transformation in household arrangements they experienced. Joel is looking at their completed Household Portrait, where most of the domestic tasks have been placed on the 50 per cent line. She tries to imagine what it would have looked like if she had completed it with her ex-husband:

> Washing the floors I'd do it all – I really hated hoovering and I did it all. . . . Tidying up – he was quite a tidy person, which I suppose is unusual. Perhaps general cleaning I'd do more of, yes, because he was at work. But he wasn't too bad around the house really (laughter) he was quite good. . . . I was quite lucky in that way. . . . Apart from the ironing he'd do most things. Apart from the cooking as well. Obviously I'd do most of the cooking . . .

> *You said he was pretty good on sort of contributing to childcare and domestic work?*

> What Neil? *Yeah.* Not childcare, no! Domestic perhaps. He wasn't very good – when Jim [their son] was very young. . . . He couldn't really cope very well, so most of the time I was left with Jim and he used to go down the pub.

The only way that she could conclude that Neil was 'quite good' was by comparing his contributions to other men rather than a female partner. Viv, too, retained gendered bench-marks for thinking back to the organization of work in her marriage:

> I don't feel [housework] is my responsibility now, whereas before in my heterosexual relationship, it was my responsibility. He was at work, so that's why I stayed at home and did the housework. There was nobody else to do it, he wouldn't come home and do the housework. I don't think many men will, quite honestly, because they're at work, whereas I was at home all day, so the least I can do is keep the house clean. . . . [Now] it's down to both of us. Whoever is at home at the time has to do whatever is necessary. It's a joint thing.

However, the space created by the absence of a male partner presented Joel and Viv with some problems. They were not educationally advantaged and had never had paid employment, so earning a living represented a challenge. Their solution was to set up a market stall and take turns in working on it. This enabled one of them to always be at home when their children returned from school. Extending into the more male territory of DIY, however, represented an even greater challenge. Joel explains:

> We've been doing a lot of maintenance work this week and quite honestly it's hard work, but it has to be done and we do it. Sometimes you could do with a bit of help. Sometimes we have to get our fathers to help us, and my brothers.

There's more to do, like maintenance, painting, decorating, carpentry – certain things that are expected of you, you know, being in this relationship, than what there is in a heterosexual one. Being married to a man, well not that he did, but most men take on the role of car maintenance and carpentry and so on. Whereas you take on these things yourself. . . . It's a joint thing, whereas, if I was married to a man, I would expect the man to do.

Here we can see how easy it is to fall into assumptions of gendered responsibility if there was a man around the home. Even though Joel's husband did not *actually* do these tasks, Joel assumes and expects 'most men' to do them. However, as two women running a household together they were forced to extend their repertoire of activities to include those that are more traditionally male activities. While difficult and challenging, they saw this experience as bringing rewards. Joel reflects on their situation:

We've taken on a male role here between us, being joint breadwinners and taking on a lot of the physical chores [that] we've never had to do. . . . Now I am having to learn . . . I get more out of my day. It's hard work, but . . . it's not just the work, it's just that I do things for myself and I get a lot of satisfaction. I have to deal with things for myself and I find that if it goes right, you know, I find it very satisfying. Things that I didn't ever think I could do, I can do now. I surprise myself.

Importantly, the more egalitarian approaches, routines and outcomes achieved by these two women in their relationship together were presented to me as being no more unusual or worthy of comment than the specialization that characterized their marriages. In both situations they were doing what seemed to them as 'natural'.

Discussion: Gender, Sexuality and 'Sameness'?

Earlier, I suggested that the boundaries drawn around gender categories create spaces for gender solidarity, and desire can be organized around 'identification and similarity rather than difference' (Connell, 1987: 182). The experience of the mothers in this study seems to bear this out. The balance they manage to achieve provides insights into a more egalitarian social world where gender seems to have lost much of its power to structure relationships along lines of difference and inequality.

Of course the idea of a passion for 'sameness' is in many ways fallacious. First, women are different from each other in all sorts of important respects (e.g., autobiography, class, ethnicity, education, employment status, income, age, degree of able-bodiedness, looks, charisma, to name but a few). However, I would argue, lesbianism is about a preference for negotiating (balancing, valuing, offsetting) differences within the solidarity that comes from experiencing the world as women. A lesbian's partner is usually her best friend, or at least one of them, and the operation of power is more likely to elaborate upon the rules of friendship (equality, support, balancing the differences, reciprocity) than the rules of heterosexual romance (the eroticization of difference, 'intimate strangers' possessing different emotional vocabularies, institutional and sexual power imbalances). Further, and related to this, is that the gender of the person one is doing gender with/for makes a real difference. As such, lesbianism is a preference for doing gender for, and being gendered by women rather than men in the social world as it is dominantly constructed. I am convinced that for women, moving beyond heterosexuality is deeply rooted in this additional gender dimension/context to the process of gendering. This is why so many of the lesbian women that I have interviewed have expressed views such as 'I cannot be *me* in relationships with men in the way that I can with women – or at least not the same *me*' (Dunne, 1997a: 113).

Secondly, to speak of 'a passion for sameness' is almost a contradiction in terms. As a phrase it is revealing because it exposes so clearly the deeply accepted and expected conjunction between passion and 'difference'. 'Sameness' conjures up images of blandness and dullness, thus revealing the exclusive power of heterosexuality to lay claim to all the necessary ingredients for generating thrilling challenges, alluring excitements. Aside from the reality of there being plenty of differences between partners in same-sex relationships to present exciting challenges in knowing and being known, the reality of a 'passion for difference' as it is lived in many women's everyday lives seriously throws into question the idea that eroticized difference is a very sound basis for sustaining long-standing relationships. One has to ask, what are we left with when difference loses its erotic power in a heterosexual partnership?[8] In answering this we are offered crucial clues into why so many women are leaving relationships with men or forgoing marriage. What it means to be a woman has radically shifted over the past 40 years, but there has not been a corresponding movement of men into women's traditional domains. The identities available to increasing numbers of women have expanded beyond wife and mother to include a more self-conscious sense of self as perhaps mothers bringing up children alone or with a partner in a separate household, as divorced or single, as feminists, as lesbians, as breadwinners and employees. As opportunities start to open for women in terms of who we can be and how we can finance our existence in the world it is less likely that women will put up with disappointment in their relationships. We are in the midst of a gender revolution and we have not yet acknowledged this let alone kept pace with the implications of this in our everyday lives. It may be that behind the 'crisis' of marriage and the traditional family lies a deeper problem that has yet to be consciously given voice – that the raised aspirations and expanded identities of many contemporary women may be in contradiction with the doing of gender through heterosexuality.

Conclusion

Meanwhile, feminism moves forward in three contradictory directions. First, the more dominant, Liberal Feminist position is about enabling women to be more like men. This involves the erosion or denial of difference but retains a masculine and capitalist view of value as defined by 'public' participation. Thus, empowerment is linked with full-time employment and occupational achievement. A problem here is that new forms of inequality emerge as, for example, others (usually working-class women) are found to fill the gaps left by the 'liberated' woman (see for example, Gregson and Lowe, 1994). This position challenges one aspect – what women (but not men) may achieve – of one dimension, *gender boundaries*, of women's disadvantage, but leaves unchallenged another central dimension, the *hierarchy of value* attached to women and men's traditional territories.

The second direction – including 'equal-but-different' and some separatist positions – recognizes and builds upon gender differences (sometimes assuming essential origins but more usually socially constructed ones). By asserting and illuminating the value of what women do, they seek to undermine the *hierarchy of value* assigned to what women and men do. Thus, women's nurturing qualities can be celebrated. The different capacities and skills of women and men may be seen to complement each other in partnerships based on equivalence – which is, of course, rather dependent on the endurance of a relationship. The problem with this approach is that *gender boundaries* are left unchallenged. Specialization, whether it be enacted in a context of inequality or equivalence, simply reinforces the traditional masculine model of employment.[9] Further, by making claims of an enduring, specifically female character, the process of socialization is reified in such a way as to leave us no further ahead than when differences have been located in nature.

A third direction is to contest both the boundaries and the hierarchies – the more challenging and difficult approach of the three, which is, however, more in keeping with the logic of feminism. When thinking about what difference gender difference makes, it is hard to come up with any which do not relate to the very structures of inequality that feminists seek to undermine. Consequently, we have a common interest in dissolving gender as a category of both content and consequence. This involves acting upon our recognition that gender has a social origin, is possessed by men as well as women and can thus be transcended by both. In practical terms, this means recognizing and celebrating the value of women's traditional areas of work and influence rather than accepting a masculine and capitalist hierarchy of value which can lead to women passing on their responsibilities to less powerful women. In conjunction with this would be the view that this valuable work is something that male peers can and should do, the aim being to facilitate and insist upon change in men's lives – enabling them to become more like women to the same degree that women have become more like men. The radicalness of this direction is that it challenges both patriarchy and capitalism. If, for example, fathers experienced parenting and domestic life in similar ways to women, then they would find the time demands of employers as unrealistic as mothers usually do. This would have serious implications for the organization of paid work and would undermine men's monopoly of economic advantage (see illustrations in Dunne, 1997b, 1998a).

Because gender and sexuality are interconnected, this suggests that the erosion of gender would undermine the meanings and circumstances that give rise to the categories heterosexual and homosexual. In this way men would lose their monopoly of women. Connell (1987: 288) draws similar conclusions in his speculations about the future for feminism. However, he pulls back somewhat from advocating this 'solution' because of concern about the loss of richness and creativity that appears to be associated with gendered culture. However, cultures survive immense change, including the erosion of other structures of domination that have given rise to art and knowledge. Further, as I have suggested, most of the differences that exist between people will not be erased by the loss of gender. They may, however, be more easily balanced between people and have less overall consequence than existing configurations of difference along gender lines.

Notes

I am extremely grateful to the following for their help and comments, and the lively, insightful debates we have had as the ideas in this chapter have emerged: Shirley Prendergast, Ginny Morrow, Andrea Doucet, Kim Perren, Esther Dermott, Jackie Beer and Sarah Oerton. I would also like to thank the editors of this book, Elizabeth Silva and Carol Smart, for providing encouragement and constructive criticism. Additionally, I am grateful to the Economic and Social Research Council for funding the project (reference no.: R000234649) and to Henrietta Moore and Bob Blackburn for their support and advice throughout.

1 The study was undertaken by the author and fieldwork was conducted during 1995 and 1996. For further details on methods see Dunne (1998a).

2 The Household Portrait was first developed by Andrea Doucet (1995, 1997) for illuminating the allocation strategies of egalitarian heterosexual couples. This technique involves both partners placing a broad range of task/responsibility tokens (colour-coded by themes such as routine domestic, household service work, childcare, etc.) on to a board offering a continuum ranging from 100 per cent partner A to 100 per cent partner B. This visual representation encourages respondents to reflect upon and discuss how their household is run, and participate in some initial analysis as patterns emerge.

3 In 40 per cent of households both partners had experienced biological motherhood.

4 While there is some evidence that men and women can form egalitarian domestic relationships (VanEvery, 1995), a distinctly asymmetrical division of unwaged labour remains the majority pattern. An unequal division of responsibilities in the home is a dominant trend in households where men are unemployed (Morris, 1995) and women are sole earners (Wheelock, 1990), among full-time dual-earner couples (Mansfield and Collard, 1988; Brannen and Moss, 1991), where both are in professional occupations (Gregson and Lowe, 1994), or the wife has a higher status job than her husband's (McRae, 1986). Gendered patterns of responsibilities remain even in countries such as Sweden and Denmark, where there is a strong political commitment to promoting equality in the employment and home lives of women and men (Borchorst, 1990; Haas, 1990). Couples who perceive themselves to be sharing in the home rarely escape the impact of gendered assumptions shaping their work strategies (Doucet, 1997).

5 For feminist critiques of heterosexuality as 'natural' see the classics, Rich (1984), Rubin (1975) and Wittig (1992). Each of these positions allows us to view lesbianism as a source of empowerment.

6 See Dunne (1997a) for a case study which attempts to explore these questions and illustrates links between lesbianism and empowerment, with particular reference to work and relationships.

7 The possibility that this passion is given voice and acted upon is limited by the existence of powerful social sanctions (e.g., representation of homosexuality as perversion, sickness) and material constraints (see Dunne, 1997a).

8 See Prendergast and Forrest (1997) for an example from contemporary teenage heterosexual relationships where difference is all that there is.

9 So long as women retain responsibility for work in the home men have the time to devote to the long paid working hours associated with 'a masculine model of employment' (Bradley, 1989) and thus retain their monopoly of employment advantages.

6

EVERYDAY EXPERIMENTS: NARRATIVES OF NON-HETEROSEXUAL RELATIONSHIPS

Jeffrey Weeks, Catherine Donovan and Brian Heaphy

Unlike the 1960s, when the questioning of traditional forms produced a search for alternatives to the family, increasingly today there is a pronounced tendency to speak of 'alternative families', differentiated by class, 'race' and ethnicity, life-cycle, single parenthood, chosen lifestyles and the like (Weeks, 1991). Yet while many of these forms have become increasingly acceptable (though not without frequent political controversy, as in the case of one-parent families), there is a continuing stigma attached to non-heterosexual (lesbian, gay, same-sex or 'queer') forms. As the pejorative term 'pretended family relationships', legally enshrined in the Local Government Act of 1988, suggests, non-heterosexual patterns are somehow not real. Perhaps it is hardly surprising, then, that the legitimacy of non-heterosexual relationships has recently become a major topic of political controversy, in debates over adoption and surrogacy (in the UK), partnership rights (in many parts of Europe), and same-sex marriage (in the Netherlands and the USA). When the queen of The Netherlands threatens to resign rather than sign into law an act legalizing 'gay marriage', and when a notoriously tardy US Congress rushes into law a bill refusing recognition of the same, something is clearly afoot in the moral undergrowth. At the same time, however, there is growing evidence that lesbians and gay men are establishing sophisticated social forms, which we describe as 'families of choice', with that sense of involvement, security and continuity over time traditionally associated with the orthodox family, and yet which are deeply rooted in a specific historic experience.

During the past generation the possibilities of living an openly lesbian and gay life have been transformed, with the construction of new spaces for everyday life (Bell and Valentine, 1995; Weeks, 1995), and the development of complex cultural patterns. The unprecedented public presence and volubility of lesbians and gays since the late 1960s is in itself an index of profound changes in the private existence of the non-heterosexual population (Plummer, 1992). In part this amounts to the construction of difference, and certainly the public presentation of homosexuality can be seen as the shaping of new narratives which affirm the distinctiveness of the homosexual experience. Not surprisingly, this has been reflected in a literature, and social and cultural stance, which asserted the importance of sexual identity, allied to a growing assertion of difference. This was supported by the emergence of a social movement which affirmed positive lesbian and gay identities, and which in turn grew out of and strengthened a concept of a distinctive lesbian and gay community (see Weeks, 1996).

Since the early 1980s, however, two marked shifts are discernible. The first is the emergence of a new discourse concerned with wider aspects of homosexual existence than simply sexuality and identity: with relationships, friendships, experiences of intimacy, homosexual parenting, as well as partnership rights and marriage, which could be described as the development of a 'relationship paradigm' (see Weeks et al., 1996 for an overview). Increasingly, political campaigns around homosexuality have extended beyond traditional preoccupations with equal rights and legal protection to embrace questions about relationships: the legal recognition of partnership rights, same-sex marriage, equal rights to adoption and the like (Sullivan, 1995).

On one level, this can be seen as an inevitable consequence of the developing cultural acceptance, and social embeddedness, of the lesbian and gay community as part of a growing pluralization of society. On another level, however, these changing preoccupations are an aspect of the second shift: a recognition of the opening up of all social identities, and what Giddens (1992) has called the 'transformation of intimacy'. On a theoretical level, the post-structuralist and post-modernist challenges to social theory have stressed the fluid, historical, negotiable, contingent nature of all social identities, including sexual identities (Weeks, 1995). Increasingly, it can be argued, identities are not pre-given; they have to be articulated in increasingly complex social circumstances. The lesbian and gay assertion of identities is only one aspect of a wider construction of identities. And if, indeed, identities are contingent, and changeable, it becomes important to understand both how and why identities emerge, how they are stabilized, and how they can be transformed. The relational possibilities – whether in the distinctive social worlds where identities are shaped and affirmed, or in the intensely personal world where intimate involvements are cemented – are keys to the understanding of personal identity. Identity is shaped in and through intimate relationships.

Modernity, Giddens (1992) has argued, is a post-traditional order in which the question 'how shall I live?' has to be answered in day-to-day decisions about who to be, how to behave and, crucially for this discussion, who and how we should love and relate to. Intimacy, in its modern form, implies a radical democratization of the interpersonal domain, because it assumes not only that the individual is the ultimate maker of his or her own life, but also equality between partners, and their freedom to choose lifestyles and forms of partnerships. Despite the particularism of the homosexual experience, one of the most remarkable features of domestic change over recent years is, we would argue, the emergence of common patterns in both homosexual and heterosexual ways of life as a result of these long-term shifts in relationship patterns (see Bech, 1996). In both, it can be argued, the central drive is the search for a satisfactory relationship as a key element in personal affirmation. The relationship, whether marital or non-marital, heterosexual or homosexual, becomes the defining element within the sphere of the intimate, which provides the framework for everyday life. It is also the focus of personal identity, in which the personal narrative is constructed and reconstructed to provide that provisional sense of unity of the self which is all that is possible in the conditions of late modernity. What Giddens (1992) calls the 'pure relationship', dependent on mutual trust between partners, is both a product of the reflexive self, and a focus for its realization. It offers a focal point for personal meaning in the contemporary world, with love and sex as the prime site for its attainment.

This can be put in another way: the transformations of intimacy, themselves the product of the breakdown of traditional narratives and legitimizing discourses under the impact of long-term cultural, social and economic forces, are making possible diverse ways of life which cut across the heterosexual/homosexual dichotomy. So alongside the discourse of difference which marks the non-heterosexual experience, we can also see the emergence of a certain logic of congruence. Non-heterosexual relationships are shaped in and through these apparently divergent tendencies.

A key aspect of these changes is that as we culturally prioritize individual choice and the acceptance of diversity, commitment becomes increasingly a matter of negotiation rather than ascription. Recent studies of family and kin obligations (Finch, 1989; Finch and Mason, 1993) suggest that although ties to family of origin remain highly significant, they cannot be assumed, and are as much a product of 'working out' as of blood. The authors prefer to use the concepts of 'developing commitments' and of a sense of responsibility that is worked out over time, so that while kin relationships remain distinctive, the extent to which they differ from other relationships, particularly friendships, is blurred. This is clearly of great significance in relationship to non-familial commitments. Nardi (1992), for example, notes that friends can provide that sense of commitment and shared responsibility which kin relationships traditionally do offer, in a 'friends as family' model. In both examples, commitments are seen as products of negotiation.

e are witnessing, we would argue, is the emergence of new
onceiving family and intimate life, which emphasize individual
.d meanings, the prioritization of intimacy as the focus of
.c arrangements, and the negotiated nature of commitment and
ι..., .ibility. Plummer (1995), among others, has conceptualized these
in terms of new narrative forms, or stories, that are significantly re-
shaping the ways in which we conceive intimate life. As Plummer puts it:

> The ceaseless nature of story telling in all its forms in all societies has come to
> be increasingly recognised. . . . Society itself may be seen as a textured but
> seamless web of stories emerging everywhere through interaction: holding
> people together, pulling people apart, making societies work . . . the metaphor
> of the story . . . has become recognised as one of the central roots we have into
> the continuing quest for understanding human meaning. Indeed culture itself
> has been defined as 'an ensemble of stories we tell about ourselves'.
> (Plummer, 1995: 5)

If this is the case, then the emergence of new ways of expressing basic
needs and desires ('new stories') may be seen as highly important. They
are indicative both of changing perceptions and of changing possibilities. New stories about sexual and intimate life emerge, it has been
argued, when there is a new audience ready to hear them in communities of meaning and understanding, and when newly vocal groups can
have their experiences validated in and through them. This in turn gives
rise to new demands for recognition and validation as the new narratives circulate. These demands may be the expressions of a minority, but
they resonate with broader changes in intimate life. It is in this context
that we can begin to understand the significance of the new stories about
non-heterosexual families of choice.

The Family of Choice

'Family' is a resonant word, embracing a variety of social, cultural,
economic and symbolic meanings. In social policy discussions, however,
it is conventionally used to denote relationships which involve the care
of children. It is striking, therefore, that the term is in common use
among self-identified non-heterosexuals to denote something broader:
an affinity circle which may or may not involve children which has
cultural and symbolic meaning for the subjects that participate or feel a
sense of belonging in and through it. These two quotations illustrate this
broadening, almost metaphoric, use of the term. The first is from a black
lesbian:

> I think the friendships I have are family. I'm sure lots of people will say this,
> but, it's very important to me because my family are not – apart from my

mother, who's *kind* of important – on the whole my family's all I've got. And my family are my friends. And I think you make your family – because I've never felt like I belonged anywhere. And it's taken me a long time to realise that it comes from me. . . . It doesn't matter where I go or who I am with, I'm not going to just suddenly be given a family, or a history, or an identity, or whatever. You don't just get it on a plate. You have to create your own. So far as I am concerned, that's how important friends are. (F02)

The second is from a white gay man:

we call each other family – you know, they're family. I'm not sure whether that's family in the sense of being gay. . . . I have a blood family, but I have an extended family . . . my friends. (M04)

There are several points that can be made about such statements. In the first place, the use of the term suggests a strong perceived need for the sort of values and comforts that the traditional idea of the family suggests (though the reality of the family of origin may be starkly different). Although some lesbians particularly disliked using the term 'family' because of its oppressive heterosexual connotations, for many others friendship circles are like the idealized family (and infinitely preferable to the real one), offering 'a feeling of belonging to a group of people who like me' (M05); 'affection, love if you like – you share the good things, and you share the bad things too' (M44); 'they support me . . . I socialize with them, talk about things that are important to me' (F01). Friendships provide the 'lifeline' that the biological family, it is believed, should provide, but often cannot or will not for its non-heterosexual offspring. For a young lesbian, the family of origin is 'homophobic', and cannot offer what friends do provide. Friends are:

supportive, and understand in a way that your family should and often doesn't. And because of people's situations, they often end up spending more time with their [friends]. . . . I think they become like family. (F43)

This brings us to the second point: the most commonly used terms applied to such relationships are 'chosen' and 'created'. For one gay man, friends are:

more important than family. . . . I take my family [of origin] for granted, whereas my friendships are, to a degree, chosen, and therefore they're created. And I feel a greater responsibility to nourish them, whereas my family will always be there. (M21)

The narrative of self-invention is a very powerful one, particularly in relation to self-identity and lifestyle. As a gay man in his late thirties put it:

> speaking from my generation . . . discovering that I was homosexual meant
> having to invent myself because there was nothing there . . . there weren't any
> role models. It may well be different for gay men coming out now. . . . But
> there's still that element of self invention. (M17/18)

This story of creating your own life is widely echoed in the theoretical
literature (e.g., Foucault, 1979; Giddens, 1992; Weeks, 1995) and reflects
(as well, no doubt, as reflexively contributing to) the perceived reality in
a post-modern world of fluid identities. It peculiarly relates, however, to
the common discourse of many lesbians and gay men who see themselves as breaking away from the constraints of traditional institutional
patterns, which denied their sexuality and identity. Heterosexuals, a gay
man suggests, 'slip into roles that are preordained and it goes along that
route. Whereas we don't have any preordained roles so we can actually
invent things as we want them' (M17/18). Or as a lesbian sees it: 'With
my family of choice it's somewhere that, you know, it's an environment
where I can be myself' (F15).

In practice, of course, there are clear overlaps between homosexual
choices and the choices of many self-identified heterosexuals. But for
non-heterosexuals the idea of a *chosen* family is a powerful signifier of a
fresh start, of affirming a new sense of belonging, that becomes an
essential part of asserting the validity of homosexual ways of life. When
a gay man was asked whether gay and heterosexual relations differed,
the reply was significant: 'Essentially, no. Strategically, yes' (M21). In
other words, by affirming the values of choice, new possibilities were
opened up for non-heterosexuals: the new type of family stands for
something different.

Identity, and thereby difference, built around sexual preferences and
choices, is confirmed through a sense of community that friendships can
provide:

> For me [family] means the gay community. (F03)

> I suppose I don't feel part of a big community, but I think there are lots of
> smaller communities . . . because I can't think of myself as being anything
> other than a gay man, having those friendships and support networks, I
> suppose, is extremely important. I think I'd be a very sad and pathetic person
> without them. (M05)

'Community', with all its historic baggage and ambiguity, nevertheless
provides the context for asserting personal values, and is also the
precondition for putting homosexuality on the public agenda.

Identity, community, choice: these are key terms in the lives of many
non-heterosexuals. They are seen as the necessary context for the
shaping (or 'invention') of what a gay man called the 'queer construct
family'. But if choice is the ruling discourse, it is also important to

recognize the limits on choice. This is the third important factor to note. It is easier for someone now coming out into the lesbian and gay social world to enter a network of friends than it would have been for someone from an earlier generation (although, of course, homosexual networks are historically well established – see, for example, Porter and Weeks, 1990). Similarly, it is easier to construct elective families in metropolitan centres than in rural areas. Political factors can also be important. One black lesbian was battling with her perception of institutionalized racism, and had made a conscious decision to shape her life choices around a community of black women. Choices are contingent on many factors, constrained by the socio-economic, cultural and historical contexts in which we live (see Allen, 1989; Weston, 1991). Moreover, these forms of interaction lack the social recognition of more traditional family patterns. The important factors, however, are not the limits, real as these are, but the ethos and values that many non-heterosexual women and men are expressing: that a sense of self-worth and cultural confidence is realized in and through the friendship networks that we describe as families of choice.

There can be no doubt of the potent meanings attached to these friendship networks by many lesbians and gay men. Do they really, however, represent something new? One way of looking at this is to compare families of choice to other recognized social forms. The most obvious is the phenomenon of friendship itself. A recent study (Roberts and McGlone, 1997) has suggested that most people still make a basic distinction between friends and kin in terms of obligation and commitment, and this is also apparent among many non-heterosexuals. However, for many lesbians and gays, their circles meant more than the term friendship usually denotes: 'For my part I don't have friendships on the level that I think heterosexuals have friendships. I think my friendships are more intense' (F43). Friendships flourish, it has been argued (Heinz Kohut, quoted in Little, 1989: 149), when overarching identities are fragmented in periods of rapid social change, or at crucial moments in individual lives, especially for lives lived at odds with social norms. This would certainly describe the context of lesbian and gay lives over the past generation. On the surface, at least, this lends credence to the idea that for many people friendships offer surrogate or 'pretend' families: substitutes for the real thing. This is not, however, how non-heterosexuals see the significance of their relationships, nor how these relationships are characterized in the recent literature. Bozett (1987), for example, sees lesbian and gay relationships as having all the significant defining features of biological families, and Nardi (1992) has described friends *as* family. Weston (1991) has concluded that in creating 'families we choose' lesbians and gays are neither involved in imitating heterosexual families, nor in necessarily replacing or substituting a family of choice for a family of origin. Like Weston's research, our own suggests strongly that for many non-heterosexuals the term 'family' embraces a variety of selected relationships that includes lovers, possibly ex-lovers, intimate friends, as well as blood relatives, and is as real as the family of origin.

A useful approach may be to conceive of elective families as something new sociologically, as an index of changing social possibilities and demands. Clearly they build on historical experience. They are in many ways like changing patterns of friendship, with much in common with the extended networks of support created by other marginalized groups. But they are also examples of what Giddens (1992) sees as the 'everyday experiments in living' that people are required to undertake in an ever more complex world. This is certainly how it is seen and expressed by a number of respondents. In this quotation a respondent is speaking about the ways in which he and his partner test the limits of what is possible:

> . . . we're constantly experimenting with just how far we want to go, and sometimes feel that we have some degree of mobility in a given situation. . . . It's not so much political flag waving, it's just doing what we want to do and trying to push the boundaries a bit, to see how people cope with it . . . (M21)

These everyday experiments are best characterized as fluid and adaptable networks, which, as we have seen, can include blood relatives, but whose core is made up of selected friends. These relationships are sometimes created across class and ethnic barriers, and may be inter-generational. They are also strikingly non-hierarchical, in the sense (in the absence of children) that there is no perceived ordering of significance along lines of age, precedence or role division – which is not to say there are not disparities of income or personal or social power, or any absence of potential conflict. Such divisions are not, however, intrinsic to the relationships. But like many friendship networks, there appears to be a tendency towards social homogeneity. Often they are single sex: a number of male respondents claim not to know many lesbians, and vice versa. In the nature of things, friendships often stretch across the homosexual/heterosexual binarism, but the inner core tend to be both homosocial and homosexual. Frequently, the inner core includes former sexual partners as well, of course, as current lovers. However, partners may have overlapping but different circles of friends. There has been a tendency in the literature to concentrate on lesbian and gay couple relationships as the exclusive focus of intimacy, and as we shall see couples are indeed important. But for many individuals who are not in long-term couple relationships, families of choice are the prime focus of emotional support. Friends may change; new people may enter the circle. But friendship networks seem permanent – certainly, individuals act on the assumption that they are.

Couples

Until fairly recently it was conventional to play down or ignore the dyadic relationships of homosexual men: a stereotype of predatory promiscuity was prevalent in the literature and in popular perceptions. By contrast, lesbians were seen as more likely to form couple relationships, and this difference was strongly related to assumptions about different male and female sexual and emotional needs (see Gagnon and Simon, 1974, for a discussion of this).

But the dominant belief in the non-heterosexual world is that lesbian and gay relationships offer unique possibilities for the construction of egalitarian relationships. This echoes wider historical studies which have indicated that the twentieth century has seen a significant shift in the traditional pattern of homosexual interactions for men and women (Abelove et al., 1993; Dunne, 1997a). There are also significant historical accounts, of course, which indicate that this is true for relations between men and women, largely as a result of the changing role of women and the 'transformation of intimacy' (Giddens, 1992; Beck and Beck-Gernsheim, 1995). The interesting feature, however, is that many lesbians and gay men have consciously shaped their relationships in opposition to assumed heterosexual models. A number of women, particularly, see their lesbianism as a conscious alternative to subordination to men. As a lesbian in her early 50s puts it:

Much more sort of helpless, weak, I think that's one of the things heterosexuality does to women. And I feel I've got stronger and stronger [since coming out as a lesbian]. And of course, some of that could be just getting older and more experienced. But I think some of it is being a lesbian. (F30)

Another woman makes a complementary, and frequently repeated, point:

[in heterosexual relationships] there is an essential power imbalance that there are certain roles, which are backed up by economics and backed up by sanctions. And also . . . men and women are socialized differently in terms of what . . . heterosexual relationships are. Yeah, I think they're very different – very. (F34)

The assumption, among men as well as women, is that, 'it's much easier to have equal relations if you're the same sex' (M31) because this equalizes the terms of the intimate involvement. Or as a lesbian says: 'The understanding between two women is bound to be on a completely different wavelength' (F33). Equal standing means that issues around, for example, the division of labour in the household, are seen to be a matter for discussion and agreement, not a priori assumption, because of 'being able to negotiate, being on an equal level to be able to negotiate in the first place' (M04); 'Everything has to be discussed, everything is negotiable' (F29).

Equality is also seen as integral to intimacy:

> I think there is . . . less a kind of sense of possession, or property, in same-sex relationships, and more emphasis on . . . emotional bonding . . . that's not quite what I mean, but they're less ritualized really. (M39)

There is plentiful evidence as well, inevitably, that egalitarian relations do not automatically develop. They have to be constantly struggled for against inequalities of income, day-to-day commitment, emotional labour, ethnic difference and the like. Inequality of income is perhaps the most frequently divisive factor, especially as for some couples sharing income or even ownership of a home was not only practically but politically difficult, as this little exchange illustrates:

> Q: Did you ever have joint bank accounts?
> A: No. No. That was too heterosexual. (M05)

Whatever the practical difficulties, however, there is a strong emphasis among lesbians and gays on the importance of building intimate couple involvement: 'being in a relationship helps to affirm one as a person and we all need that' (M44); 'I love the continuity. . . . I like the sex. I like doing some things jointly. . . . A sense that you are loveable' (F06). Affirmation through involvement in the democratic, egalitarian relationship appears to be the dominant homosexual norm, conforming closely to Giddens's definition of the 'pure relationship':

> . . . a situation where a social relation is entered into for its own sake, for what can be derived by each person from a sustained association with another; and which is continued only in so far as it is thought by both parties to deliver enough satisfaction for each individual to stay within it. (Giddens, 1992: 58)

This clearly suggests a contingency in couple relationships, which is echoed in the interviews: couples act as if a relationship might last for ever, work at making it work, but also realistically recognize that it might not:

> we said at the beginning that we'd work at it and see what happened, or something along those lines. . . . But we weren't going to make plans or a life-long commitment because . . . (M17/18)

> We've never ever said, that, you know, 'till death us do part'. But we do plan long term – while the relationship is going well, we will be planning long term. Because you can't keep planning short-term and expect long-term things to sort themselves out. (F06)

Sexual attraction is the most obvious factor that draws individuals together in the first place, and provides the basic dynamic. But sex is not in the end the decisive factor. When asked if his relationship was primarily sexual, one gay man replied:

> No. I would say it's very much more a friendship . . . we don't have a tempestuous relationship at all. I think we have a very stable relationship. Sex is obviously part of it, but . . . I wouldn't say our relationship was based on sex. (M12)

A lesbian similarly put sex in its place:

> [Intimacy] is about closeness really. And there's different degrees of it. It's about trust . . . friendship, right through to sexuality. It's about being close and trusting. (F40/41)

It is in this context that the question of sexual fidelity must be considered. For many couples, male as well as female, sexual and emotional fidelity were inextricably linked. For some, however, the most important factor was emotional faithfulness:

> Tim could sleep with somebody, and have sex with them, and I wouldn't feel that was being unfaithful. I would feel he would be unfaithful if he never told me about it. (M04)

Monogamy itself was frequently seen by men and women as something that needed both negotiation and redefinition in the changing circumstances of relationships. As a lesbian commented: 'I had to decide what was real for me, and what wasn't. So, I don't believe in monogamy. I may be monogamous, but I don't do it for its own sake' (F14).

Bauman (1993: 98) has argued that there are two characteristic strategies for dealing with the perceived flux of modern relationships, what he calls 'fixing' and 'floating'. Fixing takes place when the potential openness of what Giddens (1992) calls 'confluent love' is set firmly in place by the demands of duty. Floating occurs when the labour of constant negotiation on the terms of a relationship leads to people cutting their losses, and starting all over again. This is often the case in non-heterosexual relationships:

> . . . a lot of lesbians and gay men split up more often than heterosexuals because they're not necessarily conventionally married, and they don't have to go through all the hassle, so it is easier to split up, I think, in some cases. (F44)

This is not, however, the only pathway. Many work through the vicissitudes of their relationship, constantly re-making it, trying to 'make a go of it' by affirming their long-term commitment. Part of this may be through the creation of special rituals, celebrating together and with friends: '. . . anything we can think of, we celebrate' (F33). Some seek religious blessings or have 'gay weddings' to confirm their partnerships. Others just re-make their relationships on a day-by-day basis: '. . . just the sort of very fact of carrying on living together is a sort of . . . daily renewal of commitment' (M15). In other words, neither floating, nor fixing, but continuously confronting the challenge of relationships, 'working through' the ups and downs.

So far we have discussed same-sex couples as if they were undifferentiated. In fact, on both male and female sides there are strong perceptions of difference between lesbians and gay men. Here are comments from a lesbian woman:

> I see women's level of commitment, or emotions, more intense in their friendships. . . . I know lots of gay men would probably disagree with me . . . gay men, they talk about sex a lot . . . whereas lesbians don't. . . . Oh, this is all very varied, but I think women talk a lot more about emotional things than men do. And I don't think that's just a fallacy. I don't think that's just a myth. I think it's true. (F36)

Alongside these well-established perceptions, there is a degree of ignorance about each other's lifestyles, with both lesbians and gay men claiming not to know many non-heterosexuals of the opposite sex. Although there are differences, however, which are both political and personal, these are minor compared to the similarities in terms of life plans. Among both non-heterosexual women and men there is a similar engagement with the shaping of egalitarian, caring and enduring relationships. The role of sexual desire within these relationships varies widely, but equally important for many are wider concepts of commitment.

Care, Responsibility and Commitment

As same-sex relationships are constructed and maintained outside conventional institutional and legal support systems and structures, they are less likely to be characterized by predetermined obligations, duties and commitments. There is no lack of evidence that such issues matter to non-heterosexuals, but as part (though a critical part) of the negotiation of relationships among equals, a matter of free and conscious choice:

> I would like to think that people in gay relationships stay together because they actually want to stay together to a greater extent than people in heterosexual relationships do. (M15)

Within this sort of ethos, terms such as duty or obligation tended to be avoided by our subjects, having, as one gay man said, 'a negative connotation' (M39). Duty is 'like some kind of moral code that people use to put on you. . . . I don't think I need that kind of external thing put on me' (F04/F05). These terms were compared unfavourably with the concepts of responsibility and mutual care and commitment:

> Responsibility is something I decide to do and I keep to; obligation is when I feel I have to. (F01)

> . . . duty is something that is imposed on you . . . if you feel responsible for someone. I mean, being a parent, you're responsible for your children, then you do that because you feel you want to, not because somebody else feels you ought to. (M44)

Ideas of care and responsibility appear to be situational, dependent on the needs of parent and blood relatives, as well as of friends, but the ideas themselves are potent, organized around notions of 'the right thing to do' (M11), especially with regard to parents (see Finch and Mason, 1993). Freely chosen relationships, however, have the potentiality both to be free of imposed obligations, and therefore, more intense. For many gay men particularly the experience of the AIDS crisis has confirmed the importance of a commitment to care and mutual responsibility (see Adam, 1992): 'It makes some relationships more intense because they are inevitably going to be foreshortened' (M03).

Parenting raises questions of obligation, commitment and responsibility most sharply. Many non-heterosexuals, men and women, are involved in parenting in one way or another, as biological or adoptive parents, or as non-biological co-parents. There is evidence, moreover, that a significant generational shift is taking place in attitudes to parenting. For most gay men over 40 without previous heterosexual relationships, fathering or caring for children had appeared virtually inconceivable. Many lesbians, however, had considered having children, and for both younger men as well as women the question of children is now a live issue. This is partly the result of changing attitudes more generally, and a wider public discussion of questions surrounding non-heterosexual parenting, custody and adoption. It is partly, however, the result of an increasing interest in non-traditional ways of conceiving, especially through donor insemination (Saffron, 1994; Griffin and Mulholland, 1997; Harne and Rights of Women, 1997). A number of lesbians have been involved in discussions with gay male friends about artificial insemination, and some have conceived in this way. This raises often delicate questions about the role of the male donor in co-parenting, and is sometimes the subject of considerable anguished discussion. More traditionally, lesbian couples particularly frequently want children, to complete their relationship.

The resulting parenting arrangements can be quite complex, involving biological parents, lovers, even ex-lovers in an extended family-type arrangement. Those involved in such arrangements tend to be highly conscious of the wider cultural anxieties around such arrangements, and acutely alive, especially, to the sensitivities of the child. Take this example. Two men (M. aged 23 and G., 38) are in a couple relationship and co-parent a 12-year-old daughter with her two lesbian mothers who live nearby. The older man is the biological father through a previous heterosexual relationship and marriage with one of the lesbians:

Do you feel that you get recognition from other people as an important person in B.'s life?

M: . . . well, not in a broader sense, because at school, if I . . . go swimming, and B.'s and the school have gone, and I know not to say hello because that would cause problems, and I have to respect that, and I do. You know, I don't want to make her life difficult for her . . .
G: It's like the difference between being out personally and the fact that you're out as a family. I think we're out as individuals, but the family isn't. (M17/18)

Similarly, two lesbian parents, when asked what they most feared about being openly homosexual, replied it was 'the crap' their daughter would get:

S: I think with adolescence she's going to have a lot of problems of her own without. . . . It's more a concern, you know, for her than for ourselves really, isn't it?
J: Mm. We're already aware that she has to be secretive. (F04/05)

Yet, whatever the means of giving birth or being involved in parenting, whatever the social and personal hazards, the care and well-being of the child remains the first and ultimate responsibility of same-sex parents, over and above the relationship itself. This seems to be the common thread across the diversity of parenting practices.

The Power of New Stories

Care and legal responsibility for children raises in an acute form the legal status, and social policy implications, of the emergence of elective families and the public affirmation of lesbian and gay relationships. The evidence from European countries which have legally recognized the registration of same-sex partnerships suggests that parenting, and especially access to adoption rights, is a last taboo: characteristically, as in Denmark, when partnership rights are recognized, they exclude adoption (see Waaldijk, 1994; Bech, 1996). Attempts to give lesbian and gays full rights to marriage, as currently in The Netherlands and

Hawaii, are highly controversial precisely because they involve parenting rights also. The rights of lesbian parents, especially to custody of their children when marriages break up, have been challenged for some 20 years, often on the grounds that children need fathers for healthy development (Hanscombe and Forster, 1982; Martin, 1993; Saffron 1994), despite evidence of the success of lesbian parenting (see Tasker and Golombok, 1991, 1995, 1997; Saffron, 1996). Recent cases in Britain suggest some flexibility in legal decisions over lesbian custody (Williams, 1994), but the statutory situation remains unfavourable to lesbian and gay custody and adoption rights.

This is only one aspect of a wider lack of legal recognition of the implications of non-heterosexual domestic patterns (on the general issues, see VanEvery, 1991/92; Carabine, 1995). On a range of issues, from access of lesbians to donor insemination through parenting to immigration, health insurance, pension rights, mortgages and joint home ownership and inheritance rights, the legal status of same-sex relationships is at best ambiguous and at worst discriminatory. It is in this context that we need to consider the implications of the new narratives of non-heterosexuals about relationships and rights.

Many, if not most, self-identified lesbians and gays have a strong sense that the cultural privileging of heterosexuality inevitably denies full humanity to non-heterosexuals, and therefore fails to legitimize their most significant commitments. This is expressed by the frequent use of the terms 'homophobia' and 'heterosexism' to describe prevailing cultural norms. While there is a recognition that social attitudes had changed, often dramatically, in the past generation, making a new openness possible, there is also a strong sense that change had not gone far or fast enough. Many non-heterosexuals have experienced some form of informal discrimination, ranging from enforced self-censorship to physical attack. Above all, there is a strong sense that their most valued relationships are not given full recognition, sometimes even within families of origin, let alone the wider society.

A sense of injustice leads inevitably to a claim to rights. Essentially, non-heterosexuals wish for the same rights as heterosexuals to choose their ways of life, without being discriminated against. Many, lesbians in particular, favour full individualization of social and economic rights, which would remove the legal consequences that flow from married status, so that rights and responsibilities would belong to individuals (see Waaldijk, 1994). As a lesbian observed:

[marriage is] not going to give equal rights to everyone – it's only going to give equal rights to people who are in long-term relationships. And that doesn't seem fair to me. (F02)

Others want full access to the same couple rights as heterosexuals, including pension rights, inheritance, immigration and so on, without necessarily having formally to register a partnership. The most controversial issue, however, relates to the formal recognition of partnerships, and the question of same-sex 'marriage'. It sometimes divided couples, as this exchange indicates:

J: T. doesn't feel the need to do something like that, and I'd like to do something like that.
T: That's just your insecurity.
J: It's my insecurity, or you could re-frame it the other way round. I think we've been together now for over seven years. I think that it's appropriate that we do something that celebrates and acknowledges our relationship.
T: We don't argue on it! We just agree to disagree . . . I suppose it's conforming to the way that heterosexuals live. We're not heterosexuals. (M01/02)

On the one hand, there is the desire for the same rights as heterosexuals:

I'm totally in favour [of same sex marriage] . . . because if I met someone who I cared for that much and we couldn't make it legal in some respects, I would be so angry. . . . I mean, you don't have to have the commitment, but it's nice to have the opportunity, to actually go through the ceremony of being legally married. . . . I don't want partnership rights, I want marriage. (M10)

On the other hand, there is the discourse of difference:

I just think it's a piece of nonsense, really – not a piece of nonsense, but, I don't like saying 'aping heterosexuality' because. . . . I believe we should all be treated equally in the eyes of the law, but . . . I believe now we are not the same as straight people, that we do have differences, and that we are diverse and that we are creative, and that we take a lot more risks around a lot of things. (F36)

This leads, finally, to the question of the meaning of full citizenship in the contemporary discourse of non-heterosexuals. Plummer (1995) has suggested that historically there have been three key concepts of citizenship which have successively commanded the political agenda: political (access to equal rights in the state), social (equal access to social rights), and economic (equal access to economic opportunities). He argues that these are now being joined by a fourth claim, to intimate citizenship, which:

speaks to an array of concerns too often neglected in past debates over citizenship, and which extends notions of rights and responsibilities. . . . [I]t is concerned with all those matters linked to our most intimate desires, pleasures, and ways of being in the world. (Plummer, 1995: 151)

There are no blueprints in terms of policy or practice about how such claims to intimate citizenship should be worked through, because there is inherent in them both a sense of the contingency of all rights claims, and of the diversity of social and personal practices which they entail. Claims to intimate citizenship involve difficult questions about the relationship between private and public, about responsibilities as well as rights, about the social and political implications of any notion of complex, and different, 'equalities', about balancing a sense (and affirmation) of difference with a sense of common belonging and common values (see Weeks, 1995). The general point that can be made, however, is that these issues are, in part, on the agenda because they are being raised in the diverse interpretative communities that make up a complex society, and are being clearly articulated by lesbians and gay men. They are, in Plummer's (1995) formulation, part of 'a field of stories, an array of tellings, out of which new lives, new communities and new politics may emerge' (Plummer, 1995: 151–2).

As we have already suggested, many of the new stories of lesbian and gay lives are very close to those that might be told about rapidly changing patterns of heterosexual lives. That does not lessen the importance of the new narratives about non-heterosexual relationships. On the contrary, they underscore the significance of what is happening to our notions of 'family'. These non-heterosexual narratives of family and of choice, of care and responsibility, of love and loss, of old needs and new possibilities, of difference and convergence, are prime examples of those everyday experiments which are contributing to the creation of the 'new family'.

Note

This chapter is based on research conducted for a project funded by the Economic and Social Research Council, entitled 'Families of choice: the structure and meanings of non-heterosexual relationships' (reference no.: L315253030). The research took place between 1995 and 1996, as part of the ESRC's research programme on Population and Household Change, and was based in the School of Education, Politics and Social Science, South Bank University, London. The director of the project was Jeffrey Weeks, with Catherine Donovan and Brian Heaphy as the research fellows. The core of the research involved in-depth interviews with 48 men and 48 women who broadly identified as non-heterosexual. All the first-person quotations in this chapter come from these interviews. All female interviews are denoted by 'F', the male interviews by an 'M', each followed by a number. The numbers reflect the order in which the interviews took place. Because our respondents used a range of self-identifications – lesbian, gay, bisexual, queer, homosexual – we have preferred to use the terms non-heterosexual or same-sex throughout when referring generically to key findings.

7

THE 'NEW' PARENTHOOD: FATHERS AND MOTHERS AFTER DIVORCE

Carol Smart

Throughout the 1980s and 1990s in Britain there has been a growing debate over fatherhood, in particular the question of the role of fathers after divorce.[1] This has been conceived in terms of either a failure in fatherhood, in which it has been argued that men have not adjusted to a new role, or as a crisis in fatherhood,[2] in which it is argued that men no longer seem necessary to the family. This debate has coincided with another set of concerns which arose in the 1980s, namely a growing fear about the perceived harmful effects of divorce on children.[3] Although much of the research on which the concern about harm was based was originally North American, it was taken up in Britain and contributed to a growing alarm over a perceived increase in under-achieving and delinquent children. The link between these two sets of concerns lay in the argument that what caused this harm to children on divorce was, in fact, the lack of a 'proper' father. This argument signified a shift from previous concerns which saw the harm caused to children as arising from the poverty that so many divorced mothers and their children endured.[4] Thus we witnessed a shift from a basically socio-economic argument to a psychological argument in understanding the harms of divorce for children. Although the empirical basis of this shift is now being revised (Burghes, 1994, 1996; Kiernan, 1997), by the end of the 1980s there had become established a presumption that fatherhood was undergoing a change (or crisis) and that childhood was being irreparably damaged by a family policy which was perceived to encourage the separation of children from their fathers at the point of parental divorce. These concerns gave rise to a major change in policy on divorce in England and Wales in the shape of the Children Act 1989.

The Children Act 1989

The Children Act was the first clear statutory statement of the way in which thinking about post-divorce fatherhood had shifted. Although case law was beginning to reflect changing ideas about the importance of fatherhood after divorce, it was this Act which codified these ideas and created a clear new ethos about post-divorce parenthood (Neale and Smart, 1997). When the Children Act was passed, it created a legal situation wherein divorce no longer altered parents' legal relationship to their children. Thus the Courts no longer made orders for custody at all because it was an automatic presumption that mothers and fathers simply retained all the parental responsibility they enjoyed during marriage. The Courts could make orders for residence (where the child should live) and for contact (formerly access), but the Act made it clear that there was to be a preference for 'no orders' and that where possible parents should simply work out arrangements between themselves. This, of course, begs the questions: how are parents supposed to come to an agreement? Which principles should they follow? Should they merely continue the typically gendered arrangements they had prior to the divorce? Or should they actively create a new form of parenthood at divorce? The Law Commission (1988) report, which was the basis of the Act, envisaged something of a continuation of pre-divorce arrangements in that it acknowledged that 'clearly in most cases one parent carries a much heavier burden of responsibility than does the other' (1988: 24). However, it wanted to encourage greater responsibility on the part of fathers by removing what were perceived to be the obstacles to post-divorce fathering created by the old legislation. But this apparently simple desire that parents should make their own arrangements for raising children after divorce, just as they would have done before divorce, pays little attention to the extent to which divorce removes most of the material and also much of the emotional foundation to the parenting project which is ongoing during a marriage. It also could not possibly foresee that, rather than just engendering a little more responsibility in fathers, it might start the gradual transformation of both motherhood *and* fatherhood at the end of the twentieth century.

Mothering and Fathering in 'Intact' Families

The thinking behind the Children Act presumed that a distinction could be made between adult/adult relationships and adult/child relationships within a marriage (or cohabitation). Thus part of the argument resided in the idea that while divorce would foreclose on the spousal relationship, it need not affect the parents' relationship with the child. Thus two sets of relationships are envisaged which appear to be autonomous of one another and which can operate independently of one another. To this way of thinking, there is no reason to imagine that the parent/child relationship should be harmed or reduced because of adverse spousal relationships. This dualism is reflected in everyday thinking and speech where it is not unusual to hear it said (especially by mothers) that an individual might be a very good father but a poor husband, and so on. But I want to suggest that this is an oversimplification of parental relationships. Parents do not only relate to children, they relate to one another *as parents*, not simply as spouses (or partners). A mother's relationship to a father is not the same as a wife's relationship to a husband. Even more importantly, a father's relationship to his children may thrive simply because of his wife's mothering skills. This point is best illuminated by reference to the work of Kathryn Backett (1987).[5]

While there has been a burgeoning of studies which have looked at whether modern fathers 'do' more childcare than previously,[6] Backett's work brought to light a rather different dynamic in the relationship between mothering and fathering. Backett suggests that fatherhood is mediated through the behaviour of the mother and that it does not operate (in the main) as an independent relationship with the children. She suggests that because it is mothers who take the greatest share of the responsibility for children, fathers adopt largely a supportive role. Most significantly, to be regarded as a perfectly satisfactory father, the father did not have to participate in all aspects of childcare. It would be enough for him to deputize for the mother in her absence or to take over now and again if she was tired or stressed. Thus Backett points out that in ongoing relationships couples do not identify the good father as one who carries out 50 per cent of the childcare, or who necessarily relates in a direct and independent way with the children.

> In other words, for father involvement to be subjectively satisfactory it did not tend to be measured against some abstract set of behavioural ideals. It was negotiated and evaluated in terms of the paternal behaviour perceived as appropriate by the spouses within their own special situation at any one point in time. (Backett, 1987: 79)

In an ongoing relationship therefore, a satisfactory paternal relationship might be one in which the father has very little direct contact with the children. But Backett points out that, even where fathers have considerable contact with their children, how they relate to them is *mediated* through the mother. She explains that fathers were reliant on mothers to translate the children's moods or to interpret their needs in order that he could interact with them in a satisfactory way. Thus, in the intact family (at least in the middle-class families she studied) fatherhood could not be understood as a direct relationship with the children. Even where both parents proclaimed that they shared parenting between them, Backett argues that, in practice, fatherhood was negotiated with the mother rather than with the children.

In her study Backett found that fathers were not unhappy with this arrangement.[7] Few wanted to spend a lot more time with their children and, in the main, they recognized the limitations that a full-time caring role imposed on their wives. Thus in an ongoing marriage or cohabitation it is possible to argue that fatherhood depends upon motherhood for its satisfactory existence as a relationship (as opposed to as a biological fact). Although the extent to which a father's relationship with his children is negotiated through the mother may change as children get older, Backett suggests that it does not have an autonomous existence in the way that motherhood tends to.

This clearly has major implications for the way in which fatherhood can be enacted after divorce. If the father has relied on the mother in order to have a relationship with his children, he will find that when he no longer has a wife he no longer has the medium which provided a relationship with the children. Basically, he can no longer be a father unless he changes the nature of his relationship rather quickly. This realization was expressed very eloquently by one of the fathers in our study.[8]

Leon Holt: I hadn't really thought about it. We were still living in the house together for about a year when we were going through really difficult times, moved into separate rooms. It was a case of I'd always worked really hard, I'd come home, gone up to the study and the children were there. My role as a father was to go out to work, to bring the money in, to try and look careerwise and the children were young and it was a case of just saying 'Hello, sit on my knee, then off to bed'. And I was just there and I probably didn't pay them much attention at all. *It was only when I realized that they might not be part of my life that gave me a real shock and it made me more aware and during that year I made more effort to spend time with the children.* (Emphasis added.)

Not only does he need to alter the basis of his relationship with his children, but also with the mother of the children. He can no longer rely on her to do much of the emotional work for him because once she stops being his wife she no longer owes him that emotional labour (although she may feel that she owes it to the children). We might therefore argue that pre-divorce fatherhood is usually a poor training for post-divorce parenthood. We might further argue that post-divorce fatherhood is not simply about taking on more of the practical tasks of caring for children (although this is important) but it is about forging a new relationship with the mother, not simply ending a relationship with a wife.

If pre-divorce fatherhood ill-equips a father for post-divorce fatherhood, the question that needs to be asked is whether pre-divorce motherhood is also in some way a problematic preparation for the post-divorce situation. I want to suggest that there are significant discontinuities. It is clear, for example, that mothers find it hard to 'trust' fathers to care adequately for the children because in an intact relationship they have usually felt themselves to be the most responsible parent and also the main provider of care. In such a situation the fact that a father might only do half a job or might only participate in a restricted range of activities with children is not problematic. But as soon as the father has to be fully responsible a post-divorce mother may find it hard not to become extremely anxious and worried about his capabilities. She may also find it hard to act as mediator for the father/child relationship too. This means she might be less willing to 'cover-up' for a father who always arrives late or who fails to relate to a child in a direct fashion. This in turn might mean that the father/child relationship becomes difficult, not because she undermines it but simply because she is no longer prepared to shore it up.

The problem of the extent to which mothering in an intact relationship ill-prepares women for post-divorce family life is not simply linked to the quality of parent/child relationships however. In many respects the mother's situation is the reverse image of the father's. During the relationship or marriage he might have had an indirect relationship with his children because he maintained his status as a citizen in paid employment with access to resources and benefits which go with this status. The price that he pays for this is (often) a less close relationship to his children. For the mother the opposite is true. She has a close, direct relationship with her children but the price she pays is a diminished citizenship status. As Young argues,

> The male head of household exhibits the virtue of independence, supporting dependent mothers and children. The citizen virtue of mothers does not entail independence but, rather, the virtues of caring and sacrifice necessary for nurturing children to be good citizens. (Young, 1995: 544)

The citizen status of the mother is diminished because, as Young argues, liberal democratic societies celebrate and reward independence, while denigrating those who make themselves [*sic*] or become dependent on others. Laying claim to the citizen virtues of independence gives the head of household personal autonomy and a sense of self-confidence, both of which are denied to the dependants in a family unit. Of course, as Young points out, the independence of the head of household depends on the invisible support of a wife (see also Finch, 1983), but he still accrues the benefits of apparent self-sufficiency and self-reliance in the public sphere. He is also likely to regard himself as a citizen with rights. The mother, on the other hand, is, by virtue of her position as carer, unlikely readily to avail herself of the cultural capital embedded in this notion of the good citizen. She is unlikely to have a well-paid, secure job; indeed, she may not be in the labour market at all. The organization of the benefits system, in combination with low pay for women, may mean that she cannot hope to become a self-sufficient, independent citizen for several years. She will therefore not enjoy the self-confidence which comes from being regarded as a full citizen nor is she likely to see herself as the holder of rights. She is clearly far from powerless in terms of inter-personal relationships. Indeed, as Backett argues, her relationship to the children makes her quite powerful in relation to the father. But she remains extremely economically vulnerable and also vulnerable to a loss of self-identity and self-esteem.

It is now apparent that we need to have a much more complex picture of how relationships which are formed during a marriage or cohabitation can be reshaped or transformed after divorce or separation. It is inappropriate to imagine that parenthood simply continues as it might in an intact relationship as the Law Commission seemed to hope. Not only do we need to understand some of the material consequences of these transformed relationships, but also the gendered power dynamics and the significance of the concept of citizenship for parenthood. (Here I am using citizenship as a short-hand way of referring to a sense of legitimate selfhood which is, in turn, accorded respect and rights in contemporary society.) It is too simplistic to imagine that the difficulties facing divorced parents simply arise from personal antagonisms which can be overcome by focusing on the needs of children. Parents need to change in relation to each other as well as in relation to their children, but at the same time it is important to recognize that there are structural obstacles to change as well as emotional and cognitive ones.

I want, therefore, to pursue these ideas through the findings of our[9] empirical study of 60 parents who negotiated arrangements for their children under the new ethos of the Children Act. This study interviewed 31 mothers and 29 fathers twice over a period of two years. We were therefore able to gather a picture of the process of divorce and of making arrangements for children which spanned a time-scale from the original separation or decision to part (which was gathered retrospectively), to the point of finalizing legal matters and again some 18 months later. We were therefore able to see how the situation of the parents changed and how they adjusted to changing circumstances. We were also able to ask them to reflect upon their decisions and feelings at different moments in the whole process rather than simply establishing their reactions at one specific time. This time element was vital in establishing a more complex picture of the process of post-divorce parenting because we were able to see how parents gradually adjusted to situations which, at first, they would not tolerate or, conversely, how acceptable arrangements became unacceptable as the consequences of early decisions became clearer or as circumstances changed.

I propose to explore the issues raised above in the context of how these parents negotiated post-divorce parenthood. I will look at three interlocking issues. First, the issue raised in Backett's work about the central role of the mother and the extent to which mothers mediate fatherhood even after divorce. The key issue here is the extent to which mothers feel responsible for the children. Secondly, I will explore the question of how parents can adjust to sharing the care of children and a change in their understanding of their identity as mothers or fathers. Finally, I shall turn to the issue of citizenship and the problem of the ongoing, unresolved consequences of gender inequality in marriage and parental relationships.

Responsibility

In our sample of 60 parents, only in one family did we find a situation in which the responsibility for the children was fully shared before the divorce or separation. Although some fathers had been involved in their children's lives to a considerable extent, the overwhelmingly dominant pattern was one where the mothers had given up work or had worked part-time in order to provide the main care for the children. This gave rise to the situation that Backett describes where the father's relationship tended to be an indirect one and where the mother never felt free of a sense of responsibility for the children.

> *Linda Hewitt*: It is quite nice to wake up on a morning and think, 'Oh, I don't have to get up and go to school at half-eight' but the thing is that my life still functions around that kind of time-scale. Even if I don't have him, I'll still wake up and think 'Agh!' and even if I'm not picking him up I'll still think 'My god, it's three o'clock, I ought to be outside school!' I'm programmed to that.

This mother was sharing the care of her son on an equal basis with her former partner, but she had not been able to relinquish an overriding sense of responsibility for the child which she felt acutely while the child was away. It is worth quoting her at length because she typifies the comments of so many of the mothers we interviewed.

> *Linda Hewitt*: Yes, I worry about if he's ill whether Ivan would pick up on it because he's not very good at that. And I also discovered . . . a few months ago that he was letting David go round to some shops and cross a very busy road, which I was amazed at and said so and Ivan then said 'OK, I won't let him do it'. But he had done it in the first place.

Linda also reflected upon the way in which she was much more in tune with things which were important for her son to which his father seemed oblivious.

> *Linda Hewitt*: I mean to children it's very important that they have the right things for school or whatever and sometimes that goes sort of haywire. Like I

know that he hasn't washed his football kit and I'm the one that's saying 'Don't forget to do it' even though it's not my day and it's nothing to do with me because I know that David will get upset if it isn't done.

Not only is Linda extending her 'care work' into the time where she need not feel responsible, but she is ensuring that Ivan remains – in her son's eyes – a caring father. It is Ivan who would get the 'credit' from David for looking after his needs even though it is Linda who ensures that he does not fall short. When Linda remarks that 'to children it is very important' she is acknowledging that children and adults have different priorities and needs and that she is in tune with these. She is capable of seeing the world through her son's eyes and anticipates his emotions but she is doubtful that her former partner can do this.

The issue of responsibility would often focus on things like illness, food and clothing as these are tangible signs of caring activities. Often mothers would remark that fathers did not notice that a child was ill or that they would return them to their mothers rather than doing anything about the illness themselves.

Stella Drew: Ralph was ill and he was with Nick the day and the night, and I said to him 'If he's ill tomorrow are you going to sort something out?' and he just went mad with me on the phone. 'I am not prepared to accept that level of responsibility, it is up to you to sort that out, that is not my responsibility.' And I burst out laughing, I couldn't help it. I was annoyed at the time but it was a point I was making that I was just sick of having all the responsibility, it gets too much sometimes. I think, 'I can't take another day off work I really need the money'. I'm self-employed. But it's always me that has to do it and I just felt that was such a classic.

It is clear that this father did not want to alter the type of relationship he had had with the children during his marriage in the post-divorce situation. His relationship stayed one based on 'quality time' which is to say it embraced only fun things at weekends and holidays. Moreover, he did not even want 'children's things' to eat into his time with them.

Stella Drew: . . . it's me who does the swimming lessons, does the beavers, does the cubs, and he does complain about it if he has to do any of the children's activities when he's got them if it's too much because he feels it eats into his time.

If fathers refused to take on more responsibility after divorce, while still insisting on maintaining contact with their children, it led to real strains in the parental relationship. While mothers would often shoulder the responsibility during a marriage, they would become increasingly resentful of it once the marriage was over. This was particularly so when they found themselves living alone with the children while trying to work for a living. Former husbands often seem incapable of recognizing how much harder their wives' lives had become and how much responsibility they had to take on as lone working mothers.

> *Erica Dawson*: The first week I started on shifts he didn't want the children that day. He didn't want them early in the day. He didn't want them on Saturday, he just wanted them on Sunday. Sometimes he only wanted them on Friday night and not the weekend. I said, 'What are you doing here? I'm trying to earn a living!' and it was very difficult. It caused a great deal of upset and bad feeling and made a tremendous amount of pressure and stress. Anyway, I worked through it and shifted my hours around a little bit more and just did the best I could.

A particular bone of contention was often money and the extent to which fathers would spend money on 'frivolous' activities with the children when they were in need of new shoes, clothes or large items of expenditure.

> *Samantha Abdul*: He took them down to the arcade and he were just putting pound after pound into the machines. I said, 'It just makes me sick to see you throwing money into the machines'. They needed clothes, they needed trainers but he could spend over £30 on stupid arcade machines. I said, 'I know you don't understand but I'm on £75 a week.'

Where a father's irresponsible behaviour became damaging mothers often ceased to 'mediate' for them any more. So when a father was late or failed to turn up to collect a child, the mother might stop making excuses for him. Alternatively, she might stop 'prompting' the father to do the right thing and gradually allow the children to appreciate for themselves their father's limitations. But this was not always easy to do because the mother often wanted to protect the child.

If a post-divorce father would not, or could not, take on more responsibility for his relationship with his children, the mother was often obliged to remain his 'spouse' in the sense that one of her key roles, that of mediating, remained unchanged. In these cases divorce did not seem to bring about a new set of relationships so much as perpetuating an old relationship across different households. It seemed to produce a situation in which, to be a good mother, a woman had to remain a wife.

> *Sally Burton*: I think he thought that he could leave, have this new lover and I would still be at home to come back to, and he could come, have meals, spend time with the children and it's only very recently he's begun to realize that that isn't going to happen.

> *Meg Johnson*: I didn't feel that I had my independence or my space. While David could be away from our home and be on his own, doing his own thing, I went to live with my mother and that wasn't enough. . . . Yes, I did consider [the children's] needs, but I was thinking about myself too. That I couldn't

carry on being just mother and 'spouse' because I wasn't being a spouse and that's when I wanted to do something about it.

As these two quotations show, although some mothers were prepared to carry on as 'spouses' for a while, it was impossible for them to sustain this position for long – even for the sake of their children.

While many (although not all) of the mothers we interviewed wanted the fathers to take on more responsibility, many of the fathers were seriously annoyed that their former wives exercised this responsibility. They did not want to be 'told' to be punctual, to wash clothes, to take the children to the dentist or to be advised on what to feed the children. They saw the exercise of this responsibility as an exercise of power and they frequently became aggressive or hostile in response. Thus they were willing to allow their wives to exercise responsibility for the children during the marriage (none, for example, complained that their wives had done *too much* in relation to caring for the children), but at the point of divorce the mother's special position was interpreted as an unfair advantage (see Simpson et al., 1995).

Jack Hood: They hold all the cards and you're the one who's got to crawl back. I wanted to give her a good hiding or shake her. I couldn't even upset her. You've got no choice, you've got to go by what they say.

George Daley: I can't go up and see him any time I want to, it's got to be done through an appointment, so where does your parental rights come into it?

The fact that so many fathers at the point of divorce or separation were extremely angry with their wives/partners for having a special relationship with the children indicates the extent to which motherhood is taken for granted in most heterosexual relationships. Mothering is, in effect, invisible. It only becomes apparent when it no longer fits smoothly into space that fathering typically leaves vacant. But this anger also suggests that fatherhood is changing too. Although there may be little evidence that fathers are yet willing to take on the structural disadvantages of motherhood, it may be the case that we are witnessing a symbolic shift in fathering which means that more men want to retain an emotional relationship with their children (Beck and Beck-Gernsheim, 1995). It is in this domain that mothers become problematic, at least if they are perceived as already doing all the necessary emotional labour required to nurture children. In this scenario the mother has to be dislodged.

Adjusting to Change

Not all of the fathers in our sample wanted simply to retain the benefits of married fatherhood while being divorced. Some recognized that if they were really to remain (or become) real post-divorce fathers, they were going to have to change both in relation to the children and in relation to their former wives or partners.

> *Leon Holt*: I think at the time I felt, and probably still do, that it's still up to the father to prove that he can be a major part of the children's lives. . . . You have to prove that you are a responsible parent and you have a right of access and what you can do for them on an equal footing, then I think that will change the whole situation and actually make it more amicable in a sense that both parents realize you can talk to the other to make it work.

Leon had been a typical father during his marriage and acknowledged that he had no real relationship with his two daughters. But because he wanted to form a relationship at the point of divorce he did not seek to 'dislodge' the children's mother but to supplement her mothering as much as he could until she came to trust him and to trust her daughters in his care. He did not demand to have them half of the time as if it was his automatic right. Rather, the amount of contact he had grew over a period of months in a rate commensurate with the accumulation of trust. He knew that his wife was in a very strong position in relation to the children when they separated, but he saw this as ethically justified even though he wanted to change the *status quo*. The difference between Leon and the fathers who became aggressive and hostile at this realization is that he acknowledged his own part in the creation of the typical gendered division of labour that had been a feature of his marriage. He did not assume that it was his right to benefit from such an arrangement and that it was equally his right unilaterally to overturn it on divorce. As a consequence he was able to become a 'real' father for the first time after his marriage ended. A number of other fathers in our sample managed to achieve this also.

> *Ann Black*: Yeah [he's changed]. Obviously he doesn't see her the amount of time as when he was here, but I think he makes an effort for when they are there.

> *Colin Hanks*: I feel more of a father now. I think the most important thing for me, anyway, is to show a healthy interest in the children and a respect for the children.

> *Felicity Lessing*: They are the most important thing in his life and he has blossomed with them since we split up.

> *Jim Walters*: That's a good question! I think probably I take more responsibility as a father now than I did when I lived there, in a sense.

The question is, however, whether when the father becomes more of a father, the mother has to become less of a mother. Some mothers felt relieved that the fathers were lifting some of the burden from them and were also glad to be able to share worries and problems with the other parent. Some were also glad to have 'free' time to pursue other interests, other relationships, or simply to be alone. But it was difficult for mothers sometimes to relinquish an identity which went with being a primary carer. The case of Felicity Lessing expresses this problem with immense clarity. Felicity had given up a professional position to become a virtual full-time mother to two sons. She had taken on occasional work when the opportunity arose, but she had forgone her career prospects. Her husband Simon had continued in his career and was being very successful, but he formed a relationship with another woman at his workplace and decided to leave his wife. At the point at which they separated Simon did not have a direct relationship with his young sons. Indeed, Felicity felt that he had withdrawn from them and that he was not particularly concerned to see them after he left. But he did maintain contact with them and, at the point at which he bought a new house and moved in with his new wife, he was wanting to have the children 50 per cent of the time. This was very hard for Felicity to accept at first.

Felicity Lessing: The basic attitude was that I felt the children should have a home that was their base and that it was with me. Not just because he had left me for another woman but because that is how our roles had mapped out. That was my attitude about it and this is where we were at loggerheads because his attitude was that it was totally irrelevant who had left who from the children's point of view and that their home should be as much with him as it was with me and that my having left my career was irrelevant now since the situation was different. That was where the two of us could not see eye to eye at all.

It is clear that Felicity assumed that they had entered into an agreement when she gave up work and that her job was to be to raise the children while his was to have a career. She felt that she had made a sacrifice which should not simply be seen as irrelevant. But Simon's argument was that it was irrelevant from the point of view of the children. Ultimately, Felicity came to agree with this. She could see that from the children's point of view none of this mattered at all.

Felicity Lessing: I could have fought about things but the arguments on the other side are too strong for me. If he says, 'Well, the children need their father', then I quite agree. Why should the children see less of their father because I feel it's not fair on me?

The problem for Felicity, however, is that being a full-time mother was also her identity and not just a job. Although she gets work when she can, she cannot accept offers which clash with the time when she has the children and she can no longer travel. Simon, on the other hand, has a wife who now supports him in his childcare and who collects the children from school and deputizes for him when he cannot be there.

Yet, as Felicity herself acknowledges, she cannot really mount a case that she should have the children more of the time once it is accepted that it is in the children's best interests to spend time equally with both parents. Moreover, it is precisely because Felicity has invested so much in the welfare of her children that she cannot really pursue an argument which she feels might be the slightest bit harmful to them – even at great cost to herself.

But the case of Felicity and Simon raises some very wide questions for motherhood and fatherhood in the late twentieth century. Is it really completely irrelevant that Felicity gave up a career, pension and financial security? If so, what does this mean for women who continue to make this 'choice'?

Conclusion: The New Parenthood and Citizenship

Herein lies a major problem for post-divorce family life. The father must become a 'proper' father for which he may be ill-equipped. But if he tries, he must encroach on the sphere of mothering which was his wife's main source of self-respect and purpose – as well as an important site of emotional satisfaction. If she is to remain 'a good mother', she will relinquish her special place in relation to the children. But in making this sacrifice, she will not find that she reaps commensurate gains in terms of her citizenship status. Her weak position *vis-à-vis* the public sphere and well-paid, secure employment is not improved in any way simply because she becomes less of a mother. Her stake in the public sphere was lost at the point that she left the labour market and became a mother. It is not something that can simply be regained at the point when marriage fails (Maclean, 1991). Indeed, as Joshi (1991) has shown, at the level of income lost and benefits forgone, she will never make it up.

Entry into post-divorce family life therefore poses problems. For the father they reside in the problem of forming a direct relationship with children and winning the support of his former wife to do this. His problems are substantial. He does, however, have the full support of The Children Act, the legal profession and the mediation service if he decides on this course of action. With luck he will also have the support of his own mother and a new partner who can ensure that his enhanced fathering role does not interfere with his role as independent wage-earning citizen. For the mother the problems are of a different order. She must give up her 'special' relationship (for the sake of the children) and hence her status as a primary carer. But she must also amend her status as a dependant, earn enough money to support herself and (in part) the children, accrue benefits against the exigencies of illness and old age, and become autonomous, self-sufficient and self-confident. In other words, she must become the ideal of the independent male citizen as portrayed in liberal democratic theory (Sevenhuijsen, 1998). In this process she is unlikely to have much support from The Children Act, the legal profession or the mediation services, none of whom give priority to, or even much consideration to, the needs of mothers.

The focus on the welfare of the child and the concern to attach men to their children are both policies which have developed as correctives to what have been seen as past errors in family law policy. But because the scope of this policy is limited to the field of private law, this method of achieving 'progress' may only exacerbate other problems which are outside the remit of family law. To be specific, the current priority given by family law to children and to fathers after divorce does nothing to help the transition mothers have to make towards being treated as fully fledged citizens in modern society. In the UK it is extremely hard for women to be mothers and workers, yet it is increasingly the case that the only route to full citizenship is through paid labour and active involvement in the public sphere.[10] If mothers give up these rights in order to meet the welfare of their children, it seems a hard lesson to insist that this was an irrelevant sacrifice at the point when they divorce, especially as the routes back into this style of citizenship are so limited. The active pursuit – by family law – of equal, joint parenting *after* divorce combined with welfare and employment policies which make equal, joint parenting *during* marriage virtually impossible for the majority, gives rise to a form of disenfranchisement of motherhood rather than a new beginning for parenthood. Rather than increasing the quantum of care that children receive through the more active involvement of fathers *after* divorce, this policy may make it increasingly 'rational' for mothers to behave more like fathers *during* marriage in order to ameliorate the future deficit to their status as citizens in the context of a modern welfare state which increasingly values paid work and independence over unpaid care and commensurate dependence. Under such a scenario the 'new' parenthood may seem less desirable than once imagined.

Notes

I wish to acknowledge the contribution of Dr Bren Neale who worked with me on this project and with whom I have co-authored several papers and a book. I also wish to acknowledge the role of the Economic and Social Research Council in funding the research on which this chapter is based (reference no.: R000234582). Finally, I would like to express my gratitude to Elizabeth Silva for her comments on this chapter.

1 See Burgess and Ruxton (1996), Burghes, Clarke and Cronin (1997), Dennis and Erdos (1993), Ferri and Smith (1996), French (1993), Lewis (1986), Lewis and O'Brien (1987), Moss (1995), Simpson et al. (1995), Smart and Sevenhuijsen (1989).

2 The headline in *The Observer* on 21 April 1996 is typical. It read 'Fatherhood at crisis point'. See also 'Death of the Dad' by Melanie Phillips in *The Observer*, 2.11.97.

3 See Burghes (1994), Maclean and Wadsworth (1988).

4 The work of Kiernan (1997) has reintroduced the significance of poverty into the debate about the harms of divorce. Her research suggests that poor 'outcomes' for children are related to poverty before family breakdown rather than to the breakdown alone.

5 The significance of Backett's work is also appreciated by Simpson et al. (1995).

6 See Lewis and O'Brien (1987), Moss (1995), Burgess and Ruxton (1996). Burghes, Clarke and Cronin (1997).

7 The interesting question for the 1990s is, of course, whether more fathers do now wish to have a greater involvement with children while a marriage/relationship is ongoing. The study by Ferri and Smith (1996) is not promising in this regard.

8 This study was called 'The legal and moral ordering of households in transition' although we came to call it 'Negotiating parenthood' for convenience.

9 As I worked on the project jointly with Dr Bren Neale, I shall refer to 'we' or 'our' when I discuss the finding of the research.

10 The Blair Government has made it plain that lone mothers should enter the workforce and that the duties of the modern citizen are fulfilled through joining the labour market rather than through receiving benefits, even if they are carers.

8

GENERATIONAL TIES IN THE 'NEW' FAMILY: CHANGING CONTEXTS FOR TRADITIONAL OBLIGATIONS

Joanna Bornat, Brian Dimmock, David Jones and Sheila Peace

Judith Stacey, in her book *Brave New Families: Stories of Domestic Upheaval in 20th Century America* (1991), conjures up a picture of the modern extended family as she describes the wedding of one of her research subjects where:

> More than half of the pews were filled with members of four generations from the 'confusing tangle' of former, step-, dual and in-law relatives of Pamela and Al's divorce-extended family. (Stacey, 1991: 64)

She presents a beguiling picture of the blending of kin and step-kin as the traditional boundaries formed by blood and marriage which have marked out the territory of the family become blurred. Stacey emphasizes the scope for these 'brave new families' to foster greater social inclusion. It is, she suggests (for the USA at least) a 'democratic opportunity' to 'extend social legitimacy and institutional support to the diverse patterns of intimacy that Americans have forged (Stacey, 1991: 270). Giddens (1992) and Beck and Beck-Gernsheim (1995) suggest something similar in charting the implications of the revolution in romantic relationships. The notion of an inclusivity built on decisions rather than traditions is taken up by Weston (1991) in describing the ways in which gay men and lesbians build relationships within family frameworks (see also Dunne and Weeks et al., in this volume).

In this chapter we ask how realistic is this picture of fluidity and inclusivity and in particular how does it affect the lives and understandings of people experiencing family change in Britain today? For us, a test of the enduring strength of family bonds and of their meanings for family members is the extent to which the new extended family builds on or establishes new types of obligation and inclusivity in relation to caring between the generations. Surprisingly, this key aspect of family life is not included within Stacey's detailed investigation of family relationships.

In current debates about family change, issues relating to couple behaviour or to the quality of parent and dependent child relationships tend to predominate (Burgoyne and Clark, 1984; Gittins, 1985; Scanzoni et al., 1989; Bradshaw and Millar, 1991; Wellings et al., 1994). Contrastingly, some decades ago the intergenerational family tended to be the focus of a great deal of sociological attention in Britain (Young and Willmott, 1957, 1960; Kerr, 1958; Fletcher, 1962; Rosser and Harris, 1965; Bell, 1968). In this chapter we return to the concerns of some of those earlier discussions with our particular interest, the impact of family change on the older generation, the group whom Hagestad refers to as 'the forgotten people in divorce research' (1991: 138). Our research aim was to investigate the interaction of two statistics: the ageing of the UK population and the high incidence of divorce. In the 1990s, 15 per cent of the population was over retirement age (Family Policy Studies Centre, 1991) and should divorce rates persist at their 1993/94 levels then four in every ten marriages in England and Wales will ultimately end in divorce (Haskey, 1996). Given that family care is the preference for policy makers (Finch, 1989; Arber and Ginn, 1991; Langan, 1991; Dalley, 1996), the collision of these two statistics might be expected to produce some kind of fall-out, if not for the policy makers, then certainly for older people. We investigated this with life-history interviews in which we focused on caring relationships, intergenerational links and intergenerational transfers.[1] Our sample of interviewees was drawn from three socially distinctive areas of the town of Luton during 1994–96 and includes 60 people ranging in age from people in their early twenties to others in their late eighties.[2]

The chapter falls into two halves. In the first part we draw attention to the way in which different explanations of family relationships co-exist within family 'talk'. These differences appear to account for the co-existence of a feminist language of independence and equality in relation to partners alongside a more traditional gendered language of obligations and responsibilities in relation to intergenerational care. The second part of the chapter takes up the theme of reciprocity and obligation. With data from the Luton interviews we consider to what extent 'divorce extended' (Stacey, 1991: 64) families continue to include the older generations.

Feminist and Traditional Gendered Languages in Family Care

The family has for some time been recognized as a key battleground in social power relations, inextricably linked to gender. Gender relations within families have typically been seen as a benign manifestation of social organization (Parsons et al., 1955) or as the everyday assertion of patriarchy (Barrett and Macintosh, 1982). Data from qualitative studies provides evidence of the extent to which such models have meanings or are in any way incorporated into the language of everyday family interactions and here we focus specifically on the languages of gender and feminism while bearing in mind the reference point of generational experience.

Figures showing cohabitation and fertility rates, births outside marriage and divorce all bear witness to the remarkable transformation in assumptions about family formation that has taken place over the last 50 years (Elliot, 1996). It would be difficult to avoid the conclusion that a very significant engine of change has been the shifts in women's conceptualizations of themselves and the roles they take. In all social classes, married women with children play a larger part than ever before in the labour market and as decisions around fertility now allow for decades of women's lives to be free from childbearing (Lewis, 1984, 1992) it might be argued that we are witnessing an equalization of power between men and women within the family. Using excerpts from the interview data we illustrate how what we describe as a feminist language of independence operates in relation to certain areas of family life. This particular feminist language is identifiable in references to financial independence, cohabitation, role sharing, female authority, attitudes towards family violence, control of fertility and paid work. Adopting this feminist characterization of our women interviewees' language we are not denying the co-existence of other feminist discourses which embrace care (Tronto, 1993: 111ff.). What we note is that in talking about themselves our Luton women interviewees drew boundaries, distancing themselves from explanations of their lives which automatically and traditionally link them to care work.

The duality of their perception of course draws on real experience. Although labour market participation and fertility control may change some relationships in both public and private spheres, so far as intergenerational caring is concerned, with respect to all ages of family members, gender inequality still appears to be the rule (Ungerson, 1990; Parker and Lawton, 1994). In contrast with a feminist language analysis of the data reveals expressions which demonstrate perceptions of responsibilities as gendered. Evidence of gendered language emerges with references to women's roles, daughters' and grand-daughters' responsibilities, role segregation and expressed awareness of a need for intergenerational coping and caring strategies.

Reading through the interview data suggests that expectations of independence and equality persist alongside expectations of gendered responsibilities even under conditions where family change has disturbed the expected norms of family life. For example, Maureen Hill[3] lives with her teenage daughter, owns her own home in a middle-class area of Luton and has a successful career in the insurance industry. Since separation from her husband she has had a series of non-cohabiting relationships with men. Her perspective on the sharing of domestic tasks and on possible future relationships is distinctively independent feminist:

Would you live with someone?

I think I'd be more tempted to keep a longer-term relationship that is just that. OK, you're spending time together, but it isn't a complete live-in relationship. I'm beginning to feel that that's a much healthier option. Giving each other that independence and freedom. You can't take the mick quite as much, you know. And it keeps the roles. You know you get these defined roles where – for some reason men have got this crazy idea that women actually enjoy washing up and hoovering, I don't know, maybe it was that mother told them that. But we don't. We hate it just as much as anybody else, but at the same time you know it has to be done.

She seems to be a model of the successful woman who is 'doing it all', whose talk is shaped by ideas of independence, equality and freedom. Yet when, later, she was asked about what responsibility she feels towards her widowed mother, she adopts more traditional, gendered, explanations:

I don't know. I mean, she's so fit and strong, it's not a thought that you dwell on. But it's going to happen one day. You can't say. It depends on what happens to her, doesn't it? Ultimately the responsibility will be mine. And I don't want to make it sound like it's responsibility. But I would be the one that would have to deal with it, shall we say?

Why?

Because I just am. You know, I've got one brother living in B–, the other one living in H–. We never see the one in H– you know. Once every year, two years maybe. She gets on very well with my [brother] in B–, but I mean, he has his own worries there. My other brother is single and lives in [a few miles away], but you wouldn't call him one of life's carers. I mean, he just wouldn't know how to do it, or how to cope. So, yes, it would have to be me . . . I've got the space for her, it's not a problem, so, yes, of course she could come here. . . . Yes I would definitely be the one who would have to look after her. And I suppose, at the end of the day, I wouldn't want it any other way anyway.

Among the younger and middle-aged women, independent feminist perspectives were clearly recognizable. Women interviewed were telling modern stories that emphasized self-determination in the areas of their personal lives and careers. Alongside these notions, however, is a more traditional perspective on caring and intergenerational relationships.

Sarah Morden is bringing up her children on her own in a rented council house following separation from their violent father whom she had chosen from the start not to marry. She gains a degree of physical protection from her soldier boyfriend when he is home on leave and is taking a nursery nurse course at a local college as part of her new start in life. Like Maureen Hill, she is equally certain of her responsibilities to her mother. Her own father left home when she was a teenager and she has had little to do with him since though he visits her regularly at weekends, dropping round for a 'cup of coffee'. She thinks, 'it's just boredom on his part' as 'there's no love lost between us'. This negative attitude towards her father had been compounded recently by his decision to marry a Filipina woman whom he met on holiday and who had yet to join him in England.

Her relationship with her mother, who at 52 is still relatively young and active, seems to be one which is more emotionally determined:

I'd want her to live with me. Not because I feel I owe her, but because − I don't know, I would just − she's always been there for me, always. But not financially, because she hasn't always had the money. But she has always been there for me, and when we were kids, and like I say, when my Dad left, she worked like a Trojan. . . . I don't know if that's what she would want. I've never really asked her actually. . . . I shouldn't imagine she'd want to go into care and have people she doesn't know looking after her and things like that. Depending on why she can't look after herself. If it's − if she's just old, then she can live with me.

And your Dad?

No. No. No room at the inn, sorry. No. No, I wouldn't have him. . . . My Dad, he can rot. Well, he's got his Flip-Flop [Filipina second wife] hasn't he? She can sort him out. She's got a passport off him, so she can sort him out. That's it. . . . When my Mum gets old and if she can't take care of herself, then she could come and stay with me. Yes, that's what I'd do.

Do you think it would be you rather than anyone else?

Yes. My eldest brother, he's on his − not side, but he's the same cast as my Dad. My middle brother . . . he's in the Army. He's a fun-loving guy. And the youngest one is just a wally. He'll be 21 next month. I couldn't imagine it'd be any of them. It's always been me and my Mum, always.

Again gender seems to be operating here with the assessment of her, admittedly still young, brothers. Her phrases, 'She's always been there for me' and 'It's always been just me and my Mum, always' suggests that this is not a burdensome expectation. She is emphasizing something positive which she feels she has had in her relationship with her mother and which her brothers do not have. What we may be seeing is the feminization of the family in response to change over two generations rather than the triumph of a feminist perspective. This interpretation accommodates the position which Sarah Morden takes in relation to her

father. However negatively and bitterly accounted for, she is antici-
pating the norm of spouse care as meeting any future care needs which
he may have. To explain what we mean by 'feminization' we go on to
look at three further interviews, with a woman, a couple and a man
living on his own.

Having divorced their father, Jane Minder is bringing up her two
children on her own. She was training to be a hairdresser when she was
interviewed and was living in a privately rented flat. Again her attitudes
to the idea of caring for her parents were distinctly traditional but
complicated by the fact that her own mother had left her brother and her
father when she was young. Both her parents married again, though her
mother's marriage later broke up, leaving her alone. She sees her mother
about once a year. Her father married a woman with three children, so
Jane Minder also has three step-siblings whom she says she gets on
reasonably well with and a stepmother whom she says she likes. Her
account of her relationship with her father and mother displays some
interesting distinctions. Asked how she felt when her mother left:

> I hated her. I absolutely hated her. But then, I don't know if it was because – I
> still can't see how a woman can walk out on her kids. I don't know if that's
> because she walked out on us that I think that way, or just – I don't know. But
> I hated her, and I could never understand, and my brother can't, how she
> could walk out on us, to move in with someone, and bring up his kids – yes?
> And I think we both well, I know I hated her for years and years. And it was
> only a few years ago that she tried to sort of sit down and say – tried to
> explain the situation. And she couldn't. To me, she couldn't. No matter what
> she says will not make up for the fact of what she did.

Later she was asked, if her mother became ill, would she feel she should
help her:

> Yes, probably. It's like now, when people say to me, Well, why do you bother
> with your Mum? She's ignored you all your life, you know. She's never really
> wanted to know you when you've been in trouble and things like that. And I
> think, well, all right, yes, fine. But she's my Mum. At the end of the day she's
> still my Mum. And I can't ignore that. But then I get mad with her because she
> never wants to help herself.

And if your father became ill would you feel responsible?

> Oh, I'd do what I could to help him. If he became iller than he was now, yes.
> I'd probably be round there every five minutes. But then, he's not one of those
> people that'll accept that much help, you know. He's really stubborn. He
> won't admit to needing help, and – things. And, because my stepmum's
> registered disabled, they have a home help comes in, you know, a couple of
> times a week. . . . He was always there for me, because it got really nasty,
> things got really horrible [over her marriage breakdown], and he was always
> there for me.

Having been 'there for me' is an important consideration for both Sarah Morden and Jane Minder. A mother and a father earn a commitment that care will be available when needed because of earlier acts of kindness and support. However, even though Jane Minder's mother deserted her expected role and the family home and still appears not to be making much of a success of her relationship with her daughter, it seems that she too can expect help, if she should need it. Comparing these two accounts it seems that the maternal relationship may be more deeply culturally prescribed, surviving an encounter with reality. On the other hand, the relationship with a father seems to depend more on what he does. It is less a given.

The suggestion here that people, in this case women, could judge their fathers more harshly than their mothers contradicts other findings (Daniel and Thompson, 1996). This may be because we have higher expectations of our mothers. It may also be the case that as women grow older expectations of mothers' behaviour shifts not only in relation to their own experience of being mothers, but also in line with changing cultural expectations of what a mother's role is expected to be in the late twentieth century. This more tolerant attitude towards a mother is borne out by another interviewee, Audrey Townsend, who had suffered violence from both her father and mother who are now dead. With some of her siblings she spent time in a convent when her parents separated. She is divorced from the father of her four children and remarried some 20 years ago. She distinguishes her attitude to her violent mother, in contrast to a father who did not hit her, in terms of some form of 'inner thing that every child has got towards their Mum' which is 'stronger than a Dad thing'. Finally, she suggests that: '. . . my Mum hitting us was contact. . . . Like if she ignored us and didn't hit us, she didn't love us.'

So far we've looked at intergenerational links from the perspective of some of the women in our sample and have been drawing on the interview data to suggest that a combination of independent feminist and traditional gendered expectations concerning partnerships and caring relationships contribute towards an understanding of the family as feminized. In what follows we look at responses from some of the men in our sample to see to what extent their explanations for, and attitudes towards, family change also reveal a shift towards the feminized family.

Confirming the views of the women who were interviewed, men themselves seemed to feel less involved in intergenerational relationships than women. Dennis and Zena Cosh are a childless couple in their thirties. He has already been married once and is divorced. In their interview they both describe very 'modern' attitudes to their careers and future childcare arrangements. They both accept that her career is more important to her than his is to him. He dislikes his job and feels it has no prospects. It would seem to be a serious possiblity that he would give up work to look after the children while she carried on working.

However, when relationships with their own parents are discussed it is evident that a stronger and more traditional set of understandings survives. Her commitment to her parents would override any commitment he might have to his. This is in spite of the fact that her parents live in Germany and his in London where, from his own account, his mother and father gave him emotional and practical support when his first marriage broke up. They are both very explicit that the nature of their intergenerational relations can be explained in terms of gender, as Mr Cosh explains:

> . . . it does tend to fall on the female to look after the parents – that's just the way it is. I've got a sister. My sister lives on top of my parents. She depends a great deal on my parents, emotionally and physically, with little bits of baby-sitting for her two children, and pick up the kids here, pick up the kids there. . . . So she lives near them. And so I sort of naturally think that if there is any sort of caring to be done later it will probably fall nearer to my sister. And me as the male, that has always lived away and always been the independent one. My sister is a very dependent person, and I'm the opposite. So it will probably be payback time for my sister. By the same token, you know Zena has a brother – a younger brother. He lives in Germany and he lives two hours down the motorway from his parents. But when it comes to caring latterly it's Zena that's concerned about it. She knows that her brother, being the male, and he's just recently got married, and no doubt he'll have his own family by then, won't be expected to. I mean, I don't know, it just seems that that's the expectation isn't it?

And Ms Cosh agrees and explains this because, unlike her brother: 'I've got the emotional relationship with my parents. Even though our parents are friends to both of us.' And if her parents became ill:

> . . . that would be a major problem. Because, the way I think about it, I think I owe it to my parents to look after them, because they would look after me. . . . I would never be able to employ somebody to look after my parents. No way. I couldn't live with that, no.

Among our interviewees were a few men living on their own. Humphrey Watson is in his mid 40s and has no close contact with several successive partners and his own two sons from his early marriage who live in Luton. He has been invalided out of work, is a recovered alcoholic, and is now dependent on his mother and sister for social and practical support. His father, whom he describes as 'Victorian', and his brother, died of Huntington's Chorea, his mother caring for both of them. As he talks, he describes a situation in which he is dependent on the women in his life to maintain ties. His last partner was instrumental in getting him to contact his mother:

[last partner] . . . she made me get in touch with Mum more than I did when I was with anyone else. And I suppose because I'm not with nobody. I'm on me own. I'm saying, I'm stuck here. I suppose, you know, I tend to use the phone more. I'm not phoning her. Because I'm not speaking to nobody, I'm not – you know, because I'm all on my own, I'm talking to myself, going a bit mad, say, watching TV, non-stop or lying in bed for – you know, staying up until late at night and then staying in bed all day. So I suppose it's just contact, I suppose, you know, on the phone. You know I'll phone her later tonight. As I say, my sister comes up, and visits me, helps me out.

If your mother became ill or infirm, what would you want to happen?

Oh god – I don't know – Well – as I say, she's 71 now – I'm not sure I want to think about it actually. I know it's a thing that happens, it's going to come, but that's really – that's the only person I've got like left. I know I've got my sister, but she's got her own family, and her husband and her children to look after and that. Whereas my Mum – it's always me Mum, like. You know, I've sort of reverted back to, like all men do sometimes. Your Mum's your Mum. You've only got one – as you're told by your Mum, you've only got one Mum. *You can have many Dads, but you've only got one Mum.* (Our emphasis.)

Even though he is dependent on his sister, he makes this sound like a one-way relationship. The boundaries of her nuclear family seem to be strongly drawn. He has trouble responding to a question about what caring obligations he feels towards his mother and he clearly cannot conceive of a role reversal for either of them. His own experience is of having been some kind of Dad to two of his partners' children, though apparently not much of a Dad at all to his own. Perhaps this is why he feels it is possible to 'have many Dads'. Now, in his dependent state it seems that the significance of having a 'Mum' is not lost on him, yet, despite her years, he describes their relationship in terms of his needs and not hers.

Looking back through these six interviews we can see that independent feminist and traditional gendered languages are being used to describe different types of relationship within family groups. When the women we interviewed talk about themselves as mothers, partners and workers, they are independent and self-determining and obligations are rarely mentioned. However, when they come to talk about caring relationships with their own parents, then obligations and reciprocities come into play, but in terms which anticipate a gendered solution.

When the experience of family change is added to the picture, then the accounts begin to sound even more selective. The independent feminist perspective, with its emphasis on escape from oppression and the relinquishment of traditional role expectations, supports a self-conscious determination to do the best for oneself in new circumstances, while the gendered perspective justifies the maintenance of those ties which meet the need to preserve mother–child relationships. We hear of few fathers as having roles embedded in family ties, nor do the men describe or envisage themselves in that situation. Only those who have partners are saved from exclusion through the maintenance of caring roles. The result appears to be that in explaining intergenerational ties both women and men are talking about family relationships in which men are marginal and, though it is undoubtedly the case that some men do take responsibility for the older members of their family, what we are observing is the feminization of the family.

Caring Talk in Action

To what extent does a tendency towards the feminization of family also spread out into a wider kin structure following family change? In this section we take a closer focus and look at the way our respondents talk about their experience of intergenerational care in familes where there has been change and reconstitution. From their studies of family obligations and responsibilities, Finch and Mason draw conclusions which suggest that reciprocity based in 'mutual aid', a 'long history of reciprocal support' between women and 'a desire to facilitate continuing relationships between grandparents and grandchildren' is likely to guarantee the continuing survival of post-divorce relationships (Finch and Mason, 1990: 230; 1993: 34–5). If such principles really do operate in families which have undergone change, then, rather like the picture drawn by Judith Stacey with which we opened this chapter, there should be examples in our data of people, presumably women in the main given the feminization of the family post change, who have additional obligations and ties to ex-in-laws. We have found this to be true but only to a degree; the survival of ex-in-law relationships requires certain specific types of reinforcement. Although sympathy and moral judgements do not always favour in-laws' own children, we found from the accounts of our interviewees that for the survival of the in-law relationship obligation and reciprocity are less important than emotional and blood ties after death, divorce or separation. A number of the Luton interviewees present accounts of continuity in terms of in-law contacts. These range from enthusiastic endorsements to more measured accounts. Jane Minder, for example, presents an account which is unusual in its warmth:

My mother-in-law. Yes, she's brilliant. And I'll say to anyone – and I do say it to her – she's been more of a Mum to me than my Mum has. She treats me like one of hers. She always has done. And even my ex-husband, he says, he can't – because of the relationship I have with her, he feels that he can't talk to her, you know. He can't confide in her, because he knows how close we are, and it makes it awkward for him. But she has Amy for me, while I go to college. She'll go round and pick Amy up for me, and she looks after her, when I'm at college.

Mrs Waldon, in her eighties and one of the oldest people we inter-viewed, described cordial but not particularly deep relations with ex-in-laws which survived for years after her war-time divorce:

> Oh yes, I was friendly with one of his sisters – the sister what used to live with me . . . there's just one-two of the family, of his family left now. And one of them lives at [another town in the region] he's getting on now a bit. And I always get a birthday card, Christmas card, from them. I always get in contact with them.

Carolyn Connor describes the ending of her marriage after 22 years as 'literally out of the blue'. She too describes preserved connections with her ex-in-laws:

> I kept in touch with my in-laws, who are both dead now, but I was more family to them in terms of supporting them and doing things for them than my ex-husband, who wasn't really – and isn't really – a family man.

Perceived from the other end of an ex-in-law relationship, Vera Gorst says, of her son's ex-girlfriend, that they meet:

> Several times a week, yes. And we get on very well together. Good friends. And she can talk to me. She said at different times, when she's wanted to have a moan about my son, she's said, I can't moan to anybody else about him but you, because, she said, I can't even talk to my friends about him, because I don't want them to think any less of him. But I can talk to you, and call him anything I like, and you won't think any less of him.

Not all accounts of the ending of in-law relationships were so positive. Tamsin King has recently divorced her husband after being married just over two years:

> *What about his [ex-husband's] Mum, then, has she . . . ?*

> Never spoke to the woman from that day to this. Not one of them ever phoned to say, you know, anything. Not even when I was, like, in the refuge or anything like that. Nobody ever phoned just to say 'How are you?' But then I spoke to [ex-husband]. When we were in court, when he said he'd sign the house over . . . I said 'Why do all that? Why put somebody through all that? That you're standing here saying how much you love, and how much you miss me, and how much you want the baby, and how much you love this baby. How can you put anybody through what you've put me through?' And he said, 'Well it wasn't just me, it was my family'. But now I can well believe that. . . . Because that is just how they all are . . .

Barbara Simpson, who divorced her husband over 25 years earlier, does not see her ex-in-laws (grandparents to her daughter) who live in Luton, nor does she have any inclination to do so. She was interviewed with her grown-up daughter:

And have you stayed in contact with any of his [ex-husband's] family?

No, I haven't seen them. Elinor sees them – has to see them. But she doesn't like them, do you darling?

[Elinor] Oh no, we don't really get on. I'm a bit of a black sheep, see.

She's just like I was. They see her as me.

These two last accounts provide us with a clue as to why some relationships with in-laws persist when others fail. Each refers to a wider set of family involvement in the changes and later contacts. Where the more positive and continuing ex-in-law ties are described we heard accounts of involvements which were emotional as well as practical. In-law ties seem to persist where there is a warmth in the relationships, between daughters-in-law and their ex-in-laws and not simply as a result of obligation or continuing reciprocity. The quality of the emotional tie seems to us to be more significant. Moreover, those ties which do survive tend to be nuclear, tending to be confined to the couple and their parents. If that tie is disrupted or prevented by other members of the family, then it is unlikely to persist, as the accounts from Tamsin King and Barbara Simpson suggest. Indeed, Carolyn Connor went on to explain how her continued involvement with her ex in-laws was persistently undermined by another family member and, since their deaths, is not being maintained by other ex in-laws.

The ties which Finch and Mason (1990, 1993) describe are overloaded in terms of explanation as reciprocated need. Our respondents describe ties more in the nature of feelings and emotions rather than in terms of exchanges of childcare and informal care needs. Grandchildren do play a significant part in maintaining intergenerational ties, but more in terms of their personification of blood ties, and the intensity of those links will be determined by the quality cf the intergenerational links between the middle generation and their ex-parents-in-law. Mrs Waldon and her description of continuing low-key contacts with her wider ex-in-law family was an exception among our interviewees.

In part agreeing with Finch and Mason, and drawing on our interviews with people from three different generations, we are suggesting that for ex-in-law relationships to persist requires a particular type of emotional commitment on the part of daughters-in-law and parents-in-law and that ex-in-law relationships which do persist tend not to be extended beyond the original nucleus of children and in-laws. Drawing on the example of the families we interviewed, 'divorce extended families' are restricted in scope and dependent on the quality of ties between women if they are to persist.

Conclusion

Does the 'new' family break with tradition when issues of care and support across the generations are concerned? Our evidence is that the new family is a feminized family in which the traditional expectations of caring responsibilities and the emotions which underpin and sustain them are described and explained in terms of the quality and strength of matrilineal ties. Over 20 years ago in *The Symmetrical Family*, Young and Wilmott (1973) hypothesized that the family would become a more balanced institution and that the reliance on the matrilineal line, so much a feature of the 'classic' British kinship studies in London, Swansea and Liverpool, would diminish. Published in the early 1970s, no thought was given to what impact divorce might have on the social scene. Our evidence suggests that divorce may be strengthening matrilineality, for parents at least, if not for ex-in-laws.

However, what we cannot be sure about, given our particular methodology, is whether the independent feminist language of the younger women we interviewed is a cohort characteristic which they will retain or whether it is a life-stage characteristic which will ultimately be supplanted as they in turn grow older and a 'mature feminization' of the family takes over. Alternatively, they might be expressing themselves in a feminist language which in turn may be replaced if caring comes to be recognized as a source of political power rather than political marginality (Tronto, 1993: 175). Are they speaking in the language of the age they live in or the language of the age they are at? The gendered nature of their expectations in relation to their responsibilities towards their parents, most particularly their mothers, seems to suggest that it may be the latter. Despite changes in family composition, those expectations and emotional ties which result in caring responsibilties in later life may be non-negotiable. In contrast, expectations towards ex-in-laws seem to be governed, as ever, by factors which are more distinctively emotionally grounded. The 'divorce extended family' would not seem to be likely to bring benefits to those members of the older generation whose children are proceeding through successive partnerships or where changes have been accompanied by acrimony.

Despite these gendered and traditionally founded expectations, in all our interviews we found little evidence of intergenerational care being described as burden, even though there is a prevalence of that description in the literature relating to carers. This may be because, at the time of interview, virtually none of those interviewed described situations which were in any sense critical for them or other family members. It may also be because the long-standing English tradition of separate households (Laslett, 1997) tends to mask the effect of proximity through language which is suggestive of the need to protect independence on both sides of the generational divide.

Although our interviewees, along with ourselves as researchers, searched for their own words of explanation (Plummer, 1995) in the knowledge that the family is a flexible thing, subject to varied use and interpretation, the evidence we produce here suggests that in many respects it continues to be bound to the rhetorics of blood, to marked gender differentiation and to a degree of exclusion rather than inclusion (Borneham, 1996). For men and women in later life, the potential for widening the range of relationships needs to be seen in terms of these constraints rather than in terms of the rhetoric of the 'new' or 'divorce extended' family.

Notes

1 This study of families in Luton is one of 17 projects funded by the ESRC under their 'Population and Houshold Change' Programme. This had the aim of stimulating research into the 'interrelationship between household living arrangements and broader demographic change in the United Kingdom'. The initiative clearly reflects a certain amount of anxiety about contemporary social change and families. Other funded projects include investigations into lone parenthood, absent fathers, teenage motherhood, migration and changing communities.

2 A more detailed account of our research methods is included in J. Bornat, B. Dimmock, D.W. Jones and S.M. Peace, 'The impact of family change on older people: the case of stepfamilies', in S. McRae (ed.), *Household and Population Change*. Oxford: Oxford University Press (forthcoming).

3 All interviews have been given pseudonyms to ensure confidentiality. Tapes and transcripts have been deposited at the ESRC Qualidata Resource Centre at the University of Essex, subject to participants' individual permissions.

9

BROTHERS AND SISTERS, UNCLES AND AUNTS: A LATERAL PERSPECTIVE ON CARIBBEAN FAMILIES

Mary Chamberlain

The dysfunctionality of the West Indian family has been a consistent theme in the scholarly and popular literature on the Caribbean family, resurfacing again in 1991 after the United Kingdom census revealed a higher proportion of single-mother-headed households among the African-Caribbean community in Britain (Phoenix, 1996b). This, it has been argued, correlates with the apparently high levels of 'welfare dependency' and social deviance within this community (see, for instance, Dench 1996).

This interpretation is neither new nor original. By the mid-nineteenth century the concept of family in Britain was perceived as nuclear, patriarchal and hierarchical, and members of the family were defined by their primary relationship to the conjugal couple (see Davidoff and Hall, 1987). Discrete family units, headed by a male breadwinner, became the hallmark of both civilized society and stability, and the means to achieve it. Deviation from this family model – through, for instance, over-crowding or illegitimacy – was regarded as evidence of savagery, or as a quick route towards it. This model of the family had, by the mid-nineteenth century, assumed a normative role within British society and, by extension, its colonies. Within that mix of paternalism and steel which characterized British Imperial rule, Britain, as the Mother Country, saw herself as the ultimate arbiter of domesticity, and the bearer of a grand 'civilizing' mission (Elton, 1945).

In the West Indies, the former slaves, viewed either as savages or insouciants, were considered incapable of achieving, or ignorant of, the moral sensibilities of family life. Collectively, they were regarded as unstable, individually as promiscuous or insensitive, ill-suited to raising children with propriety or maintaining the appropriate hierarchy of the family. Such views motivated the activities of the evangelical missionaries in the colonies, and informed the views of the colonial authorities. 'The late census', remarked the Governor of Jamaica in 1844, 'will be of service if they [sic] direct attention to the moral and sanatory condition of the inhabitants.'[1]

It was not only the former slaves who attracted such opprobrium. It came to be applied equally to the indentured labourers from China and, in particular, India, brought to the West Indies after the abolition of slavery. Marriages, other than those made under Christian rites and law, were not recognized by the colonial authorities and, as a result, most children were classified as illegitimate, and most wives as concubines. Indeed, nineteenth-century colonial authorities were obsessed by what they considered domestic instability, the low rates of marriage and the high rates of illegitimacy, both of which were regarded as clear threats not only to family formation but to the concept of citizenship and to moral and social progress. Instances of civil unrest, such as the Morant Bay Rebellion in Jamaica in 1865, or the Federation Riots in Barbados in 1875, could be cited as evidence of the moral degeneracy of the West Indians, the root cause of which was domestic instability. As in Britain, focus on the family as the cause of civil ills and poverty deflected attention away from economic and political inequality. Within the colonial imagination, the link between illegitimacy and good citizenship was inseparable. In 1891 the Registrar General of Jamaica (whose views were echoed by his counterpart in Trinidad) bemoaned the prevalence of 'illegitimacy', for 'the foundational elements of good citizenship are thus lacking and the progress of the State is hindered'.[2]

Such views retained their proscriptive and prescriptive powers well into the twentieth century. The Moyne Commission, for instance, reporting on the widespread disturbances throughout the Caribbean in the 1930s, found one explanation of social disturbance to lie at the heart of family form, while trained scholarly observers of the twentieth century continued to repeat similar assumptions. Thomas Simey, the British pioneering scholar/practitioner of social welfare, argued that the prevailing family structure was 'loose', family relationships accordingly 'very casual' (Simey, 1946). The Western European family (nuclear, 'patriarchal' and with the conjugal union at its centre), became the norm, the 'natural' structure of families against which all else could be measured. Against this, black British West Indian families proved deviant and by implication unstable.

Once established as deviant, the quest for explanation, classification, and derivation began. It is not the point of this chapter to review the literature or revisit the debates on the Caribbean family. Much of it focuses on the African-Caribbean family where a primary concern has been with conjugal and union status, and within that on the role of women in childrearing and family support. The emphasis has been on matrifocality and its corollary, male marginality, although in recent years the concept of household broadens some perspectives on and definitions of the Caribbean family (Clarke, 1957; Solein, 1960; Greenfield, 1966; R.T. Smith, 1988; for an overview of the literature, see Barrow, 1996). It is, however, important to suggest that many of the contemporary features of Caribbean families in Britain (such as a high incidence of single-mother-headed households) reflect both historic patterns and contemporary trends within the Caribbean. Such formations may deviate from the British norm, but not necessarily from the Caribbean (Baylies, 1996).

One feature of Caribbean families in Britain which has, for the most part, been neglected is the impact, and the implications, of migration on the family. The early literature on West Indian migration to Britain placed economic determinants as the primary motive in migration and concerned itself with the nature of the 'race problems' generated by black migration to Britain. Indeed, the dominant perspective was from that of the metropole. The role of migration itself as a powerful dynamic within culture and the family, the ways in which the family supported and enabled migration, the role of migration in supporting the family (Richardson, 1983; Thomas-Hope, 1992; Fog Olwig, 1993) and as a continuing dynamic within families has only recently engaged the research imagination of migration scholars (Chamberlain, 1995, 1997). Regarding migration and the family from the perspective of the Caribbean, however, begins to shift the analytic framework away from what is perceived as abnormality, to points of cultural survival and retention.

This chapter, based on research undertaken by Harry Goulbourne and myself on 'Living Arrangements, Family Structure and Social Change of Caribbeans in Britain', within the ESRC Programme on 'Population and Household Change', aims to explore an aspect of Caribbean family life in Britain. Our research is based on approximately 180 life-story interviews across three generations of 60 families who originated in Jamaica, Trinidad/Tobago and Barbados and who migrated to Britain in the 1950s and 1960s.[3] The use of transgenerational lifestudies may reveal many nuances in family life and the processes by which values, attitudes and behaviour are transmitted and transformed across generations, and across the oceans. Our research is pointing clearly to the importance of families in migration, and in particular, to the vibrancy and strength of what Brodber (1986) first identified as the 'transnational' family, suggesting not only the importance of transgenerational links but also intragenerational links, in particular those of siblings and affines (Chamberlain and Goulbourne, forthcoming; Goulbourne, forthcoming). These findings affirm our belief that the conventional frameworks for understanding the formation and transformation of Caribbean living arrangements and family structure in the points of destination are inappropriate tools for understanding the complexities and dynamics of Caribbean families. The conjugal relationship may not always be the focus of a family unit, nor the most important one, and may marginalize the role and place of siblings and collaterals, the roles of family members (and memories) located elsewhere, and the importance and nature of families dispersed.

This chapter will focus on the role of siblings and the extension of the sibling role as a metaphor for social behaviour. There are problems in any studies of siblings. They raise definitional problems which are short-circuited in other family relationships. The relationship of a husband and wife, parent and child is, on the whole, relatively clear cut, albeit dependent on cultural circumstances and historical moments. Beyond the conjugal, blood (or social) ties, it is assumed that particular functions, rights and responsibilities relate to these roles and relationships and failure to perform or conform is, in both social and legal terms, measurable. Siblings and collaterals may, however, claim membership simultaneously of several families, both of origin and creation. While children who share a parentage are related as brothers and sisters, the definitions from there on begin to shade into degrees. There is similarly a problem over location, and identification. It is assumed that siblings share a common experience of parenthood and childhood, and common structures of identification such as race, ethnicity, class and social status, and that, gender aside, they will be broadly equal. Such assumptions, as Leonore Davidoff (1995) indicates, assume a two-parent norm, an experience not necessarily relevant to a West Indian context where half and step-siblings and membership of multiple nuclear families is not uncommon.

The sibling relationship itself is, moreover, often fraught. It may change over the life-cycle of the family and of the individual, it may imply competition and exclusion as much as, or as well as, co-operation and inclusion, and the status, nature and meaning of a sibling relationship may well in due course influence the role over siblings' children, and among cousins. Birth order and colour can also affect the nature of the relationship between siblings, and the direction of family resources, and can, and often does, result in fierce rivalry and even estrangement as well as determining individual life chances. Indeed, the passions evoked by sibling rivalry can often mould the attitudes, behaviour and personality development and may in many ways be a more powerful force than parental influence.

Three further factors need to be introduced. First, demographic change may have an impact on the role and position of siblings. The move from larger to smaller families means that individuals have fewer brothers and sisters, and the subsequent generation will have a smaller number of uncles, aunts and cousins. Secondly, migration reduces the physical presence of siblings although their role as providers may not necessarily have been diminished. For migrants, and in particular for their children, the day-to-day influence of brothers and sisters, uncles and aunts may not be as powerful a factor as it was for their parents' generation, although in time this may change. Thirdly, rural and urban neighbourhoods in the West Indies survive and function according to a sibling model of the family, as adults assume an avuncular and quasi-parenting role and children, in turn, learn to defer to their 'natural' authority. It is tempting to speculate, at this stage, whether, and with what effect, a notion of behaving 'like' family, of living arrangements which readily incorporate what outside observers may perceive as strangers, influences the actual creation and organization of families and, further, whether and to what extent those alternative family models were translated into survival strategies of migration (both for the migrants and those left behind) and continue to be transmitted to subsequent generations of migrant families.

This chapter uses three case studies from families drawn from our data to illustrate the complexities of family relations. One family originated in Jamaica, two in Trinidad. However, as with many Caribbean families, there are trans-national as well as often trans-ethnic and racial connections. One family is African-Caribbean, one mixed race, and one of East Indian origin. Elder members of these families were all born and brought up in the Caribbean. A necessary focus of each case study is the importance of socialization in the Caribbean and the ways in which family relations, or migration, influence subsequent family formations. Shifting the centre of analysis away from the conjugal relationship may reveal other important dynamics in family life.

Family 1

Maude was born in 1935 in Mandeville, Jamaica, the first daughter but the fifth child of her mother's eight children. Her father was an 'agriculturer', farming rented land, her mother a 'higgler' (hawker). Her parents lived together, but did not marry until the children were grown up. Maude shared paternity with seven of her siblings. Her eldest brother, George, her mother's first son, was the child of a white man, distinguished from his (half) siblings by colour. Nevertheless, he 'grew up as part of the family'.

George migrated to the USA and from there 'was responsible for paying for my education . . . in all ways, *he was my parent, really, in a sense.* And to this day, he is special. Very, very special to me . . . he shaped a lot of my thinking' (JI 028).[4] The role George plays was similar to that performed by her parents' siblings whose brothers and sisters, on both sides, had also migrated, to Panama, Cuba and the USA, 'sending back' both money and clothes to help support those left behind. These remittances were an essential ingredient of the family economy. The pattern of sibling support in, and through, migration, and the importance of sibling networks for the migrant, has been an established feature of Caribbean migration (Fog Olwig, 1993; Chamberlain, 1997). At the same time, through the return of remittances, migrant family members retained their claim to family, and in particular, sibling membership, for it was that relationship which held the promise of long-term reciprocal support, particularly on return. In family chronology, siblings can expect to survive the parents.

The neighbourhood in Mandeville was peppered with relatives who were in close and regular contact, and 'would sort of make sure that we were looked out for' (JI 028), providing physical shelter, financial support and moral guidance. '[M]y [childhood] was shaped by a lot of these people.' But the classification of 'sibling' itself became a powerful metaphor within the neighbourhood, and governed the roles of parental peers – godparents, friends and neighbours – who became, in essence, fictive siblings. It governed, equally, the behaviour and attitudes of children towards these adults.

> They would scold me, but most of all . . . I remember the love . . . it was a crucial part of my childhood and I think it has made me into a whole person. That, I remember, the community love. People just loved you . . . the community had a parenting responsibility . . . they protected me . . . you just knew that they were there for you . . . that was very, very comforting. (JI 028)

Of the eight children, Maude was the one, as she saw it, to be privileged. She was 'cherished', 'let off' family chores to pursue an education. This preferential status was confirmed and reinforced by her parents' peers in the community, who 'nurtured me too and *wanted me to become a special young woman*. In other words, I was a role model and didn't even know it' (emphasis added). Her father mortgaged the house to raise the money to send her to England to train as a nurse. It is not clear why Maude was singled out within the family for preferential treatment. It may be related to her position as the first daughter, or to an estimation within the family that she would benefit most from education, or to her relationship with her eldest brother whose colour, and links with his white paternal family, privileged him in a society where class, race and colour were broadly coterminous. The favouritism, however, caused 'resentment and anger' among her siblings who 'did not have access to education like I did . . . my sister and myself are estranged almost totally. I see my [other] brother sometimes, but . . . we're not close.' This estrangement has repercussions for her own daughter, Laura.

For many West Indian migrants, coming to England meant that day-to-day contact with siblings in the Caribbean or elsewhere was reduced for themselves and, particularly, for their children, although many families continue to retain vibrant and supportive links with kin abroad. Maude married a Trinidadian, one of 13 children, most of whom migrated to North America. Laura and her brother had relatively little contact with their grandparents which, as Laura says 'is really sad. I think it's one of the sad things about West Indian parents, or West Indians coming to Britain, because I've never really known my grandparents, not on a daily basis' (JI 063).[5] Laura also grew up distanced from regular contact with her father's siblings through geography, and from those of her mother's siblings in England as a result of 'this family politics'.

In marked contrast to her mother, whose 'counsel' was provided by aunts and other significant female members of the neighbourhood, and who was singled out as a role model, 'to be a special young woman', there was no such 'counsel' available for Laura, nor was she held up or expected to be a role model. As the eldest of only two children, sibling experience and support was limited. Equally, the family was isolated in the predominantly white neighbourhood in which they lived, and from the daily influence of other family members and even family friends who might have provided additional or alternative guidance and models. Laura describes her father as 'Victorian' in his views on women: 'I was a female and, you know, there's a whole thing about protecting your girl children and not wanting to get pregnant and the whole of that. . . . My brother didn't have all that stress and aggravation. . . . Inequality, yeh' (JI 063). Laura became a nurse, like her mother, but, unlike her mother, left after six years, went to Italy where she worked (as an au pair, and then an English teacher) for two years, and on her return, secured a place at university to study languages. She is married, to a man of mixed Guyanese/Jamaican parentage and plans, in due course, to have her own family. Laura's trajectory, in England, was in many ways far more autonomous and self-defined than that of her mother from Jamaica and the concept of family which she espouses far more numerically limited and nucleated. Her mother had been earmarked for upward social mobility. Laura had no such collective direction or confirmation in her life choices, and no favourite sibling to 'cherish' her sense of self. Laura has become a Born Again Christian, and this has also been an influence in how she imagines and how she will institute her family. She disapproves of her brother, who lives with his girlfriend and their child, and is critical also of her father who has an 'outside' child in Trinidad, whose existence she did not discover until she was in her teens.

Laura's discourse of family accords more centrally with what is regarded as a 'traditional' European Christian marriage, even though this is at variance with her own parents' and her grandparents' experience of marriage and family. This 'double' discourse is not, however, unusual in our sample, though in this example it is revealed across, rather than within, a generation.

Family 2

Arianne was born in Trinidad in 1931, the eldest of five children as well as 'quite a lot of half-sisters', who originated in the first marriages of both her parents. Arianne's grandmother came from Venezuela, trading goods in Trinidad until eventually settling there. Arianne's father was born in Trinidad, of (African) Venezuelan parents, although her family was ethnically diverse, 'pure, pure [Amer]Indian . . . we grow with them . . . on the father's side, we have Chinese . . . we have Assyrian . . . we're all kind of people in our family . . . oh, it was . . . colourful' (TM 098).[6]

Her mother, though born in Venezuela, was brought up in Trinidad (while *her* mother was travelling) by her elder siblings, in particular 'the eldest . . . [who] used to see after the smaller ones. So my mother stay here and she went to school here in Trinidad' (TM 098). The parenting role of siblings in this family continued across the generations. Arianne grew up with her seven siblings, including two from her mother's first marriage, and a cousin, 'like sisters'. Her father died when Arianne was 15, and when she was 18 her mother; her aunt, who was also her godmother, assumed the role of parent, looking after Arianne, her brothers and sisters and by this time another nephew. The family was surrounded by aunts and uncles and, as with Maude's experience, the metaphor of family extended throughout the neighbourhood, from material support ('anything we give . . . this is for Mr Joe, this is for this body, this is [for those] less fortunate . . . there's so much in this giving . . . they have something, they will send something to give') to control.

> You hardly could have misbehaved really long ago, you know, because . . . family, and the neighbours . . . want to know what going on. Why you here? Who you know, what you know. If they see you talking to anybody that they know, well, let us say, a loose person, somebody whom, you know, bad to the parents. . . they would call you and tell you 'Listen, you must not keep that person's company, because they would lead you astray'. (TM 098)

Moral and practical guidance in sexual matters was assumed to be the province of older women in the neighbourhood, 'I always have older people friend . . . my mother hadn't any course to tell us anything, but she used to tell us . . . everything. Everything. . . . What to do, what not to do, what we mustn't do, what to expect'. Arianne became pregnant when she was 20 and gave birth to her only child, Clarissa, in 1951. She did not marry Clarissa's father and although he supported Clarissa when he could, Arianne had to work to keep them both, moving from the country to a suburb of Port-of-Spain in order to do so. Arianne's siblings remained in Rio Claro. Although Arianne was not the oldest in the family (her half-siblings preceded her) she was the eldest girl and was 'always . . . responsible for everybody . . . everyone turned to her. . . . If they had problems . . . anything at all, it's "Auntie Ari would sort it out"' (TM 055).[7]

As a child Clarissa spent her holidays with her grandparents, who owned a cocoa plantation, and her aunts and uncles where 'all the children would be growing up together'. Her grandfather played the quatro in a Parang (traditional folk) band and 'we would go round with him as well, to all the houses . . . he liked all his grandchildren'. Clarissa describes her father as a 'lady's man'. It was not until she was in her teens that Clarissa discovered that she had eight other brothers and sisters and 'last year, I found I had another one'.

Clarissa was her mother's only child although, in addition to her siblings through her father, Clarissa also had a number of step-siblings, the children of the man with whom her mother eventually lived during Clarissa's adolescence. Prior to that, however, Arianne shared a house-hold with another family in Lavantille, replicating here her 'siblings' left behind. It was there that Clarissa spent her formative years as a singleton child.

> . . . we grew up together . . . we were never alone. We were either with Aunty Iris, as I call her, or Mum was there, and Mum would have the two girls, or Auntie Iris would be looking after us. . . . They're in America at the moment. They're all married with their families in America . . . [we are] like sisters . . . we had people like Aunt Iris and friends who had their own families and who were . . . sort of like sisters . . . they were that close. . . . It was like having aunties, really . . . you felt as part of the family. . . . I was always treated like one of the family. . . . I really had a lot of influences from the families. And basically, you know, had a lot of family life. (TM 055)

Arianne's 'way of life' incorporated not only the creation of substitute families, but within that, replicated the role of elder sister: 'my mother . . . was always being called upon to do something for everyone, and so I've had loads of aunts and uncles, by virtue of being friends of hers . . . there have always been people around' (TM 055).

Clarissa came to England to train as a nurse, and had a child by a Barbadian 'who turned out just like my father, really'. She did not marry him and, like her mother, found herself having to work and bring up a child alone, removed (like her mother) from broader family networks. It may have been that earlier childhood experience of co-parenting which inspired her own choice of childrearing pattern. Clarissa re-created a communal home, first with her aunt whom she describes as a

> respectful aunt, not family aunt. She is someone I met when I first came over, one of my friends . . . because we're Trinidadians together, we all sort of cottoned on . . . so at the time when I got pregnant I stayed with her. (TM 055)

And then with her daughter's childminder which was:

> extremely convenient. I didn't have to go anywhere, to take [my daughter] anywhere, I just leave and go to work and come back. And that seemed to work out well enough. . . . [She] *was, to be honest, like another mother.* She . . . really loved [my daughter]. [She] was the life and soul of her . . . she loved children. (TM 055)

Such a pattern may be seen as a variant of 'child shifting' (see Gordon, 1987: 423–7), although in the case of both Arianne and her mother, they remained present in the household. It may also be seen as an example of co-mothering, common in Latin America and now emerging as a recognized pattern in some Latin American regions, and African American communities in the USA (Forna, 1997). Three generations had migrated, Arianne's mother from Venezuela, Arianne from the country to the city, and Clarissa from Trinidad to England, and all adopted strategies which incorporated collaterals – blood or 'respectful' – in a co-parenting role. 'I was', as Clarissa says, 'quite happy to bring [my daughter] up the way I was brought up' (TM 055).

Family 3

Mrs Ramlakan was born in Trinidad in 1926. Her father was born on the boat which brought his parents from India to Trinidad at the turn of the century. As indentured labourers, the family lived in barracks until the indentures were expired when they moved out to farm their own land. Mrs Ramlakan's grandfather, however, returned, suddenly and secretly, to India:

> I see my father crying . . . many times, when we were small, my father used to tell me. He used to cry and tell me, he say 'My father gone back to India and leave me alone in Trinidad. And I have nobody, only three children I have. (TH 102)[8]

Her mother's parents were also East Indian, though born in Trinidad. Her parents' marriage, according to Hindu custom, was an arranged match. Her father indentured himself on a sugar estate and lived in plantation barracks until able to move out and build a house of their own.

Mrs Ramlakan was one of three daughters, her mother the eldest of nine children. As adults, her mother's siblings and their families lived on, or close to, her parents' land in Monkey Town. Mrs Ramlakan's mother and father worked as agricultural labourers. Her father, however, 'did a little kind of hasty' (quick tempered) and as a result was often out of work. On one of these occasions, he secured a job in Moruga:

> . . . my mother had she nice little house already . . . and my grandparents, everybody not too far, and all she brothers and everybody near . . . we know everybody. Well, when my father tell my mother he want to go there to live . . . my mother start to cry . . . she don't want to go . . . she own a little house and she don't want to go. My father say . . . she had to go. . . . He sell the house . . .

she don't want to come, so she crying . . . my father make mother pack up. They pack everything . . . my mother crying, crying. (TH 102)

The family moved but after a while Mrs Ramlakan's mother fell sick and, leaving her husband, returned with her children to Monkey Town to be close to her brothers and sisters. Her husband was forced eventually to follow her and it was there that Mrs Ramlakan spent the rest of her childhood, recalling, as with Arianne and Maude, the familiality of the village. In this case, the village had both East Indians and Africans:

They used to live nice, the creole [African Caribbean] people in the village was nice people. We had good respects for them, because we used to call some of them 'grandmother', 'grandfather', 'grandpapa', 'grandmama', the old people then, right?. . . . So these aunts of we, and live like we're the same of it . . . if you go by them, they used to give you food to eat . . . they used to treat we good, the negro people where we lived nearby . . . we live well with them. And we still have some of . . . those great-grandparents children still alive. We have of the boy living down the road here. He does call me 'Tanty' up to now. If he come up the road . . . if he come here, he does call me 'Tanty', he said because he know his grandparents and my mother and them was friends, *so we live like family*. (TH 102)

Mrs Ramlakan lived close to her grandparents, sleeping there on many occasions, and to her uncles in the village. When Mrs Ramlakan was 17, her parents arranged her marriage. She was, however, married in a Christian Church, rather than according to Hindu rites. On marriage, following common patterns within this community, she and her husband went to live with his family, first with her mother-in-law, before they eventually built a house on land next to her and her husband's brother. Mrs Ramlakan had six children. Although on marriage she moved away from her own family, she nevertheless remained very close to her two older sisters, 'I respect my sister a lot, because they, my sister really love me the most. . . . If I want anything, and I go and tell her, she give me. Any, any problem I have, I used to go to my sister . . . any little thing . . . I used to send and call she, and she always come.' One of this sister's children was sickly, and came to Mrs Ramlakan:

This child only sick, I know what to do. Well, you have so much children, four children, and your child, nothing do happen to them. 'Take this child for me.' So I say 'Alright.' So I pay she, and I take the child. . . . Money, a little money now . . . she say 'Alright . . . this child is your child from today.' And he get better . . . I didn't bring him home. I say 'Well, he is my child from today' but he stay with the mother, because she nurse him . . . she used to always tell him 'I'm not your mother, your mother live in Lengua.' Always, always used to say 'Your mother live in Lengua.' So he always say 'Yes, who is my mother?'

. . . And he come up big man, and he do still say 'Who is my mother?' Yeh.
(TH 102)

Although Mrs Ramlakan qualified the 'buying' by saying that 'me and
she sister', she did in fact 'buy' three more children, two of whom
belonged to neighbours. She explained it by arguing that if a child falls
sick:

> I say 'This is my child from today' and I take it from you. And he get better . . .
> just for he get better is the reason why I do it. And they really get better. Look
> my neighbour, nobody would have a sick child, and I went and buy the child
> from the lady and the child get better . . . you have to consider the child. You
> does have to consider the child. This one over there is call me 'Ma' up to now,
> does call me 'Ma' . . . this one over here does call me 'Ma', the little boy. (TH
> 102)

The 'one over there' was her nephew, Sureth, who migrated to Britain in
1972, joining two of his cousins who had arrived earlier. His mother,
Mrs Ramlakan's sister, worked first on the land and then in her own
shop, employing relatives to look after her children while she did so.
'Family. Cousins. Because some of my cousins had . . . very large
families, nine, ten children. So I think it was a help for them, to send
someone to stay with us' (TH 051).[9] The family was, according to Sureth,
'very close', although the boundaries were clearly demarcated. His
father was at times estranged from his younger brother for, as the eldest
son,

> . . . you are the eldest son, you are the favourite and you are left in charge . . .
> my dad got, like me, got what was supposed to be the best. All the property
> and so . . . he [uncle] wasn't too please and there was always a bit of friction
> among them. (TH 051)

Moreover, his father's 'playboy' style resulted in two half-sisters, whom
Sureth did not meet until an adult, and whose existence was not
condoned by his mother or her family. Nevertheless, the closeness with
his mother's family Sureth tries to maintain in Britain: 'My two cousins
will tell you, every Christmas I try to get them here, to try and re-enact
what we used to have at home.'

Although the neighbourhood in many ways replicated an idea of the
family – 'Because we're so small a society . . . the neighbours, we forget
some of them is not even our family and we grow up as family' – it was
not to neighbours, but to her sister that Sureth's mother turned in need,
particularly when:

> He [Sureth's father] was violent. He used to beat her too. Many occasion he
> broke her arm . . . [then] she would go to her sisters, the first thing she'll do is
> go to her sister. I don't think she go to any neighbours or anything. She will go

to her sister. When he hit her, she will leave home and go to her sisters. I remember, as children, about three occasions she pack her bags, and we trailing off to some aunt or somewhere. And then he will come back after a couple of weeks, and beg us to go back. (TH 051)

The bond between Sureth and his aunt and her children is tight. Mrs Ramlakan has come to Britain, staying with Sureth and his family, and Sureth remains in close contact with his cousins in Britain, and his siblings and other family in Trinidad, feeling strongly that his children must be made aware and proud of their heritage and parentage. He was, however, brought up as a privileged elder son, in a family in which the women were strongly protective of each other and of each other's children, where siblings played a vital role in providing support and sanctuary and where other collaterals offered closeness and companionship, a condition which Sureth attempts to replicate for his own children in Britain:

I try to bring them up like home, to some extent. Not quite like home, but I make them aware of what I am from, and what I am, to know my culture, my background . . . the family closeness, I get my cousins, my nephews and nieces to come here, that they be together and close, more so than they do their parents . . . keep them close . . . to give them their cultural heritage. (TH 051)

Conclusion

This chapter has described some of the features of sibling and collateral support in West Indian family life. It has stressed, in particular, the role siblings have played in childhood and childrearing and how a concept of social responsibility and the inculcation of such concepts in the West Indies was not considered to be the sole prerogative of parents, but of the wider family and neighbourhood although the emphases may differ between ethnic groups, and urban/rural context. Smaller family size, and a generation not brought up in the close proximity of a 'neighbourhood family' may have an impact on the development and formation of those families in Britain, as the first case study suggests. On the other hand, although demographic change is clearly a powerful variable in family behaviour, family culture remains equally powerful in determining attitudes and behaviour, as suggested by the third case study. Much further work is clearly required to support, expand and analyse its importance in the British context and to explore how, if at all, migration has altered or adapted the role of siblings and collaterals, particularly as Caribbean families begin to extend into the second and third generation and where living arrangements and family structure continue to conform to those common in the Caribbean itself. Certainly, with the first generation of migrants, the role of kin and fictive kin was a powerful factor in determining migration and settlement, as suggested by the second case study, replicating in the UK the 'neighbourhood' families of the Caribbean. There is some evidence, from this and earlier studies (Chamberlain, 1995), that the replication of Caribbean family forms is not only permissible as this community extends into its second and third generation, but is becoming in itself a powerful statement of cultural identity.

Perhaps the use of the lateral family as a metaphor for social organization and support may also be a useful tool in exploring contemporary living arrangements of Caribbeans in Britain. Black-led churches, regional solidarities, as organizations are vibrant features of West Indian communities and it may be that one explanation for their creation and survival, at least in the form in which they have emerged as offering particular fraternal support, may lie in the cultural roots in the Caribbean which saw the lateral family as a powerful symbol and model for informal, fluid and non-exclusive social organization and support. It may be that the symbolic form of 'family' is the feature which retains a resilience, transmits its influence, and shapes forms of social support across generations and cultures. In any case, to look at the Caribbean family through a particular conjugal prism may not offer the most useful perspective for understanding Caribbean family life, and may simply replicate what Platt (1980, though in a different context) argues as the 'categorical error' which sees, and has seen, Caribbean families as anarchic and dysfunctional.

Notes

1 CO 140/133. Governor's speech to Governor's Council and Assembly, 25 October 1844, St Iago de la Vega, Jamaica.

2 CO 140/208. Appendix to papers of Legislative Council of Jamaica, 1891.

3 This research has been funded by the ESRC as part of the programme on 'Population and Household Change'. All primary references, unless otherwise stated, are to the interview data collected in this research. The data will be deposited with the ESRC Qualidata Resource Centre at the University of Essex. Pseudonyms have been used throughout the chapter to protect the identity of the informants.

4 JI 028/2. Tape 1, pp. 8–13.

5 JI 063/3. Tape 1, pp. 2–9.

6 TM 098/1. Tape 1, pp. 5–11.

7 TM 055/2. Tape 1, pp. 4–23.

8 TH 102/1. Tape 1, pp. 6–29.

9 TH 051/2. Tape 1, pp. 3–29.

10

RECONSIDERING CHILDREN AND CHILDHOOD: SOCIOLOGICAL AND POLICY PERSPECTIVES

Julia Brannen

After many lean years, family life research in the UK has become something of a boom area. A focus on parenting, especially in the context of changing family forms, is a popular policy and academic topic. Even more recently there has been a surge of interest in childhood, especially work which examines the world from the perspective of children. Recently, research funding bodies have followed one another's example in supporting research in this area and with this perspective. The study of 'normal' childhoods, not only the problematic childhoods of the few, constitutes a growth area especially within sociology.[1]

Sociologists' new interest in childhood has emphasized children's agency in the outside world, as well as inside families and other adult-dominated institutions. In reaction to the deterministic concept of socialization, these sociologists have sought to uncouple children from the nuclear family and to re-frame them conceptually both as subjects of research and as subjects who construct their own consciousness and life trajectories. They have argued that sociology's refusal, until recently, to consider children as an active and distinctive group of research subjects lies in its theoretical assumptions concerning children. These assumptions have failed to question the dominant developmental paradigm of childhood as a state of 'becoming' (Frankenberg, 1993) and have located children in the originary contexts of family life, assigning them dependency status under the umbrella of the moral and economic responsibility of their parents. This positioning of children has obscured them rather than made them visible (James and Prout, 1990; Alanen, 1992). In methodological as well as theoretical terms, this means that, rather than speaking for themselves, others have spoken on children's behalf, with parents and other adults acting as children's chief spokespersons (Oakley, 1994).

In focusing on children's agency, the new study of children may come to resemble the study of youth which has long treated young people as a distinctive social category and which has theoretically accorded young people the possibility of self-determination. Paradoxically, however, as young people's transitions to adulthood have been arrested in the UK by changes in the labour market and public policy, a somewhat radical departure in youth research has been to study young people in the context of family relationships (see, for example, Jones and Wallace, 1992; Brannen et al., 1994). By contrast, the new direction in childhood research is to divorce children from such contexts.

The developmental and socialization paradigms, which have for so long captured childhood, have assisted in a generally unproblematic portrayal of children within the 'age' and generational orders. These orders are not fixed. Adolescence has extended up the age hierarchy so that young people enter the labour market later but adolescence also starts earlier and has moved down the age hierarchy. It is salutary to remember that even biological maturity is subject to changing social and economic conditions; for example, in some parts of Europe, from the first half of the nineteenth century, the female menarche was brought forward by more than four years (Mitterauer, 1992). Childhood should not be conceptualized without considering the impact of the shifting boundaries of youth and adolescence, the other main portions of the life course.

Current age hierarchies are couched in the modernist paradigm of chronological and quantifiable time and are founded on values which privilege the notion of the 'march to progress' (Novotny, 1994). They also derive from the hegemony of adult generations and are ways of conceptualizing the world which are convenient to adults (Harris, 1983). The hegemony of age hierarchy is therefore likely to obscure the many cultural and contextual nuances which shape the multi-faceted experience of childhood. While we may not be able to understand childhood without first understanding adulthood, so the opposite also applies. As Jenks notes, 'it becomes impossible to produce a well-defined sense of the adult . . . without first positing the child' (Jenks, 1982: 10). The question 'what is a child?' needs to be addressed, therefore, in relation to the reconstitution of generational boundaries and also in relation to the ways in which these boundaries are negotiated in particular contexts. A child may be constituted as a young adolescent in one context and with respect to a particular generational order and quite differently in another; for example, depending upon country, culture, class and gender, for one child, work may be constituted as employment while, for another, it is a form of social learning.

Just as childhood is constituted differently in relation to the generational order, so it is valued differently depending upon the social and historical context. Typical conceptualizations of children today turn on their 'relational' significance to society since their immediate economic worth has diminished in industrialized societies – in Zelitzer's terms 'the priceless' but economically 'worthless' child (Zelitzer, 1985). As marriage and co-residential parenthood become less common, children are increasingly significant to the symbolic order of family life (Jenks, 1996; Smart and Neale, forthcoming).

In this chapter, I shall attempt to put this new interest in the sociology of childhood into perspective. I will first outline the main theoretical frameworks which, in recent years, have conceptualized children and childhood, indicating some of the continuities and changes in emphasis concerning children's agency and reflecting on the political values which may underlie these. Next, I consider the UK policy context in which research is carried out and which increasingly shapes the research agenda generally, not only in this field. I consider four major policy concerns likely to drive research on childhood. These developments are evident at different levels and differ in their legitimacy in the UK context. In order to show how theoretical and political perspectives can be differently combined, I shall compare the UK with Scandinavia.

Paradigms for the Study of Children

Research which has been largely 'on' or 'about' children has viewed children through a number of theoretical paradigms: (1) the framing of a child as a developing individual and/or in a dependent status within a family; (2) the conceptualization of the child in other settings and between contexts; and (3) the child as a social category and social actor. Each paradigm varies in the importance it places on social structure and social agency. As I shall indicate, the concept of children's agency has a place in all three paradigms but greater importance is placed upon it within the third paradigm. I shall also argue that underlying each theoretical perspective are political values. In the new sociology of childhood, children's 'right' to be treated as reflexive, social actors is a political viewpoint, not only a theoretical perspective. Indeed, in a similar way to the feminist project which identified as its goal the pursuit of knowledge for women, the values of the new sociology of childhood clearly identify as its goal the creation of a body of knowledge which is not only about children but *for* children. This goal both reflects and contributes to the arrival of children and childhood on the political stage as the new minority group.

(1) Child as Developing Individual or Unit of Socialization

The psychology of child development has dominated the research field of children's socialization; the child is conceptualized individualistically in relation to his or her age and 'stage' in the life span of biological, cognitive and emotional development. Governed by strong normative notions of what constitutes 'proper' development, children's location in the family context is generally taken as given (and still considered desirable if family life is problematic). However, under the powerful influence of psychoanalysis, child development also accords children agency but offers little analysis of the conditions under which it is engendered. For, within this paradigm, the opportunities and constraints of gender, class, race, culture and ethnicity are context- rather than person-centred and therefore excluded from the frame. Instead, family relationships, notably the attachment of the child to the mother, are seen as the main influence on children's development (Bowlby, 1951). Although some suggest that theories of learning and education view children as passive – 'to be controlled, taught and tested' (Denzin, 1977: 20, cited in Mayall, 1996), children are also considered to be active participants in decision-making. Indeed, the way in which children develop initiative and competences is the chief process by which they do, and indeed should, grow to maturity (Phoenix, 1996a). Moreover, if children fail to learn that they can control the world, this is said to disrupt the developmental process (Erikson, 1968). However, as Mayall argues, within this paradigm children's learning is devalued since it is adults who lay claim to the knowledge about children's development and become the experts (Mayall, 1996: 54).

By contrast, sociology has viewed children's 'socialization' rather more deterministically, often within a functionalist framework. In national census and large-scale survey enquiries, children have been relegated to the status of household 'dependent'. In intensive studies of family life mothers are the principal agents of social transmission and social control and children are conceptualized as receptacles of their care rather than contributors who are mutually involved in the socialization project. Feminist sociology has sought to reveal women's hitherto hidden productive contribution to family life, and therefore highlighted mothers' rather than children's agency. A consideration of the implications of feminist analysis for children's agency is therefore needed.

It is helpful, at this point, to consider that political values underpin child development and socialization theories. While theoretical perspectives differ, their political values need not however be antithetical. In most Scandinavian societies, children's needs, which have been met through publicly supported daycare, have been closely connected to mothers' entry into the labour market but, unlike in the UK, these different sets of interests and associated value perspectives have been accommodated. Indeed, the period in which mothers' employment escalated in countries like Sweden and Norway coincided with a growth in public sector jobs which have been concentrated in the human services, including the expanding daycare services (Waerness, 1994). This helped to forge political alliances between mothers and the Scandinavian welfare states (Hernes, 1987; Leira, 1992). Coherence between the political goal of gender equality and the need to provide for children's interests has been achieved. As Dahlberg (1997) documents for Sweden, early childhood education and its institutions were historically linked to the creation of modern democratic life and associated ideas of the child as central to the wider solidaristic community, at the same time as contributing to national economic growth by supporting mothers' employment. Although these political discourses have changed over the years, Swedish children are still considered to be the shared responsibility of parents and of the state, with their own freedoms and legal rights.

In Scandinavian societies, relative coherence has also been achieved in the research field, that is among the different disciplines involved in the study of gender and the study of child development and pedagogy, albeit that the research is carried out on separate but parallel tracks. Some Swedish researchers have even managed to bridge both perspectives, for example Dahlberg and the psychologist Philip Hwang, who combined research interests on parental employment with the study of children in daycare (Broberg and Hwang, 1991; Hwang and Haas, 1995).

In the UK, child development has had more influence than other disciplines on policy and professional practice concerning children, through its alliances with medicine and education. Drawing on attachment theory (Bowlby, 1951; Ainsworth and Wittig, 1969), it has sustained the policy view that young children ought to be with their mothers. Indeed, since the war, UK government policy has ignored the needs of working parents and, similarly, those of their children. Conservative governments' ideological stance during the 1980s and 1990s maintained that these matters ought to be private responsibilities, in effect that the 'proper' place of mothers and young children was in the home (Moss, 1992). By contrast, the notion of 'home' within the Swedish policy context acquired both public and private connotations and has been historically fundamental in the creation and representation of the welfare state as the 'People's home' (*Folkhemmet*) in which both mothers' and children's needs were central (Dahlberg, 1997).

(2) Children's Social Interaction in other Settings and between Contexts

The second paradigm concerns children's social interaction in different, mainly institutional contexts, and, unlike child development, does not simply take these as given. It cuts across disciplines, notably social psychology and social psychiatry, social policy, sociology and education. Some of this work has accorded children agency. While positivistic studies have focused on child 'outcomes' in relation to institutional care, other work has examined the social processes by which children, as active agents, learn, develop and interact with the adults who care for, educate them and control them (see studies in Bernstein and Brannen,

1996). But because of the institutional focus, the agency of children is often underplayed.

Sociological work which has taken account of children's agency includes the work of Bernstein (in the 1960s and 1970s) and Walkerdine's research (in the 1980s) on children's social interaction in schools and family life. These researchers place considerable theoretical weight, however, on the structural processes and contextual factors which shape children's agency. Moreover, it is important to note that their approaches take issue with dominant psychological perspectives, and deconstruct the modernist notion of the autonomous child or young person. Bernstein's work identifies and analyses social trends whereby children's autonomy is normatively prescribed – the trend towards 'self-regulation' and the ways in which it is shaped by social class. In developing notions of visible and invisible modes of social control, Bernstein's work reveals how covert surveillance, notably via particular modes of communication, give rise to self-regulation (Bernstein, 1971, 1975). Walkerdine and Lucey (1989) address the gender contradictions in this modern process of self-regulation, namely that it is mothers who seek to engender a sense of power in their children when their own access to power and resources is limited.

> A libertarian analysis of mother–child relations stresses 'freedom' for the child. Freedom from repression so that the child can be free to discover individuality and autonomy, free to learn self-regulation – the only luggage needed on the conflict-free path to democracy. But the picture of harmony is a fantasy, one which ignores and denies the possibility of resistance and power. (Walkerdine and Lucey, 1989: 29)

The political values which underpin the research within this paradigm are clearly highly variable. The work of Bernstein (1971, 1975) and Walkerdine and Lucey (1989) conceptualizes children as social actors but problematizes children's autonomy. While assuming children's agency, they examine the import and social construction of autonomy and the constraints upon it. In this endeavour, they mount a radical critique of modern democracy so that what appears on the surface to constitute freedom and autonomy, in practice disguises subtle forms of resistance and constraint. Other research in this paradigm is more likely to be underpinned by a reformist policy agenda, for example concerning the protection of children 'in need'. Its theoretical assumptions posit 'the family' as being centrally important for children and hence the need to compensate children for the loss of it through the provision of other families.

(3) *Children as Sociological Agents*

The first basic tenet of the new sociology of childhood is 'the idea of children as a social group on whom social forces operate to condition the character of childhood' (Mayall, 1996: 2). This work places central importance on children's agency rather than on the constraints within which children's agency is negotiated. Once children are considered to be, or consider themselves to be, reflexive social actors, the conditions exist for them to be treated as a social category or collectivity whose interests should be considered separately from those of parents and other adults. Children are thereby liberated from the conceptual confines of developmentalism. The social categorization of children is an important step in the process by which a group claims power and contests the distribution of resources. Freed from the hidden, ancillary position of dependency upon households, that is parents, children become units of analysis in official statistics, bringing into question dominant definitions of 'child' and 'young person'. Once childhood is considered a status rather than a transitory period and once children constitute a visible social group, it is possible to value children's productive contribution in the social, economic and emotional division of labour through their activity in schools, households and elsewhere. Children also become visible as consumers and clients of services.

The rethinking of childhood also reveals how children's lives are organized 'under the eye of adults' and their daily experiences in time and space (Mayall, 1996). It addresses the fact that children's lives are lived out in child-defined as well as adult-defined contexts (Ambert, 1992). These different contexts have different implications for their agency, albeit safe, institutional contexts reserved only for children are created by adults to protect children from the dangerous adult world (Dencik, 1989; Frones, 1994). On the other hand, these environments may also seek to provide a liberal environment in which children are free to make some individual choices.

The new childhood studies also aim to address the complexity in children's identity, and challenges the assumption that children have a unitary identity (James and Prout, 1996). Rather, children's identities are multi-layered and are shaped by the different contexts which children inhabit. Drawing upon post-modern theories of individualization, children, like young people, are seen to develop strategies which help them to negotiate and move between different contexts and to construct their own lives accordingly (Andenaes and Haavind, 1993; Dahlberg, 1996).

In the UK, this paradigm of childhood is relatively new and is therefore still in the initial phase of identifying and asserting childhood as a social category. In Scandinavian countries, it has a longer history and theoretical links have been made which have led to much greater conceptual differentiation in the category 'child', especially in relation to gender and social class (Andenaes and Haavind, 1993; Dahlberg, 1996). Moreover, like Bernstein and Walkerdine, these researchers have problematized notions of autonomy in understanding the ways in which children, as reflexive agents, contribute to their own socialization.

Politics of Childhood and Children's Rights

More significant than the emergence of a new paradigm of childhood in bringing children to the fore is the fact that childhood has itself become a cause for concern. The world is changing rapidly. Time itself is taking on new meanings for those in the 'rat race' of dwindling employment opportunities, increased uncertainty and the growth of consumerism. The project of parenting has become more unclear as parents are increasingly perplexed as to how to prepare children for an uncertain future. British society has become increasingly unfriendly to children. All these changes have significant implications for children's lives. The political values underpinning the new sociology of childhood reflect this state of affairs.[2]

The values of this new seam of childhood research reside in the emergent UK politics of children's rights rather than in the policy agenda of child protection, which is still currently pre-eminent in UK public policy, or in the earlier politics of critical social analysis. In Beck's terms, there is a movement occurring in childhood and youth away from 'internalizing the spirit of democracy' (socialization) and the 'loyalties' of gender, family ethnicity and social class, towards the 'experience of deeds' involving questions of power and, above all, political participation. The process is marked by distinctions between the concepts of active rather than passive freedom which arise in the context of loosening ties with families of origin and the increasing flexibility of the labour market (Beck, 1997b: 157). The right of children and young people to have and to demand 'a life of their own' is said to involve the displacement of conventional forms of participation on the part of young people, via the 'provision' of conventional welfare organizations, towards the pursuit of political activity based upon children and young people taking initiative (Beck, 1997b: 166). This process also implies a move away from the notion of rights as forms of entitlement to welfare – involving the equitable distribution of provision via the bureaucracy of the state – towards the notion of rights to political participation, and associated responsibilities, in which the onus is on the individual to make rights claims.

But despite the attractions of individualization, this concept does not adequately address the issue of adult obligation. For while children should have rights to protection, care and participation, so also adults must have obligations to children which are also fundamental (Smart and Neale, 1999). Nor does it address the experiences of all groups of children and young people. Challenges remain in analysing differences among children, including the ways in which childhood is shaped by 'age' (capacities), gender, class and race. It is understandable that the new paradigm of childhood studies has not yet adequately differentiated the social category of children (in the UK). In focusing on children's agency, there is a need to treat the notion of agency cautiously and not to confuse it with notions of autonomy and independence.

Moreover, notions of children's autonomy and rights are ethnocentric assumptions which are part of a liberal rights discourse which may not be acceptable to all cultural groups, particularly in respect of beliefs about controlling children (Roche, 1996). Children's rights are also gendered, as Gilligan (1982) has argued, especially with respect to ethics of care. Gender norms concerning what is appropriate behaviour for boys and girls interact with cultural beliefs; for example, the meaning of adolescence and the expectations of autonomy, connectedness and care may differ among groups of different cultural origin and according to the gender of young people (Brannen, 1996). While being sympathetic to the overall project and the need to re-focus on children's agency, it is important therefore not to forget past research and to consider its particular contribution to the understanding of the distribution of power and the processes by which power is enacted both overtly and covertly. We should not lose sight of what we have gained from an understanding of gender and patriarchy.

Ultimately, if the new sociology of childhood is to exist *for* children, we need to look at what this means and in what way children constitute a class not of but for itself (Oldman, 1994). It seems unlikely that, in a political sense, children as a collectivity will ever be able to speak and act for themselves without adult support or intercession, in the way that other political groupings based on class and gender do (Oakley, 1994). Those who urge respect for children's rights must address not only children but those whose actions affect children (O'Neill, 1989).

Politics of Childhood and the Research Agenda

In the UK, policy has increasingly influenced research agenda. There are general as well as specific reasons for this. At a general level, many research funding bodies have increasingly preferred applied or interventionist studies and have often set the research agenda according to current, and frequently short-term, policy concerns. Research centres, programmes and initiatives now address specific policy-related themes which control a large portion of the research money available. This is happening in the context of a general 'marketization' of research in which researchers compete in the market-place and orientate their research proposals to a variety of different 'users' of research. These users of research have power not only to decide which proposals receive funding but which topics are chosen for research, and how the research is carried out, disseminated and evaluated. The generation and admin-istration of research programmes on childhood are no exception to this process (Brannen and Edwards, 1996).

More specifically, childhood is coming more to the fore in the UK as a focus for research (and is likely to do so even more in the future) not only because social scientists have suddenly woken up to children's invisibility as social actors but because of increasing policy concern with childhood and generational matters. Four major policy concerns related to children are evident at national, international and European levels. These are now driving, or will in the future drive, the research agenda on childhood. Not all are currently manifest or expressed in public debate in the UK and are therefore not yet reflected in the funded research. The first theme relates to concern about the 'break up' of family life which is much discussed in the UK and has been translated into a concern about 'parental responsibility' (see Smart, in this volume). The second, more pre-eminent at the international than the national level, relates to growing poverty among children, while the third debate, evident elsewhere and at an international level, is about children's rights. The fourth concerns two debates, discussed mainly elsewhere in Europe, which relate to the future of coming generations, on the one hand concerning a life-course imbalance in the distribution of employment ('the compression of work') and, on the other, a demographic generational imbalance between the young and old.

In the UK context, the most prominent policy debate in recent years, which shows no sign of disappearing even with a change of government, concerns fears about declining parental responsibility and the 'inadequate' socialization of children; these are pre-eminently seen to arise from the high level of 'family breakdown'. Parenthood (that is, motherhood) is problematized (in the way that working-class motherhood was targeted in the nineteenth century) so that major policy solutions are directed at inculcating 'parenting skills'. Beyond this, the state's role in engendering greater parental responsibility (see the 1989 Children Act) is largely confined to guidance and advocating partnership between parents and professionals, for example teachers, daycare workers, social workers and other 'child professionals'. This policy concern refers to children only indirectly and addresses parental responsibility for children's behaviour in a variety of domains, including the education system, the law and divorce. Moreover, despite the emphasis placed by the private sector and by government in recent years on individual consumers rather than producers (for example, the Citizen's Charters), children as a significant consumer group have been ignored despite their obvious importance.

Contiguous with the UK policy emphasis on 'private' (parental) responsibility for children, the state retains a residual concern for families who are 'in need' or, in the language of the Labour Government, 'socially excluded'. Here there is much public concern, with new revelations of child abuse occurring daily and most recently in the public childcare sector. Again, the public discourse addresses children indirectly, focusing instead on professionals, although in the Children Act there is an important provision for children 'looked after' by the state to be consulted about decisions concerning their care. In public policy terms, need is defined individualistically and material resources which parents require in fulfilling their obligations to their children are excluded from the policy frame. Instead, child protection policy aims to prevent children from being wrested from their families; 'family is best' even when particular family situations fail, while the parents of children taken into care 'share' responsibility with the state (via social services).[3] As Oppenheim and Lister (1996) conclude, in further endorsing parental responsibility UK policy has relinquished society's responsibility for children and has, in some senses, privatized childhood with the result that it is peripheral to a politics dominated by the concerns of the market.

A second policy debate, more apparent at the international than the national (UK) level, is the growth of poverty among children which, in the majority world context, manifests itself in the high rates of child labour frequently involving the exploitation of children through the labour market. Economic inequality has also grown dramatically in the UK over the last decade and a half but, because of the overriding policy concern with parental responsibility, it has not attracted much public debate. A number of British studies and reports have, however, drawn attention to the poor and declining material position of families with young children in contrast to those without children (Kumar, 1993; Goodman and Webb, 1995; Holtermann, 1995; Kennedy et al., 1996). For example, there is a substantial increase in the proportion of children living in households with half the average income and of those living in households with no earner (Department of Social Security, 1996), while trend data for 1984–94, based on the Labour Force Survey, indicate a substantial increase in the proportion of 'work poor' families with dependent children in the UK and, at the other end of the socio-economic spectrum, 'work rich' families with two full-time earners have increasingly become the norm (Brannen et al., 1997).

Within this broad theme, the cost to the state of family breakdown and lone mothers, the majority of whom depend upon state support, is a more dominant policy concern in the UK. The consequences of living on social security benefits for children and lone mothers have been much less significant. The effect upon family relationships of chasing children's fathers for financial support, especially children's relationships with their fathers, are therefore also overlooked. Even though some of the consequences of divorce and lone parenthood may negatively affect children (Richards, 1996), the major thrust of UK policy concern and policy solutions continues to lie in getting lone mothers back into the labour market with much less regard for the needs of children and the state of childhood in Britain.

A third policy debate concerning children's rights is evident in the 1989 United Nations Convention on the Rights of the Child. The UN Convention covers children's rights to provision, protection and partici-pation (Franklin and Franklin, 1996). The acquisition of participatory rights covered by Article 12 of the UN Convention constitutes a later rather than an earlier development in the children's rights discourse and is the most contentious. Children's participatory rights include the right to freedom of association, the right to freedom of expression and the right to be listened to. Much of the thrust related to the UN Convention may have less to do with children and more to do with a critique of liberal democracies which have permitted the exclusion of a number of groups from full political status and citizenship (Alanen, 1992: 69). A further important impetus behind the Convention has been the need to redress the poor conditions of many children in the majority world where childhood tends to be short and where the transition to adulthood occurs more abruptly and at earlier ages than in the Western industrialized world. Thus in the majority world, many 'maturing' or 'mature minors' are in a position partly analogous to adult oppressed groups with the result that the rhetoric of rights may help them secure political recognition and a greater share of their societies' resources.

While the UK government has been a signatory to the Convention since 1991, it has been remarkably slow in implementing it and has been heavily criticized for this. Unlike the UK, some North European countries have long treated children as citizens with a legal status in some respects independent of their parents, Sweden being the most progressive country in this regard (Dencik, 1989). For example, the Swedish state provides maintenance benefits and legal assistance to children. Its laws prohibiting corporal punishment have been in existence for a long time. Moreover, if Swedish parents find that their circumstances are such that they cannot manage to give their children all the personal care they need, children can appeal to the state which is statutorily required to look after children who are in need of welfare assistance (Dencik, 1989). Moreover, since 1973 children have been able to appeal directly to the state through the special Children's Ombudsman (this is also so in Norway).

The fourth issue of public policy concern which I highlight and which has implications for the research agenda on children is largely manifest at European level or in other European countries. This is really two debates: on the one hand, a concern about the growing imbalance in the life course and a consequent shrinkage in the period given to employment and, on the other, a concern about the demographic imbalance between older and younger generations. In the first case, there are significant effects on children's lives since the period of parents' maximum economic activity typically coincides with childbearing and childrearing, resulting in what Hochschild terms 'a time famine' for parents and a hurried pace of life for children (Hochschild, 1997). In the second case, the increasing imbalance between the diminishing size of the younger generation versus the increasing size of older generation has major consequences for the funding and structuring of the welfare state. A heightened policy awareness is emerging concerning the implications of changing life-course patterns and the changing demographic profiles of de-industrializing countries. Currently, these policy questions are not directed at children *per se*. But there is some public concern expressed about children's lives being increasingly pressurized by parents' employment (of course, in the UK large numbers of children have no parent in work). There is also some concern about young people's values, in particular their willingness to care and provide for older generations, in the context of diminishing employment opportunities and welfare benefits for themselves, especially pensions (Wilkinson and Mulgan, 1995).

I am suggesting that there is an interplay between policy concerns and the kinds of funded research carried out on children and childhood. Such interplay arises in the context in which research is funded. As the UK funding process is linked more closely to policy, practitioner and other 'user' concerns, research increasingly reflects this. A good deal of UK research funding on matters which touch children's lives has supported, and continues to support, studies which address the first policy concern around parenthood and questions related to ('inadequate') parental responsibility, the 'breakdown' of family life, the 'problem' of lone parents, declining family values, as well as more specific policy questions. The second policy debate I considered, namely the growing poverty and inequality which exists among children (and their parents) in Britain, has attracted little UK-funded research. This is because the debate and the very discourse of inequality have been politically unacceptable in Britain throughout the 'Thatcher' years and hence have remained undercurrents, largely considered subversive of market forces. Furthermore, from my own experience and from those of other people concerned with these issues, I can vouch for the difficulty of getting funding bodies to address the connections between the workings of the labour market and the welfare and experiences of children and their families. The possibility of discovering negative effects of the politically desired 'economic project' of employability and economic competitiveness upon children and family life looks as if it will continue to be a very unwelcome message to public policy-makers and politicians.

To some extent, a burst of research which is now beginning to occur in Britain under the umbrella of the emergent childhood studies, with its emphasis on children's agency and children's perspectives, testifies to the increasing significance of the third policy concern (more current at an international level and elsewhere in Europe) around children's rights. This debate is now rapidly gaining ground in the UK, in part at least because of the new political emphasis on the responsibilities of citizenship in the context of the need to restructure the welfare state, and on active forms of 'participation' as a way of countering political alienation, especially among young people. To some extent the political values of the new childhood studies 'fit' with these new political agendas; whether childhood as a policy concern and as a focus of study will find support in the market-place of research 'users' is another question. By contrast, childhood research has for many years been commonplace in Scandinavian and some other European countries where the policy climates have long recognized children's citizenship.

The fourth two-pronged policy debates which I highlighted, concerning the life-course imbalance regarding the distribution of employment and the impending generational imbalance, have yet to be widely debated in the UK, although they are current at European level and in some other European countries. They have little direct impact on current policy thinking relating to children in the UK, although their indirect effects are likely to be considerable. On the issue of the imbalance in the parents' employment careers, one might note young children's currently inequitable experience of (privately provided) daycare, while on the question of the generational imbalance the effects of a restructured welfare state lie in wait.

The ways in which children and young people view their current and future lives, in the context of these generational imbalances, are not, as yet, a popular area for UK-funded research. Nor are they likely to be unless they have short-termist policy implications which are politically acceptable. Concerns relating to the future may look a long way off from the perspectives of younger generations. However, the ways in which people in general think about the future is in a process of transformation (Harvey, 1990; Novotny, 1994; Adam, 1995; Kumar, 1995). The present is marked by excessive 'busyness', 'an intolerance of waiting', with the result that the present extends into the future or rather expectations of what can be achieved in the present overtake experience (Novotny, 1994). As Nilsen puts it, 'the future as a category is abolished and a "perpetual present" or an "extended present" takes the future into the here and now' (1997: 1). This tendency combines with an (early) life-course phase to make young people's concern with the future more rather than less remote. These matters pale into insignificance compared with the many individualized decisions of the present which, if Beck is correct (Beck, 1997b), children and young people today see themselves as responsible for making: the need to get a 'good' education, and the need to find ways into and through an increasingly uncertain labour market, not to mention the vast array of lifestyle opportunities and choices which beckon to those fortunate enough to have the resources.

Conclusion

This chapter has considered the emergence of a sociology of childhood in the UK which involves rethinking a field of knowledge which has hitherto treated children's definitions and perspectives as invalid or unreliable. The first part of the chapter discussed the ways in which children and childhood have been theorized according to three paradigms. These paradigms include: the socialization of the child in the family; the secondary socialization of the child in organizations and other institutional settings; children as a social category and as individualized social actors who shape their own identities. Childhood needs to be understood in relation to all three paradigms and in relation to the interplay between children's agency, adults' obligations to children, and the contexts and constraints of adult- and child-dominated institutions. In discussing these paradigms, I have tried to indicate how each differs in the emphasis it gives to social structure versus social agency, but also, more fundamentally, I have suggested that different sets of values underpin each paradigm. The third paradigm, the new sociology of childhood, represents a move towards creating a politics *for* children in which children are the central actors. How this is to be achieved is unclear but might surely depend upon those with greater power to speak for them. The creation of such a body of knowledge is a necessary step in claiming power and contesting resource distribution. This paradigm represents a different political vantage point from those embedded in the other paradigms, whether these relate to New Right or communitarian values about the responsibilities of parenthood, professional and expert knowledge of what a 'normal' child should be, the critical analysis of social inequality or the politics of feminism.

In the second part of the chapter I examined the conditions – or policy 'push' – under which this new interest in childhood is occurring. I noted increasingly close links between research and policy agenda in the UK, signified by the prioritizing of 'users' in the funding process. Next, I outlined four major policy areas of debate, some dominant at national, some at European and some at international level. I suggested that these are either currently driving research agenda on childhood and bringing children to the fore, or are likely to do so in the future. I argued that, in the UK, the debate has been 'stuck' for some time in the politics of parental responsibility, despite the considerable evidence of the growing material disadvantage experienced by many British children and their families. I also suggested that the debate around 'children's rights' – in particular the extension of participatory rights to children – is beginning to gain ground in Britain and is now fuelling the new childhood studies, albeit filtered through the well-established work in this field conducted elsewhere, notably in Scandinavia. I noted that childhood as a separate domain has long been part of the political and research agenda there. The conditions for the growth of a children's rights discourse in the UK may prove more fertile ground in the current political climate than the redress of social inequality, if only because the children's rights discourse places emphasis upon the active agency of the individual rather than placing the onus upon the bureaucratic apparatus and costliness of the welfare state. At the same time, the public policy concern with child protection in the UK looks set to continue. Finally, I signalled some of the emergent policy debates which may drive future research in the UK: the politics around an increasing imbalance in the distribution of employment over the life course and its consequences for children's experience of time, and the politics concerning the increasingly problematic 'generational pact'. Whether research will follow in the wake of these concerns in the shorter term may to some extent be affected, at the national level, by how far it is acceptable to criticize the dominance of market forces and how far and how quickly the welfare state is restructured.

Notes

1 The Economic and Social Research Council Programme *Children 5–16*, funded in 1996, is a particular case in point together with a range of other research initiatives.

2 For example, it was precisely such concern which led to the refocusing of a proposal for an ESRC Research Programme from parenting to childhood (Brannen and Edwards, 1996).

3 Moreover, foster care, rather than residential care, is increasingly the preferred care solution for these children since it is regarded as the closest approximation to 'proper' family life. Consistent with the concept of parental responsibility, foster carers are significantly no longer defined as substitute parents but are referred to as 'carers' (Rhodes, 1995).

BIBLIOGRAPHY

Abelove, H., Barale, M.A. and Halperin, D.M. (eds) (1993) *Lesbian and Gay Studies Reader*. London: Routledge.

Adam, B. (1995) *Timewatch: The Social Analysis of Time*. Oxford: Blackwell.

Adam, B.D. (1992) 'Sex and caring among men', in K. Plummer (ed.), *Modern Homosexualities: Fragments of Lesbian and Gay Experience*. London: Routledge.

Ainsworth, M.D.S. and Wittig, B. (1969) 'Attachment and exploratory behaviour of one year olds in a strange situation', *Determinants of Infant Behaviour*, 4: 113–16.

Ainsworth, M.D.S., Blehar, M., Waters, E. and Wall, S. (1978) *Patterns of Attachment*. Hillsdale, NJ: Erlbaum.

Akrich, M. (1992) 'The de-scription of technical objects', in W. Bijker and J. Law (eds), *Shaping Technology/Building Society*. Cambridge, MA: MIT Press.

Alanen, L. (1992) *Modern Childhood? Exploring the 'Child Question' in Sociology*. Juyväskylä: Institute in Educational Research. Publication Series A. Research Report 50.

Allen, G. (1989) *Friendship: Developing a Sociological Perspective*. Boulder, CO: Westview Press.

Ambert, A.M. (1992) *The Effect of Children on Parents*. New York: Haworth Press.

Andenaes, A. and Haavind, H. (1993) 'When parents are living apart: challenges and solutions for children with two homes', in A. Leira (ed.), *Family Sociology – Developing the Field*. Report 93: 5. Oslo: Institute for Social Research.

Arber, S. and Ginn, J. (1991) *Gender and Later Life: A Sociological Analysis of Resources and Constraints*. London: Sage.

Arber, S. and Ginn, J. (1995) 'The mirage of gender equality: occupational success in the labour market and within marriage', *British Journal of Sociology*, 46 (1): 21–43.

Aries, P. (1980) 'Two successive motivations for the declining birth rate in the West', *Population and Development Review*, 6: 645–50.

Backett, K. (1987) 'The negotiation of fatherhood', in C. Lewis and M. O'Brien (eds), *Reassessing Fatherhood*. London: Sage.

Barrett, M. and Macintosh, M. (1982) *The Anti-Social Family*. London: Verso.

Barrow, C. (1996) *Family in the Caribbean: Themes and Perspectives*. Kingston (Jamaica): Ian Randle Publishers; Oxford: James Currey Publishers.

Bauman, Z. (1993) *Postmodern Ethics*. Oxford: Blackwell.

Baylies, C. (1996) 'Diversity in patterns of parenting and household', in Elizabeth

B. Silva (ed.), *Good Enough Mothering? Feminist Perspectives on Lone Motherhood.* London: Routledge.

Beardsworth, A. and Keil, T. (1992) 'The vegetarian option: varieties, conversions, motives and careers', *Sociological Review*, 40 (2): 253–93.

Bech, H. (1996) *When Men Meet: Homosexuality and Modernity.* Cambridge: Polity Press.

Beck, U. (1992) *Risk Society: Towards a New Modernity.* London: Sage.

Beck, U. (1997a) *The Reinvention of Politics: Rethinking Modernity in the Global Social Order.* Cambridge: Polity Press.

Beck, U. (1997b) 'Democratization in the family', *Childhood*, 4 (2): 151–69.

Beck, U. and Beck-Gernsheim, E. (1995) *The Normal Chaos of Love.* Cambridge: Polity Press.

Beck, U., Giddens, A. and Lash, S. (1994) *Reflexive Modernization: Politics, Traditions and Aesthetics in the Modern Social Order.* Cambridge: Polity Press.

Bell, C. (1968) *Middle Class Families: Social and Geographical Mobility.* London: Routledge & Kegan Paul.

Bell, D. and Valentine, G. (1995) *Mapping Desire: Geographies of Sexualities.* London: Routledge.

Benjamin, O. and Sullivan, O. (1996) 'The importance of difference: conceptualizing increased flexibility in gender relations at home', *Sociological Review*, 44 (2): 225–51.

Berk, S.F. (1985) *The Gender Factory: The Apportionment of Work in American Households.* New York: Plenum.

Bernardes, J. (1987) '"Doing things with words": sociology and "family policy" debates', *The Sociological Review*, 36 (2): 267–72.

Bernardes, J. (1997) *Family Studies: An Introduction.* London: Routledge.

Bernstein, B. (1971) *Class, Codes and Control*, Vol. 1: *Theoretical Studies Towards a Sociology of Language.* London: Routledge & Kegan Paul.

Bernstein, B. (1975) *Class, Codes and Control*, Vol. 3: *Towards a Theory of Educational Transmissions.* Routledge & Kegan Paul.

Bernstein, B. and Brannen, J. (eds) (1996) *Children, Research and Policy.* London: Taylor & Francis.

Blumstein, P. and Schwartz, P. (1985) *American Couples.* New York: Pocket Books.

Borchorst, A. (1990) 'Political motherhood and childcare policies: a comparative approach to Britain and Scandinavia', in C. Ungerson (ed.), *Gender and Caring: Work and Welfare in Britain and Scandinavia.* London: Harvester Wheatsheaf.

Borneham, J. (1996) 'Until death do us part: marriage/death in anthropological discourse', *American Ethnologist*, 23 (2): 215–38.

Bourdieu, P. (1977) *Outline of a Theory of Practice.* Cambridge: Cambridge University Press.

Bourdieu, P. (1996) 'On the family as a realized category', *Theory, Culture and Society*, 13 (3): 19–26.

Bowlby, J. (1951) *Maternal Care and Mental Health.* Geneva: World Health Organization.

Bozett, F.W. (1987) 'Preface', in F.W. Bozett (ed.), *Gay and Lesbian Parents.* New York: Praeger.

Bradley, H. (1989) *Men's Work, Women's Work.* Cambridge: Polity Press.

Bradshaw, J. and Millar, J. (1991) *Lone Parent Families in the UK.* Department of Social Security Research Report No. 6. London: HMSO.

Brannen, J. (1996) 'Discourses of adolescence: young people's independence and autonomy within families', in J. Brannen and M. O'Brien (eds), *Children in Families: Research and Policy*. London: Falmer Press.

Brannen, J. and Collard, J. (1982) *Marriages in Trouble: The Process of Seeking Help*. London: Tavistock.

Brannen, J. and Edwards, R. (1996) 'From parents to children: the generation of a research programme', in J. Brannen and R. Edwards (eds), *Perspectives on Parenting and Childhood*. London: South Bank University.

Brannen, J. and Moss, P. (1991) *Managing Mothers: Dual Earners Households after Maternity Leave*. London: Unwin Hyman.

Brannen, J., Dodd, K., Oakley, A. and Storey, P. (1994) *Young People, Health and Family Life*. Buckingham: Open University Press.

Brannen, J., Moss, P., Owen, C. and Wale, C. (1997) *Mothers, Fathers and Employment: Parents and the Labour Market in Britain 1984–1994*. Sheffield: Department for Education and Employment.

Broberg, A. and Hwang, P. (1991) 'Swedish childcare research', in E. Melhuish and P. Moss (eds), *Day Care for Young Children*. London: Tavistock.

Brodber, R. Wiltshire (1986) 'The Caribbean transnational family'. Paper presented to UNESCO/ISER Eastern Caribbean Sub-regional Seminar, University of the West Indies, Cave Hill, Barbados.

Burgess, A. and Ruxton, S. (1996) *Men and Their Children*. London: Institute for Public Policy Research.

Burghes, L. (1994) *Lone Parenthood and Family Disruption: The Outcomes for Children*. London: Family Policy Studies Centre.

Burghes, L. (1996) 'Debates on disruption: what happens to the children of lone parents', in Elizabeth B. Silva (ed.) *Good Enough Mothering? Feminist Perspectives on Lone Motherhood*. London: Routledge.

Burghes, L., Clarke, L. and Cronin, N. (1997) *Fathers and Fatherhood in Britain*. London: Family Policy Studies Centre.

Burgoyne, J. and Clark, D. (1984) *Making a Go of It: A Study of Stepfamilies in Sheffield*. London: Routledge & Kegan Paul.

Butler, J. (1990) *Gender Trouble: Feminism and the Subversion of Identity*. London: Routledge.

Carabine, J. (1995) 'Sexuality and social policy'. Paper given at Social Policy Association, Women's Interest Group.

Chabaud-Rychter, D. (1994) 'Women users in the design process of a food robot: innovation in a French domestic appliance company', in C. Cockburn and R. Fürst-Dilic (eds), *Bringing Technology Home*. Buckingham: Open University Press.

Chabaud-Rychter, D. (1995) 'The configuration of domestic practices in the designing of household appliances', in K. Grint and R. Gill (eds), *The Gender-Technology Relation: Contemporary Theory and Research*. London: Taylor & Francis.

Chamberlain, M. (1995) 'Family narratives and migration dynamics', *New West Indies Guide/Nieue West-Indische Gids*, 69 (3/4): 253–75.

Chamberlain, M. (1997) *Narratives of Exile and Return*. London: Macmillan.

Chamberlain, M. and Goulbourne, H. (forthcoming) *New Perspectives on Caribbean Families*.

Chisholm, L. and du Bois-Reymond, M. (1993) 'Youth transitions, gender and social change', *Sociology*, 27 (2): 259–79.

Clarke, E. (1957) *My Mother who Fathered Me*. London: George Allen & Unwin.

Cockburn, C. (1997) 'Domestic technologies: Cinderella and the engineers', *Women's Studies International Forum*, 20 (3): 361–71.

Cockburn, C. and Ormrod, S. (1993) *Gender and Technology in the Making*. London: Sage.

Connell, R.W. (1987) *Gender and Power*. Cambridge: Polity Press.

Cowan, R.S. (1983) *More Work for Mother: The Ironies of Household Technology from the Open Hearth to the Microwave*. New York: Basic Books.

Coward, R. (1992) *Our Treacherous Hearts: Why Women Let Men Get Their Way*. London: Faber.

Dahlberg, G. (1996) 'Negotiating modern childrearing and family life in Sweden', in J. Brannen and R. Edwards (eds), *Perspectives on Parenting and Childhood*. London: South Bank University.

Dahlberg, G. (1997) 'From the "people's home" – folkhemmet – to the enterprise: reflections on the constitution and reconstitution of the field of early childhood pedagogy in Sweden', in T. Popkewitz (ed.), *Educational Knowledge: Changing Relationships between the State, Civil Society and the Educational Community*. Albany, NY: The State University Press of New York.

Dalley, G. (1996) *Ideologies of Caring: Rethinking Community and Collectivism* (2nd edn). Basingstoke: Macmillan.

Daniel, G and Thompson, P (1996) 'Stepchildren's memories of love and loss: men's and women's narratives', in S. Leydersdorff, L. Passerini and P. Thompson (eds), *Gender and Memory: International Yearbook of Oral History and Life Stories* (Vol IV). Oxford: Oxford University Press.

Davidoff, L. (1995) 'Where the stranger begins: the question of siblings in historical analysis', in L. Davidoff (ed.), *Worlds Between: Historical Perspectives on Gender and Class*. Cambridge: Polity Press.

Davidoff, L. and Hall, C. (1987) *Family Fortunes: Men and Women of the English Middle Class 1780–1850*. London: Routledge.

Davidson, C. (1982) *A Woman's Work is Never Done: A Social History of Housework 1630–1950*. London: Chatto & Windus.

De Cooman, E., Ermisch, J. and Joshi, H. (1987) 'The next birth and the labour market: a dynamic model of births in England and Wales', *Population Studies*, 41: 237–68.

Dench, G. (1996) *The Place of Men in Changing Family Attitudes*. London: Institute of Community Studies.

Dencik, L. (1989) 'Growing up in the post-modern age: on the child's situation in the modern family, and on the position of the family in the modern welfare state', *Acta Sociologica*, 32 (2): 155–80.

Dennis, N. and Erdos, G. (1993) *Families Without Fatherhood*. London: Institute for Economic Affairs Health and Welfare Unit.

Denzin, N.K. (1977) *Childhood Socialization*. San Francisco: Jossey-Bass.

Department of Social Security (1996) *Households below Average Income: A Statistical Analysis 1979–1993/4*. London: HMSO.

DeVault, M.L. (1991) *Feeding the Family: The Social Organization of Caring as Gendered Work*. London and Chicago: University of Chicago Press.

Doucet, A. (1995) 'Gender differences, gender equality and care: towards understanding gendered labour in British dual earner households'. PhD dissertation. Faculty of Social and Political Sciences, University of Cambridge.

Doucet, A. (1996) 'Encouraging voices: towards more creative methods for collecting data on gender and household labour', in L. Morris and S. Lyons (eds), *Gender Relations in Public and Private: Changing Research Perspectives*. London: Macmillan.

Doucet, A. (1997) '"You see the need perhaps more clearly than I": seeing, measuring and theorising domestic responsibility'. Paper presented to the Canadian Association of Sociology and Anthropology, Memorial University, Saint John's, Newfoundland, June.

Duncombe, J. and Marsden, D. (1996) 'Can we research the private sphere? Methodological and ethical problems in the study of the role of intimate emotion in personal relationships', in L. Morris and S. Lyons (eds), *Gender Relations in Public and Private: Changing Research Perspectives*. London: Macmillan.

Dunne, G.A. (1992) 'Differences at work: perceptions of work from a non-heterosexual point of view', in H. Hinds and J. Stacey (eds), *New Directions in Women's Studies in the 1990s*. London: Falmer Press.

Dunne, G.A. (1997a) *Lesbian Lifestyles: Women's Work and the Politics of Sexuality*. Basingstoke and London: Macmillan.

Dunne, G.A. (1997b) 'Why can't a man be more like a woman? In search of balanced domestic and employment lives', London School of Economics Gender Institute Discussion Paper Series, 3. London: LSE.

Dunne, G.A. (1998a) '"Pioneers behind our own front doors": towards new models in the organization of work in partnerships', *Work Employment and Society*, 12 (2): 273–95.

Dunne, G.A. (1998b) 'Add sexuality and stir: towards a broader understanding of the gender dynamics of work and family life', in G.A. Dunne (ed.), *Living Difference: Lesbian Perspectives on Work and Family Life*. Birghampton, NY: Harrington Park Press.

Dunne, G.A. and Doucet, A. (forthcoming) 'Who essentially cares? Towards a reformulation of gender dynamics of care giving', in A. O'Reilly and S. Abbey (eds), *International Perspectives on Mothers and Daughters*. Toronto: Rowman & Littlefield.

Elliot, F. Robertson (1996) *Gender, Family and Society*. Basingstoke: Macmillan.

Elton, Lord (1945) *Imperial Commonwealth*. London: Collins.

Erikson, E. (1968) *Identity: Youth and Crisis*. New York: W.W. Norton.

Ermisch, J.E. (1983) *The Political Economy of Demographic Change*. London: Heinemann.

Family Policy Studies Centre (1991) *An Ageing Population*. London: FPSC.

Fenstermaker, S., West, C. and Zimmerman, D.H. (1991) 'Gender inequality: new conceptual terrain', in R.L. Blumberg (ed.), *Gender, Family and Economy: The Triple Overlap*. London: Sage.

Ferri, E. and Smith, K. (1996) *Parenting in the 1990s*. London: Family Policy Studies Centre.

Finch, J. (1983) *Married to the Job*. London: George Allen & Unwin.

Finch, J. (1989) *Family Obligation and Social Change*. Cambridge: Polity Press.

Finch, J. and Mason, J. (1990) 'Divorce, remarriage and family obligations', *Sociological Review*, 38 (2): 219–46.

Finch, J. and Mason, J. (1993) *Negotiating Family Responsibilities*. London: Routledge.

Fletcher, R. (1962) *Britain in the Sixties: The Family and Marriage – An Analysis and Moral Assessment*. Harmondsworth: Penguin.

Fog Olwig, K. (1993) 'The migration experience: Nevisian women at home and abroad', in J. Momsen (ed.), *Women and Change in the Caribbean*. Kingston (Jamaica): Ian Randle.

Forna, A. (1997) 'The girl with three mothers', *Independent on Sunday*, 8 June.

Foucault, M. (1979) *The History of Sexuality*, Vol. 1: *An Introduction*. London: Allen Lane.

Fox Harding, L. (1996) *Family, State and Social Policy*. London: Macmillan.

Frankenberg, R. (1993) 'Trust, culture, language and time', Consent Conference No. 2. Young People's Psychiatric Treatment and Consent. London: Social Science Research Unit, Institute of Education.

Franklin, A. and Franklin, B. (1996) 'Growing pains: the developing children's rights movement in the UK', in J. Pilcher and S. Wagg (eds), *Thatcher's Children? Politics, Childhood and Society in the 1980s and 1990s*. London: Falmer Press.

French, S. (ed.) (1993) *Fatherhood*. London: Virago.

Frones, I. (1994) 'Dimensions of childhood', in J. Qvortrup, M. Bardy, G. Sgritta and H. Wintersberger (eds), *Childhood Matters: Social Theory, Practice and Politics*. Aldershot: Avebury.

Gagnon, J. and Simon, W. (1974) *Sexual Conduct*. London: Hutchinson.

Gardiner, J. (1997) *Gender, Care and Economics*. Basingstoke: Macmillan.

Garnsey, E. (1982) 'Women's work and theories of class and stratification', in A. Giddens and D. Held (eds), *Classes, Power and Conflict: Classical and Contemporary Debates*. Basingstoke: Macmillan.

Gershuny, J. (1983) *Social Innovation and the Division of Labour*. Oxford: Oxford University Press.

Gershuny, J. (1992) 'Change in the domestic division of labour in the UK, 1975–1987: dependent labour versus adaptive partnership', in N. Abercrombie and A. Warde (eds), *Social Change in Contemporary Britain*. Cambridge: Polity Press.

Gershuny, J., Godwin, M. and Jones, S. (1994) 'The domestic labour revolution: a process of lagged adaptation', in M. Anderson, F. Bechhofer and J. Gershuny (eds), *The Social and Political Economy of the Household*. Oxford: Oxford University Press.

GHS (1995) *General Household Survey*, Office of Population Censuses and Surveys. London: HMSO.

Giddens, A. (1992) *The Transformation of Intimacy: Sexuality, Love and Eroticism in Modern Societies*. Cambridge: Polity Press.

Gilligan, C. (1982) *In a Different Voice: Psychological Theory and Women's Development*. Cambridge, MA: Harvard University Press.

Gillis, J.R. (1997) *A World of their Own Making: A History of Myth and Ritual in Family Life*. Oxford: Oxford University Press.

Ginn, J. et al. (1996) 'Feminist fallacies: a reply to Hakim on women's employment', *British Journal of Sociology*, 47 (1): 167–74.

Gittins, D. (1985) *The Family in Question: Changing Households and Familiar Ideologies*. Basingstoke: Macmillan.

Glover, J. and Arber, S. (1995) 'Polarization in mothers' employment', *Gender, Work and Organization*, 2 (4): 165–79.

Good Housekeeping (1997) Issues of October, November and December. London: National Magazine Company.

Good Housekeeping Institute (1955) *The Happy Home*. London: National Magazine Company Library.

Goodman, A. and Webb, S. (1995) *The Distribution of UK Household Expenditure 1979–1992*. London: Institute of Fiscal Studies.

Gordon, S. (1987) 'I go to "Tanties": the economic significance of child-shifting in Antigua, West Indies', *Journal of Comparative Family Studies*, 18 (3): 427–43.

Gordon, T. (1990) *Feminist Mothers*. London: Macmillan.

Goulbourne, H. (forthcoming) 'The transnational character of Caribbean kinship in Britain', in Susan McRae (ed.), *Population and Household Change* (provisional title). Oxford: Oxford University Press.

Greenfield, S. (1966) *English Rustics in Black Skin: A Study of Modern Family Forms in a Pre-Industrial Society*. New Haven, CT: Connecticut College and University Press.

Gregson, N. and Lowe, M. (1994) *Servicing the Middle Classes: Class, Gender and Waged Domestic Labour*. London: Routledge.

Griffin, K. and Mulholland, L.A. (eds) (1997) *Lesbian Motherhood in Europe*. London: Cassell.

Gubrium, J.E. and Holstein, J.A. (1990) *What is Family?* Mountain View, CA: Mayfield Publishing.

Haas, L. (1990) 'Parental leave in Sweden', *Journal of Family Studies*, December.

Hagestad, G.O. (1991) 'The ageing society as a context for family life', in N. Jecker (ed.), *Ageing and Ethics*. New York: Humana Press.

Hakim, C. (1996) *Key Issues in Women's Work: Female Heterogeneity and the Polarization of Women's Employment*. London: Athlone Press.

Hanscombe, G. and Forster, J. (1982) *Rocking the Cradle: Lesbian Mothers – A Challenge in Family Living*. London: Sheba Feminist Publishers.

Harne, L. and Rights of Women (1997) *Valued Families: The Lesbian Mothers' Legal Handbook*. London: The Women's Press.

Harris, C.C. (1983) *The Family and Industrial Society*. London: Allen & Unwin.

Harrop, A. and Moss, P. (1995) 'Trends in parental employment', *Work, Employment and Society*, 9 (3): 421–44.

Harvey, D. (1990) *The Condition of Postmodernity*. Oxford: Blackwell.

Haskey, J. (1996) 'The proportion of married couples who divorce: past patterns and current prospects', *Population Trends*, 83: 28–36.

Heaphy, B., Donovan, C. and Weeks, J. (1997) 'Sex, money and the kitchen sink: power in same-sex couple relationships'. Paper presented to the British Sociological Association Annual Conference, 'Power/Resistance', University of York, April 1997.

Hernes, H.M. (1987) *Welfare State and Women Power*. Oslo: Universitetsforlaget.

Hochschild, A.R. (1989) *The Second Shift*. New York: Avon Books.

Hochschild, A.R. (1996) 'The emotional geography of work and family life', in L. Morris and S. Lyons (eds), *Gender Relations in Public and Private: Changing Research Perspectives*. London: Macmillan.

Hochschild, A.R. (1997) *The Time Bind: When Work becomes Home and Home becomes Work*. New York: Metropolitan Books.

Holtermann, S. (1995) *All Our Futures: The Impact of Public Expenditure and Fiscal Policies on Britain's Children and Young People*. London: Barnados.

Housewife (monthly magazine) Issues of February 1954 and October 1957. London.

Humphries, J. and Rubery, J. (1984) 'The reconstitution of the supply side of the labour market: the relative autonomy of social reproduction', *Cambridge Journal of Economics*, 8: 331–46.

Humphries, J. and Rubery, J. (1992) 'The legacy for women's employment: integration, differentiation and polarization', in J. Michie (ed.), *The Economic Legacy 1979–1992*. London: Academic Press.

Hutton, S. (1994) 'Men's and women's incomes: evidence from survey data', *Journal of Social Policy*, 23 (1): 21–40.

Hwang, P. and Haas, L. (1995) 'Company culture and men's usage of family leave benefits in Sweden', *Family Relations*, 44: 28–36.

Irwin, S. (1995a) *Rights of Passage: Social Change and the Transition from Youth to Adulthood*. London: UCL Press.

Irwin, S. (1995b) 'Social reproduction and change in the transition from youth to adulthood', *Sociology*, 29 (2): 293–315.

Irwin, S. (1995c) *Gender and Household Resourcing: Changing Relations to Work and Family*. GAPU Working Paper 12, School of Sociology and Social Policy, University of Leeds.

James, A. and Prout, A. (1990) *Constructing and Reconstructing Childhood: Contemporary Issues in the Sociological Study of Childhood*. London: Falmer Press.

James, A. and Prout, A. (1996) 'Strategies and structures towards a new perspective on children's experiences of family life', in J. Brannen and M. O'Brien (eds), *Children in Families: Research and Policy*. London: Falmer Press.

Jenks, C. (1982) 'Introduction: constituting the child', in C. Jenks (ed.), *The Sociology of Childhood: Essential Readings*. London: Batsford.

Jenks, C. (1996) 'The postmodern child', in J. Brannen and M. O'Brien (eds), *Children in Families: Research and Policy*. London: Falmer Press.

Jones, G. and Wallace, C. (1992) *Youth, Family and Citizenship*. Buckingham: Open University Press.

Jordan, B., Redley, M. and James, S. (1994) *Putting the Family First: Identities, Decisions, Citizenship*. London: UCL Press.

Joshi, H. (1991) 'Sex and motherhood as handicaps in the labour market', in M. Maclean and D. Groves (eds), *Women's Issues in Social Policy*. London: Routledge.

Joshi, H. and Hinde, P.R.A. (1993) 'Employment after childbearing in post-war Britain: cohort study evidence on contrasts within and across generations', *European Sociological Review*, 9 (3): 203–27.

Kennedy, P., Whiteford, P. and Bradshaw, J. (1996) 'The economic circumstances of children in ten countries', in J. Brannen and M. O'Brien (eds), *Children in Families: Research and Policy*. London: Falmer Press.

Kerr, M. (1958) *The People of Ship Street*. London: Routledge and Kegan Paul.

Kiernan, K. (1997) *The Legacy of Parental Divorce*. CASE Paper 1. London: London School of Economics.

Kumar, K. (1995) *From Post-industrial to Post-modern Society: New Theories of the Contemporary World*. Oxford: Blackwell.

Kumar, V. (1993) *Poverty and Inequality in the UK: The Effects on Children*. London: National Children's Bureau.

Langan, M. (1991) 'Who cares? Women in the mixed economy of care', in M. Langan and I. Day (eds), *Women, Oppression and Social Work*. London: HarperCollins.

Lash, S. (1994) 'Reflexivity and its double: structures, aesthetics, community', in U. Beck, A. Giddens and S. Lash (eds), *Reflexive Modernization: Politics, Traditions and Aesthetics in the Modern Social Order*. Cambridge: Polity Press. pp. 110–73.

Laslett, P. (1997) 'The increasing independence of older people from their families: from the 16th century to the 21st century, and from the Third Age to the Fourth'. Paper given at the 16th Congress of the International Association of Gerontology, Adelaide, Australia.

Law Commission (1988) *Family Law Review of Child Law: Guardianship and Custody*. Law Commission No. 172. London: HMSO.

Lefaucher, N. (1995) 'De la stabilité à la mobilité conjugale', *Politis la revue*, 8: 19–23.

Leira, A. (1992) *Welfare States and Working Mothers*. Cambridge: Cambridge University Press.

Lesthaeghe, R. (1995) 'The second demographic transition in western countries: an interpretation', in K. Mason, V.K. Oppenheim and A.-M. Jensen (eds), *Gender and Family Change in Industrialized Countries*. Oxford: Clarendon Press.

Leto, V. (1988) '"Washing, seems it's all we do": washing technology and women's communication', in C. Kramarae (ed.), *Technology and Women's Voices*. London: Routledge & Kegan Paul.

Lewis, C. (1986) *Becoming a Father*. Milton Keynes: Open University Press.

Lewis, C. and O'Brien, M. (eds) (1987) *Reassessing Fatherhood: New Observations on Fathers and the Modern Family*. London: Sage.

Lewis, J. (1984) *Women in England 1870–1950: Sexual Division and Social Change*. Hemel Hempstead: Harvester Wheatsheaf.

Lewis, J. (1992) *Women in Britain since 1945: Women, Family, Work and the State in the Post-war Years*. Oxford: Blackwell.

Little, G. (1989) 'Freud, friendship and politics', in R. Porter and S. Tomaselli (eds), *The Dialectics of Friendship*. London: Routledge.

Machin, S. and Waldfogel, J. (1994) *The Decline of the Male Breadwinner*. Suntory and Toyota International Centres for Economics and Related Disciplines Discussion Paper WSP/103, London School of Economics.

Mackenzie, D. and Wajcman, J. (eds) (1985) *The Social Shaping of Technology: How the Refrigerator Got its Hum*. Milton Keynes: Open University Press.

Maclean, M. (1991) *Surviving Divorce*. Basingstoke: Macmillan.

Maclean, M. and Eekelaar, J. (1997) *The Parental Obligation: A Study of Parenthood across Households*. Oxford: Hart Publishing.

Maclean, M. and Wadsworth, M.E. (1988) 'The interests of children after parental divorce: a long-term perspective', *International Journal of Law and the Family*, 2: 155–66.

McCracken, E. (1993) *Decoding Women's Magazines: From Mademoiselle to Ms.* London: Macmillan.

McRae, S. (1986) *Cross-class Families: A Study of Wives' Occupational Superiority*. Oxford: Clarendon Press.

McRae, S. (1991) *Maternity Rights in Britain*. London: Policy Studies Institute.

McRae, S. (1997) 'Household and labour market change: implications for the growth of inequality in Britain', *British Journal of Sociology*, 48 (3): 384–405.

McRae, S. (ed.) (forthcoming) *Household and Population Change*. Oxford: Oxford University Press.

Mansfield, P. and Collard, J. (1988) *The Beginning of the Rest of Your Life: A Portrait of Newly Wed Marriage*. London: Macmillan.

Martin, A. (1993) *The Guide to Lesbian and Gay Parenting*. London: Pandora.

Martin, J. and Roberts, C. (1984) *Women and Employment: A Lifetime Perspective*. London: HMSO.

Mason, J. (1996) 'Gender, care and sensibility in family and kin relationships', in J. Holland and L. Atkins (eds), *Sex, Sensibility and the Gendered Body*. Basingstoke: Macmillan.

May, J. (1997) 'Square deal', *Red Pepper*, 39: 26–8.

Mayall, B. (1996) *Children, Health and the Social Order*. Buckingham: Open University Press.

Mitterauer, M. (1992) *A History of Youth*. Oxford: Blackwell.

Morgan, D.H.J. (1996) *Family Connections*. Cambridge: Polity Press.

Morgan, P. (1995) *Farewell to the Family?* London: Institute of Economic Affairs.

Morris, L. (1990) *The Workings of the Household: A US–UK Comparison*. Cambridge: Polity Press.

Morris, L. (1995) *Social Divisions: Economic Decline and Social Structural Change*. London: UCL Press.

Moss, P. (1992) 'Introductory essay: EC perspectives', in C. Hogg and L. Harker (eds), *The Family Friendly Employer: Examples from Europe*. London: Daycare Trust.

Moss, P. (ed.) (1995) *Father Figures: Fathers in the Families of the 1990s*. Edinburgh: HMSO.

Mott, F.L., Statham, A. and Maxwell, N.L. (1982) 'From mother to daughter: the transmission of work behaviour patterns across generations', in F.L. Mott (ed.), *The Employment Revolution: Young American Women in the 1970s*. Cambridge, MA: MIT Press.

Murray, C. (1990) *The Emerging British Underclass*. London: Institute for Economic Affairs.

Nardi, P. (1992) 'Sex, friendship and gender roles among gay men', in P. Nardi (ed.), *Men's Friendship*. London: Sage.

Neale, B. and Smart, C. (1997) 'Experiments with parenthood?', *Sociology*, 31 (2): 201–19.

Nicholson, L. (1997) 'The myth of the traditional family', in H.L. Nelson (ed.), *Feminism and Families*. London: Routledge.

Nilsen, A. (1997) 'Where is the future? Time and space as categories in the analysis of young people's images of the future'. Paper presented at the European Sociological Association Conference, August 1997.

Novotny, H. (1994) *Time: The Modern and Postmodern Experience*. Cambridge: Polity Press.

Oakley, A. (1994) 'Women and children first and last: parallels and differences between children's and women's studies', in B. Mayall (ed.), *Children's Childhoods: Observed and Experienced*. London: Falmer Press.

O'Brien, M. (1987) 'Patterns of kinship and friendship among lone fathers', in C. Lewis and M. O'Brien (eds), *Reassessing Fatherhood*. London: Sage.

Oerton, S. (1997) '"Queer housewives?": some problems in theorising the division of labour in lesbian and gay households', *Women's Studies International Forum*, 20 (3): 421–30.

Office for National Statistics (1997) *Social Focus on Families*. London: HMSO.

Oldman, D. (1994) 'Childhood as a mode of production', in B. Mayall (ed.), *Children's Childhoods: Observed and Experienced*. London: Falmer Press.

O'Neill, O. (1989) *Constructions of Reason: Explorations of Kant's Practical Philosophy*. Cambridge: Cambridge University Press.

Oppenheim, C. and Lister, R. (1996) 'The politics of child poverty 1979–1995', in

J. Pilcher and S. Wagg (eds), *Thatcher's Children: Politics, Childhood and Society in the 1980s and 1990s*. London: Falmer Press.

Oppenheimer, V.K. (1994) 'Women's rising employment and the future of the family in industrial societies', *Population and Development Review*, 20 (2): 293–342.

Ormrod, S. (1994) '"Let's nuke the dinner": discursive practices of gender in the creation of a new cooking process', in C. Cockburn and R. Fürst-Dilic (eds), *Bringing Technology Home*. Buckingham: Open University Press.

Parker, G. and Lawton, D. (1994) *Different Types of Care, Different Types of Carer*. London: HMSO.

Parsons, T., Bales, R.F., Olds, J., Zelditch, M. and Slater, P.E. (1955) *Family, Socialization and Interaction Process*. New York: Free Press.

Peace, H.F. (1993) 'The pretended family – a study of the divisions of domestic labour in lesbian families', *Leicester University Discussion Papers in Sociology*, No. S93/3. Leicester: Leicester University Press.

Peattie, L. and Rein, M. (1983) *Women's Claims: A Study in Political Economy*. Oxford: Oxford University Press.

Phillips, M. (1997) *The Sex Change State*. Memorandum no 30, October. London: Social Market Foundation.

Phillips, M. (1998) 'A man's job is to win the bread: a woman's job is to spread it . . .', *The Observer*, 22 March: 25.

Phoenix, A. (1996a) 'Participation and autonomy in child development'. Paper presented to the Institute of Public Policy Research, London.

Phoenix, A. (1996b) 'Social constructions of lone motherhood: a case of competing discourses' in Elizabeth B. Silva (ed.), *Good Enough Mothering? Feminist Perspectives on Lone Motherhood*. London: Routledge.

Platt, Gerald (1980) 'Thoughts on a theory of collective action: language, affect and ideology', in M. Albin (ed.), *New Directions in Psycho-History*. Lexington, MA: Lexington Books.

Plummer, K. (ed.) (1992) *Modern Homosexualities: Fragments of Lesbian and Gay Experience*. London: Routledge.

Plummer, K. (1995) *Telling Sexual Stories: Power, Change, and Social Worlds*. London: Routledge.

Political and Economic Planning (1945) *The Market for Household Appliances*. London: PEP and Oxford University Press.

Porter, K. and Weeks, J. (1990) *Between the Acts: Lives of Homosexual Men 1895–1967*. London: Routledge.

Prendergast, S. and Forrest, S. (1997) 'The hieroglyphics of the heterosexual', in L. Segal (ed.), *New Sexual Agendas*. Basingstoke: Macmillan.

Rhodes, P. (1995) 'Charitable vocation or proper job? The role of payment in foster care', in J. Brannen and M. O'Brien (eds), *Childhood and Parenthood*. Proceedings of the International Sociological Association Committee for Family Research Conference, 1994. London: Institute of Education.

Rich, A. (1984) 'On compulsory heterosexuality and lesbian existence', in A. Snitow, C. Stansell and S. Thompson (eds), *Desire: The Politics of Sexuality*. London: Virago.

Richards, M. (1996) 'The socio-legal support for divorcing parents and their children', in B. Bernstein and J. Brannen (eds), *Children, Research and Policy*. London: Taylor & Francis.

Richardson, B. (1983) *Caribbean Migrants, Environment and Human Survival on St Kitts and Nevis*. Knoxville, TN: University of Tennessee Press.

Roberts, C. and McGlone, F. (1997) 'Kinship networks and friendship: attitudes and behaviour in Britain 1986–1995', Population and Household Change Research Programme, *Research Results No. 3*. Swindon: ESRC.

Roche, J. (1996) 'The politics of children's rights', in J. Brannen and M. O'Brien (eds), *Children in Families: Research and Policy*. London: Falmer Press.

Rodger, J.J. (1996) *Family Life and Social Control: A Sociological Perspective*. Basingstoke: Macmillan.

Rosser, C. and Harris, C. (1965) *The Family and Social Change: A Study of Family and Kinship in a South Wales Town*. London: Routledge & Kegan Paul.

Rubery, V. (1996) 'The labour market outlook and the outlook for labour market analysis', in R. Crompton, D. Gallie and K. Purcell (eds), *Changing Forms of Employment: Organisations, Skills and Gender*. London: Routledge.

Rubin, G. (1975) 'The traffic in women: notes on the "political economy" of sex', in R.R. Reiter (ed.), *Towards an Anthropology of Women*. London: Monthly Review Press.

Ruddick, S. (1980) 'Maternal thinking', *Feminist Studies*, 6 (2): 342–67.

Saffron, L. (1994) *Alternative Beginnings*. London: Cassell.

Saffron, L. (1996) *What about the Children? Sons and Daughters of Lesbian and Gay Parents Talk about their Lives*. London: Cassell.

Scanzoni, J., Polonko, K., Teachman, J. and Thompson, L. (1989) *The Sexual Bond: Rethinking Families and Close Relationships*. Newbury Park, CA: Sage.

Schor J.B. (1993) *The Overworked American: The Unexpected Decline of Leisure*. New York: Basic Books. (First edn 1992.)

Scott, J. (1997) 'Changing households in Britain: do families still matter?', *Sociological Review*, 45 (4): 591–620.

Scott, J. and Brook, L. (1997) 'Family change: demographic and attitudinal trends across nations and time', *Research Results*, No. 1. ESRC Population and Household Change Research Programme.

Sevenhuijsen, S. (1998) *Citizenship and the Ethics of Care*. London: Routledge.

Seymour, J. (1992) '"Not a manly thing to do?" Gender accountability and the division of domestic labour', in G.A. Dunne, R.M. Blackburn and J. Jarman (eds), *Inequalities in Employment, Inequalities in Home-Life*. Conference Proceedings for Cambridge Social Stratification Seminar 9–10 September 1992.

Siltanen, J. (1994) *Locating Gender*. London: UCL Press.

Silva, E.B. (ed.) (1996) *Good Enough Mothering? Feminist Perspectives on Lone Motherhood*. London: Routledge.

Silva, E.B. (1997a) 'The cooker and the cook in the making of gender', School of Sociology and Social Policy, University of Leeds. Mimeo.

Silva, E.B. (1997b) '"This is the way we wash. . .". Laundry and dish washing in Britain: 1900–1990s', *GAPU Working Paper No. 17*, School of Sociology and Social Policy, University of Leeds.

Silva, E.B. (1998) 'Changing households and housework: washing technologies in Britain'. Paper presented at the Gender, Work and Organization Conference, Manchester, January.

Silver, H. (1987) 'Only so many hours in a day: time constraints, labour pool and demand for consumer services', *Service Industries Journal*, 7 (4): 26–45.

Simey, Thomas (1946) *Welfare and Planning in the West Indies*. Oxford: Oxford University Press.

Simpson, B., McCarthy, P. and Walker, J. (1995) *Being There: Fathers after Divorce.* Newcastle upon Tyne: Relate Centre for Family Studies.

Sly, F., Price, A. and Risdon, A. (1997) 'Women in the labour market: results from the Spring 1996 Labour Force Survey', *Labour Market Trends*, March.

Smart, C. (1997) 'Wishful thinking and harmful tinkering? Sociological reflections on family policy', *Journal of Social Policy*, 26 (3): 301–21.

Smart, C. and Neale, B. (1999) *Family Fragments?* Cambridge: Polity Press.

Smart, C. and Neale, B. (forthcoming) '"I hadn't really thought about it": new identities/new fatherhoods', in J. Seymour and P. Bagguley (eds), *Relating Intimacies: Power and Resistance*. London: BSA/Macmillan.

Smart, C. and Sevenhuijsen, S. (eds) (1989) *Child Custody and the Politics of Gender.* London: Routledge.

Smeds, R., Huida, O., Haavio-Mannila, E. and Kauppinen-Toropainen, K. (1994) 'Sweeping away the dust of tradition: vacuum cleaning as a site of technical and social innovation', in C. Cockburn and R. Fürst-Dili (eds), *Bringing Technology Home. Gender and Technology in a Changing Europe.* Buckingham: Open University Press.

Smith, D. (1987) *The Everyday World as Problematic: A Feminist Sociology.* Toronto: University of Toronto Press.

Smith, R.T. (1988) *Kinship and Class in the West Indies: A Genealogical Study of Jamaica and Guyana.* Cambridge: Cambridge University Press.

Social Focus on Women (1995) Central Statistical Office. London: HMSO.

Solein, N. (1960) 'Household and family in the Caribbean', *Social and Economic Studies*, 9 (1): 101–6.

Stacey, J. (1991) *Brave New Families: Stories of Domestic Upheaval in Late Twentieth Century America.* New York: Basic Books.

Stones, R. (1996) *Sociological Reasoning: Towards a Past-modern Sociology.* Basingstoke: Macmillan.

Strasser, S. (1982) *Never Done: A History of American Housework.* New York: Random House.

Sullivan, A. (1995) *Virtually Normal: An Argument about Homosexuality.* London: Picador.

Sullivan, O. (1997) 'Time waits for no (wo)man: an investigation of the gendered experience of domestic time', *Sociology*, 31 (2): 221–39.

Tasker, F.L. and Golombok, S. (1991) 'Children raised by lesbian mothers', *Family Law*, May: 184–7.

Tasker, F.L. and Golombok, S. (1995) 'Adults raised as children in lesbian families', *American Journal of Orthopsychiatry*, 65 (2): 203–15.

Tasker, F.L. and Golombok, S. (1997) *Growing up in a Lesbian Family: Effects on Child Development.* New York and London: Guilford Press.

Tasker, F.L. and Golombok, S. (1998) 'The role of co-mothers in planned lesbian-led families', *The Journal of Lesbian Studies*, 12: 4.

Thomas-Hope, E. (1992) *Explanation in Caribbean Migration.* London: Macmillan.

Tronto, J.C. (1993) *Moral Boundaries: A Political Argument for an Ethic of Care.* New York/London: Routledge.

Ungerson, G. (1990) *Gender and Caring: Work and Welfare in Britain and Scandinavia.* London: Harvester Wheatsheaf.

VanEvery, J. (1991/92) 'Who is "the family"? The assumptions of British social policy', *Critical Social Policy*, 11 (3): 62–75.

VanEvery, J. (1995) *Heterosexual Women Changing the Family: Refusing to be a 'Wife'!* London: Taylor & Francis.

VanEvery, J. (1997) 'Understanding gendered inequality: reconceptualizing housework', *Women's Studies International Forum*, 20 (3): 411–20.

Van Krieken, R. (1997) 'Sociology and the reproductive self: demographic transitions and modernity', *Sociology*, 31 (3): 445–71.

Voysey, M. (1975) *A Constant Burden: The Reconstitution of Family Life.* London: Routledge & Kegan Paul.

Waaldijk, K. (1994) 'Homosexuality: European Community issues', in G. Zijlstra and A. Clapham (eds), *Family? Partners? Individuals?* Amsterdam: RoseLinks.

Waerness, K. (1994) 'Women and the welfare state: common and conflicting interests in the 1990s', in L. Simonen (ed.), *När Gränserne Flyter: En Nordisk anthologi om vård och omsorg.* Jyväskylä: Jyväskylä University Press.

Wajcman, J. (1991) *Feminism Confronts Technology.* Cambridge: Polity Press.

Walby, S. (1997) *Gender Transformations.* London: Routledge.

Walkerdine, V. and Lucey, H. (1989) *Democracy in the Kitchen: Regulating Mothers and Socialising Daughters.* London: Virago.

Ward, C., Dale, A. and Joshi, H. (1996) 'Combining employment with childcare: an escape from dependence?', *Journal of Social Policy*, 25 (2): 223–47.

Warde, A. (1997) *Consumption, Food and Taste.* London: Sage.

Webb, S. (1993) 'Women's incomes: past, present and prospects', *Fiscal Studies*, 14 (4): 14–36.

Weeks, J. (1991) 'Pretended family relationships', in J. Weeks (ed.), *Against Nature: Essays on History, Sexuality and Identity.* London: Rivers Oram Press.

Weeks, J. (1995) *Invented Moralities: Sexual Values in an Age of Uncertainty.* Cambridge: Polity Press.

Weeks, J. (1996) 'The idea of a sexual community', *Soundings*, 2 (Spring): 71–84.

Weeks, J., Donovan, C. and Heaphy, B. (1996) *Families of Choice: Patterns of Non-heterosexual Relationships – A Literature Review.* Social Science Research Papers No. 2. London: South Bank University.

Wellings, K., Field, J., Johnson, A.M. and Wadsworth, J. (1994) *Sexual Behaviour in Britain.* Harmondsworth: Penguin.

West, C. and Zimmerman, D.H. (1987) 'Doing gender', *Gender & Society*, 1: 125–51.

West, C. and Zimmerman, D.H. (1991) 'Doing gender', in J. Lorber and S.A. Farrell (eds), *The Social Construction of Gender*, Newbury Park, CA: Sage.

Weston, K. (1991) *Families We Choose: Lesbians, Gays and Kinship.* Albany, NY: Columbia University Press.

Wheelock, J. (1990) *Husbands at Home: The Domestic Economy in a Post-industrial Society.* London: Routledge.

Wilkinson, H. and Mulgan, G. (1995) *Freedom's Children: Work, Relationships and Politics for 18–24 year olds in Britain Today.* London: Demos.

Williams, F. (1994) 'Lesbian couple granted parental rights', *Gay Times*, 191, August: 29.

Wittig, M. (1992) 'One is not born a woman', in M. Wittig (ed.), *The Straight Mind and Other Essays.* Hemel Hempstead: Harvester Wheatsheaf.

Young, I.M. (1995) 'Mothers, citizenship, and independence: a critique of pure family values', *Ethics*, 105 (April): 535–56.

Young, M. and Willmott, P. (1957) *Family and Kinship in East London.* London: Routledge & Kegan Paul.

Young, M. and Willmott, P. (1960) *Family and Class in a London Suburb*. London: Routledge & Kegan Paul.

Young, M. and Willmott, P. (1973) *The Symmetrical Family: A Study of Work and Leisure in the London Region*. Harmondsworth: Penguin.

Zelitzer, V.A. (1985) *Pricing the Priceless Child: The Changing Social Value of Children*. New York: Basic Books.

Zmroczek, C. (1992) 'Dirty linen: women, class and washing machines, 1920–1960s', *Women's Studies International Forum*, 15 (2): 173–85.

INDEX